VICTORIA'S HEIR

The Education of a Prince

"It is pleasant to be transferred from an office where one is afraid of a sergeant-major into an office where one can intimidate generals, and perhaps this is why History is so attractive . . . The captains and the kings depart at our slightest censure, while as for the 'hosts of minor officials' who cumber court and camp, we heed them not, though in actual life they entirely block our social horizon. We cannot visit either the great or the rich when they are our contemporaries, but by a fortunate arrangement the palaces of Ujjain and the warehouses of Ormus are open for ever. . . ."

E. M. FORSTER, *Abinger Harvest*

The rare, the rather awful visits of Albert Edward, Prince of Wales, to Windsor Castle.

(By kind permission of Sir Max Beerbohm and Messrs. William Heinemann Ltd).

VICTORIA'S HEIR

The Education of a Prince

by

GEORGE DANGERFIELD

With a Frontispiece
by
Sir Max Beerbohm

CONSTABLE & CO. LTD.
London

First English Edition January 1942
Reprinted . . May 1942

To
My Mother and Sister, with Love

PRINTED IN GREAT BRITAIN BY
LOWE AND BRYDONE PRINTERS LIMITED, LONDON, N.W.10

FOREWORD

I AM sure that the greatest compliment that a reader could pay to this book would be to want to do more reading or re-reading about the same period.

Those who wish for an adequate bibliography covering the literature of the period will find it at the end of two volumes of the Oxford History of England: *The Age of Reform, 1815-1870*, by E. L. Woodward, and *England, 1870-1914*, by R. C. K. Ensor.

I have not attempted to. put a bibliography at the end of this book. The list would be long and I think it would look quite impressive; but I cannot see that it would have any real value as a bibliographical apparatus. The selection has—of necessity in a book of this kind—been an arbitrary one; only a fragment of the historical literature of the English nineteenth century has been necessary for my purposes.

I should like, however, to mention with especial gratitude and ·admiration two brilliant and comparatively unsung monographs: *1851 and the Crystal Palace* by Christopher Hobhouse (London, J. Murray. 1937), and *La Vie Parisienne* by Sacheverell Sitwell (London, Faber and Faber. 1937).

I believe that the reader could do worse than have recourse

once more to what are still the four chief treasure houses of nineteenth century English history: *The Greville Memoirs*, *The Letters of Queen Victoria*, Monypenny and Buckle's *Life of Benjamin Disraeli*, and Morley's *Life of Gladstone*. From these the curiosity can proceed to further explorations—political, economic, biographical—for all four are full of suggestion. And the files of more and more public libraries are well equipped to deal with such an adventure.

In this respect, I should like to express my gratitude (which is shared, I am sure, by thousands upon thousands of other readers there) for the courtesy and efficiency of that great institution, the New York Public Library, where a great deal of the reading for this book was done.

G. D.

CONTENTS

Prologue

CORN AND CLASSES

JANUARY, 1901. The trumpets sounded, the heralds in their chivalrous coats recited proclamations in marvelous English. Queen Victoria was dead, and Edward VII reigned in her place.

Soon after Edward VII's accession, England was flooded with illustrated supplements and books of photographs, which pursued him through every phase of his career. There was the later Prince of Wales, the ripe fruit of wealth and easy living, perpetually smiling as he led in a Derby winner or opened a Colonial Exhibition. There was Disraeli's "Prince Hal," too plump for his age, putting an Order round a maharajah's neck. Backwards went the procession of photographs and engravings to more remote and yet more remote days—to the era of the *cylindre* and the Paris of Napoleon III, to his wedding—days when people's very faces were, in some subtle and indefinable way, already part of history. Then he was shown as a bachelor, innocent, arrogant, and perplexed, with a vaguely Hanoverian look, lost in the Age of Palmerston. He was a small boy in kilts, holding the Queen's hand, among the pomps of the Crystal Palace. He was a very little boy, idealized by Winterhalter, or caught by the more truthful daguerreotype in the preposterous clothes of early Victorian childhood.

At last the procession comes to rest in Hayter's picture of his christening at Windsor in 1842, with Sir Robert Peel, the Duke of Wellington, Lord Melbourne; with a youthful Prince Albert, a slim Victoria. The Archbishop of Canterbury, who wears a wig, is about to name the child ALBERT EDWARD; he has already declared, as the liturgy prescribes, that all men are born in sin, but he has cautiously introduced this statement with the remark "May it please Your Majesty." There is something in every detail of the group— the curl of a whisker, the shape of a collar, the falling of a gown from the shoulders—to remind us that these august people are standing in the earliest twilight of modern England. They smile (with the exception of the royal parents); after all, it is a christening; but fancy gives them a certain wistfulness, as though they were momentarily looking back not forward, to a world which most of them had known so well: to the days of the Regent, to Waterloo, to Badajos and Torres Vedras, and the smoke and the thunders of Trafalgar.

One element in Edward VII's swift rise to popularity can be detected in these pictures. His life, like Queen Victoria's, seemed to stretch back into a very distant past. He, too, was an example of something which the English especially cherish—the persistence of their traditions. When he came to the throne, however, many people wondered if England would ever really take to him. He was in his sixtieth year, he was too old to change. Was not his past one long tale of idleness and dissipation, punctuated by trivial public services?

4

If premonitions were founded upon perspicacity, large numbers of human beings would be prophets; but this is rarely the case; and it was not the case in 1901. Those who indulged in these gloomy thoughts had not taken into account another very important fact. During the past two decades, a new spirit had crept into English life, and it was now openly manifest in the person of the new king. It was an amused and expansive spirit, much too fond of luxury, and inclined to strain against the inhibitions and decorums of the previous decades. None the less, it was not itself indecorous. The sprightly people, for example, who had clustered around King Edward when he was Prince of Wales moved—it was only to be expected—into the new court circles: but they had to behave. Edward VII was the grandson of a martinet; he was so fanatically punctual that every clock in his residences was kept thirty minutes fast; and his eye, which was preternaturally quick to detect some error in the wearing of a decoration, took in other details as well. At a dinner party, early in his reign, one of his guests, the charming daughter of an admiral, appeared in a dress that showed an inch or so of ankle. Edward VII summoned her and said, in his husky voice, rolling his r's—and with a smile, for he never could resist a pretty face—"I'm afraid you must have made a mistake. This is a dinner, not a tennis party." It was always unwise to assume that the King's behavior took after his morality. Only the latter was loose.

The new spirit, in fact, was one that worked inside and not outside the solid forms of Victorian respectability. It was not merely to be found in high circles: it was everywhere. In 1890, there was a great outburst of rage against Albert Edward, who had appeared in court as a witness in a law-suit

5

arising from a card scandal. The outburst died away, and it was noticed that the Prince was rather more popular than before. The crowds at the races—a fair touchstone of the lighter side of public opinion—greeted him with a quizzical satisfaction, with cheers and laughter. He had been going the pace, and, on the whole, they approved.

After he became King, the approval continued and increased, but it was of a more serious kind. The swelling optimism of the Diamond Jubilee had given way to a mood of doubt and disillusionment. The Boer War still dragged on; what could the matter be? Were the Boers, after all, so very wrong? Were they not—perhaps—right? In any case, the war had torn a rent in the protective fabric of the nineteenth century Empire, and chilly fogs and mists were beginning to leak in from the outside. But there was the King, a supremely self-confident man. With his short stout body, his smile, and his cigar, he looked like a sporting banker, a living testament to the fact that the nation's credit was still sound. The light that beat down upon the throne seemed to bring his good qualities—his amazing affability, his consummate tact—into sharp relief, and to throw his less pleasing ones into the shadow. As for his past, no doubt he *had* gone the pace; but what of that? The sins of the throne were, in a way, an excuse for the sins of the people.

Between the real and the apparent king—between Edward as he was, and as the public believed him to be—there yawned a sizeable chasm. If he had conformed to the educational schemes of his father, he might have acquired, among other things, some knowledge of the way in which the vast majority of his subjects lived and worked. But no, his education, such as it was, had been of a very different kind. It was casual, it was haphazard, it was the effect of exalted birth, a prodigious memory for faces, a taste for travel, and an endless curiosity about the intimate lives of eminent or amusing people. When he came to the throne, he was a living encyclopedia of information concerning the tastes and habits of monarchs, diplomatists, and politicians, and of more ambiguous people who pulled the strings in the world's capitals. Contrary to popular belief, he was not a statesman: both Lord Balfour and Lord Grey have testified to the fact that he never initiated a policy. But he was a sensitive instrument in statecraft; he knew his way, none better, through the social mazes of Europe. And so it came about that his one important historical rôle—of a positive kind—was played in four days, in an astonishing personal triumph in Paris. On the negative side, he did something to increase the mutual distrust of England and Germany.

Such were his achievements as King. And yet, it may be, his real place in history is of a more indefinite nature. If Queen Victoria in her last years became a Universal Mother in the eyes of her people, there was something—it has quite rightly been said—of the Universal Uncle about King Edward. This was the faintly disreputable, the very benevolent idea which—less than forty years ago—reigned in the imagination of England. It was not, to be sure, the most kingly of rôles, but it was something. It was something to have flitted for a few years, like an agreeable, affectionate, and amusing thought, through the mind of a great people.

Albert Edward, Prince of Wales, passed through great historical incidents on his way to becoming Edward VII. These

7

incidents helped to form his character: they also—what is perhaps more important—helped to form the world in which we live today. The first of them was a political struggle which took place some five years after his birth, and without some knowledge of which we cannot hope to understand either the man or his times. This political struggle—a vitally significant event in history—was, as it were, a curtain-raiser to the whole rich drama of Victorian England. It had an effect upon the lives of all who dwelt in the nineteenth century. As for Albert Edward, who was born into a world of Aristocracy and lived to become conspicuously a part of the world of Wealth, he may almost be said to have been shaped by it. It is known as the Repeal of the Corn Laws, and its leading actor is Sir Robert Peel.

II

Sir Robert Peel could never bring himself to utter the word "potato." It signified, no doubt, a necessary vegetable, but that did not mean that a gentleman need admit it to his vocabulary. And Sir Robert was a gentleman in a very English way. His own education, his inherited baronetcy, obscured the fact that his grandfather had been born in humble circumstances; an extreme stiffness of manner did the rest. In a time when educated English speech was not so uniform as it is today, his slight Lancashire accent aroused little comment. Indeed, with his handsome presence and his icy manners, his wealth and his title, he was well equipped to play a leading part in Tory politics. The Tories themselves, who were not disposed to make concessions where birth was in

question, were prepared to accept Sir Robert's cotton-spin-
ning ancestry with merely the faintest sniff of polite suspicion. But Sir Robert's ears were abnormally sensitive. He
could detect a sniff, even a very little sniff, even a sniff that
had hardly been sniffed at all: and the formal hedge with
which he surrounded himself on public occasions was doubtless the result of this sensitivity.

It was, therefore, rather odd to find this successful gentleman, in the summer of 1845, peering with uneasy excitement
at the barometer. Upon the verdict of that instrument much
depended. If the rains were to continue, a bad harvest would
follow; and then Peel might be obliged to break with the
gentlemen of England. He was Prime Minister, he had been
in office for nearly four years; and it was, to say the least,
ironical that the humble potato should play (as very soon it
did) a part in his affairs—should, indeed, help to crown with
triumphant catastrophe a career that might have ended in
honor and in peace.

And yet, perhaps, there was something appropriate in this.
The fates often suit their pattern to the inner rather than the
outer man; and the inner Sir Robert was quite at odds with
the outer. In his behavior towards the political beginner, the
chance acquaintance, the unknown admirer, he was harsh
and cruel; his true feelings towards mankind expressed themselves in secret. The begging-letter writer, that touchstone
of early Victorian generosity, ranked him, as a ready giver,
next only to Queen Adelaide and Mr. Charles Dickens. In
other and more important ways, the essential paradox of his
nature can be discerned. He prided himself upon his high
connections, and never to the end of his days questioned his

9

right to be the member of a privileged class; yet, sometimes in the aridity of his speeches, sometimes in his private correspondence, one can detect an almost haunted concern for the underprivileged poor. He needed the sanction of fact before he would accept a theory; but, for all his caution, he was a visionary as well. Above all—and this was, perhaps, the consequence of all his other qualities—he loved fame. He loved it more than office, more than honor, more even than rank. Such was the man who, in the summer of 1845, was nerving himself to break the Tory party.

In order to appreciate Sir Robert's predicament, it is necessary to turn back to 1841, when, for the second time, he became Prime Minister. He was the head of a party that represented, though it did not exclusively contain, the landed wealth of England. It believed in the protection of agriculture, and, by inference, in the protection of everything else. The Whig government which preceded that of Sir Robert had, however, left behind it a considerable deficit: it had not been extravagant, but Lord Melbourne had been at its head, and, as so often happened where Lord Melbourne was concerned, things had somehow or other become very muddled. In order to discover new sources of national income, Sir Robert was faced with two alternatives: he could either raise the duties or lower the duties, and he chose the latter alternative. An increase in consumption followed, but it was not large enough: Sir Robert, therefore, forced a reluctant Parliament to agree to an income tax. The tax, it is true, seemed to favor agriculture at the expense of industry, but even then a number of old-fashioned gentlemen shuddered at the introduction of such a revolutionary measure. Sir Robert, they told themselves, was a sound man, none sounder; the tax was undoubtedly the child of necessity not of invention. But still they shuddered, and well they might; for they were standing already in the chilly dawn of Free Trade.

These changes produced, as was only natural, a disturbing effect upon the members of Peel's government. They were ınen of acumen; they knew that they were playing a part in no ordinary administration; and the exalted but vague uncertainty which attended this knowledge was to pursue some of them for the rest of their lives. One man in particular, a very junior minister, thought things over with an extraordinary seriousness. William Ewart Gladstone had always been a serious thinker; but in 1832, when he first entered Parliament, his chief political preoccupation had been with the relative merits of Pedro, Miguel, and Donna Maria in respect to the throne of Portugal. He was also much exercised about the state of Poland. As for domestic affairs, he found them irksome; in fact, he paid very little attention to them at all: and since, among ambitious young Tories, this was the fashionable approach to the problem of governing England, he cannot altogether be blamed for it.

In 1841, however, as Vice-President of the Board of Trade, he was required to look into the tariff system, an unreformed relic of the eighteenth century, for the purpose of reducing or abolishing some of the existing tariffs. He looked—at first reluctantly—he had hoped for some more romantic post; he was astonished; he looked again. The influences of Eton and Oxford, his party loyalty, his deep conservatism—all were shaken: and those mercantile origins, which he shared with Peel, began in a curious way to assert themselves. Details which had once seemed tedious and vulgar now cast a spell upon his subtle intellect. For here, spread before him, complicated and unregenerate, here was the economy of the landed class. He might almost have been looking into its mind. It was not merely that raw materials, the very life-blood of manufacture, were heavily taxed; even stranger discoveries awaited him. Food, for instance, was scarce; yet the tariffs on food were fantastic. He found among other things that each kind of fish had a special import rate—with two exceptions, turbot and lobster. These delicacies, the traditional food of aldermen and noblemen, were allowed to enter the ports without a duty. He recommended a uniform duty upon all fish, but the protest from certain eminent quarters was so loud that on one crucial point he was obliged to yield. . . . Lobsters continued to enter the country duty-free.

After such an experience, it is hardly surprising that his faith in protection should have been undermined. The upheaval, however, was slow and agonizing. Gladstone's conscience was a peculiar organ: it was not so much a conscience as a conspiracy against his peace of mind. To those intricate rational processes in which he delighted it added a perverse, a fanatic, an irrational element. Throughout his long career, it never left him alone. Now, an able administrator at the Board of Trade, a man whose prospects were generally admitted to be very bright, he was assailed by doubts. The Government's attitude towards the opium trade filled him with uneasiness; but more alarming still was its equivocal position in the matter of the possible union between the two Welsh dioceses of Bangor and St. Asaph. But these evasions were useless: the tariff remained. In 1842, he almost resigned because he felt that the Cabinet's wheat scale was "virtual protection," and the negative character of his talk with Peel on that occasion left him with a chilly and ineffaceable memory. In 1843, his attitude had grown so extremely delicate that it was said that his arguments were in favor of free trade and his parentheses in favor of protection. At last a political crisis of his own choosing threatened to relegate this inner debate to some more private sphere. It was proposed to raise the annual grant to the Catholic seminary at Maynooth from £9000 to £26000; and amidst the sectarian frenzies which proposals of this nature were apt to arouse in early Victorian England, Gladstone suddenly resigned. It was a most inopportune step; the Government needed all the support it could muster: he was most sorry to leave it. But what could he do? He wrote a letter of explanation to Peel, and, as was frequently the case when Gladstone took his pen in hand, the mystery deepened. Was he opposed to this measure? On the contrary, he was prepared, he said, "in opposition to my own deeply cherished predilections, to give a deliberate and even anxious support to it." But it so happened that in 1839 he had published a book called *The State in its Relations with the Church*, in which he had given vent to his deeply cherished predilections in a manner which, for Mr. Gladstone, was positively lucid. Few people, it is true, had perused *The State in its Relations with the Church* and fewer still, it may be, remembered it: but Gladstone felt that he could no longer remain in the Cabinet. His colleagues were puzzled and exasperated. It seemed that his political career was finished: and he himself was of this opinion. No more need he worry over Free Trade and Protection. In a characteristic speech, lasting well over an hour, he unbosomed himself to the House of Commons. "What a marvellous talent is this!" exclaimed Richard Cobden, as Gladstone at last sat down. "Here have I been listening with pleasure to this explanation, and yet I know no more why he left the Government than before he began." Benjamin Disraeli had also been listening with pleasure—but with pleasure of another kind. "Gladstone may have an *avenir*," he wrote his sister afterward, "but I hardly think it." Here, however, Mr. Disraeli was wrong.

While Gladstone thus wrestled with his conscience, Peel was reaching his own conclusions in his own less vexatious way. In 1842, in spite of his great "Free Trade" Budget of that year, he was still a protectionist. He had reduced to a nominal amount the duties on raw materials and half-manufactured articles; his income tax, even though it made no distinction between earned and unearned income, was also a free trade measure; yet he had merely nibbled at the duties on wheat, and the sugar duties he had left untouched. His pledge to the country gentlemen of England, his ideal of a country that could support itself in time of war, an obstinate belief in the theory that wages fell with the price of food—they all held him back. He was not like Gladstone, he did not allow the problem to intrude into his public life; he continued on his way, calmly and prudently: but those who knew him best would have been surprised at the inner excitement that possessed him. At last, in 1844, he made a startling and decisive discovery. Examining the statistics for the years 1839-41 he saw that while prices for food were high in those years, wages were low; a further set of figures, relative to the trade revival year of 1843, showed, on the other hand, that while food was cheap, wages were high. "I cannot resist the conclusion," he said, "that wages do not vary with the price of provisions." Once he found a conclusion to be irresistible, Peel was not the man to turn his back upon it. His last objection to Free Trade had vanished; before him there loomed —malign and majestic—that stronghold of Toryism and Protection . . . the Corn Laws.

These laws had been founded upon the exigencies of the Napoleonic Wars, and were subsequently maintained in the interests of a rather small and most distinguished class of quite rapacious persons. The laws had undergone various metamorphoses between 1804 and 1842, but the effect was the same: their restrictions upon the import of foreign wheat and other grains made every bad harvest a source of appalling misery to large numbers of the English people. The parsons, the tenant farmers, and, above all, the landlords were much concerned in maintaining these laws. The landlords! The great Reform Act of 1832 had been prophetic rather than practical; it foreshadowed, it did not put into effect, the political triumph of the manufacturing class. The landed interest still dominated the Lords, still packed the Tory back benches in the Commons. Peel did not regard these gentry with unmixed approval: too many of them, he complained, spent their time in eating and drinking, hunting and shooting, gambling, horse-racing; and among the worst offenders in this respect was his own Secretary for War and Colonies, Lord Stanley. They seemed to believe—and a solid body in the Church of England, still yawning from its long Georgian sleep, supported them in this—that some divine approval manifested itself in the rent-rolls; and that theorists such as Ricardo were approaching if not passing the verges of downright blasphemy. If the poor suffered from lack of bread, that was the will of an inscrutable Providence—they must suffer in helpless silence: or, perhaps, when the pangs of hunger became too acute, they might try to alleviate their agony with a pinch of curry-powder mixed with water. This remedy was, indeed, most sympathetically suggested by the Duke of Norfolk, one of the wealthiest landowners in the country. But Peel's Toryism was not as the Duke's. He believed, strange to say, that some more sustaining diet was in order; that, in fact, the poor might actually be given bread. After 1844 all but the most obtuse of his followers began to suspect that sooner or later he would advocate the repeal of the Corn Laws.

It was a horrible suspicion. The protectionists sincerely believed that if the Corn Laws were repealed, agriculture would be ruined; the sincerity of this belief was not diminished by the fact that, if agriculture were ruined, their incomes would suffer accordingly. And there had arisen to plague them an exasperating organization called the Anti-Corn Law League, an odious and vulgar set of manufacturers and radicals which increased in voice and numbers every day. These men did not propose to stop at the repeal of the Corn Laws: no, they had more drastic ambitions; they wished to gain a proper representation for themselves in Parliament. It was intolerable. And yet—after all—were their arguments entirely without foundation? The economics of foreign trade are difficult and complex; but from the endless considerations advanced by the Anti-Corn Law League, one at least emerged in a most simple form. Trade in the '40's was bad—and it would continue to be bad, it would positively grow worse, if foreign countries were not allowed to exchange their surplus food for English manufactures. The protectionists were dismayed. Might there, perhaps, actually be some truth in this? But what, after all, did the future of trade signify? They brushed the inconvenient thought aside. A fact of infinitely more importance was the terrible hypocrisy of the free traders. They pretended to care for the working classes; and yet one had merely to visit one of the new manufacturing towns to see how little the well-being of the working classes counted in their employers' scheme of things. One had merely to contemplate those rows of base brick hovels, unventilated, undrained, huddled back-to-back; one had merely to observe the wretched creatures who emerged from them, to work preposterously long hours for preposterously low wages . . . and then, pray, what became of the humanitarian arguments of the Anti-Corn Law League? This criticism was not exactly relevant; but it happened to be true; and the manufacturers could only reply that the agricultural laborer was in little better shape than the factory worker. And all this washing of dirty linen seemed merely to prove that neither side was really interested in the condition of the poor. The conflict was not, in fact, a conflict between Protection and Free Trade: more obscure and more profound issues were at stake. The old ruling class was fighting desperately against the new. Land was arrayed against Capital—it was one more phase in that strange warfare which had been foreshadowed, in England by the Reform Act of 1832, in France by the usurpation of Louis Philippe, and which, years later, was to plunge the United States of America into one of the most appalling periods of carnage in the history of man.

The unenfranchised masses, though they listened with a certain pleasure to the eloquence of the free traders and the objurgations of the gentry, had little interest in this quarrel. Their thinkers were involved in the more universal causes of the People's Charter, whose revolutionary provisions, with their attendant unrest, supplied the Corn Law battle with a somber and heroic background. Once again, as in 1832, the choice seemed to lie between revolution and reform; once again, English history was moving towards one of its great crises. The leaders of the Anti-Corn Law League hoped to bring the Chartists over to their side, but in vain: the latter perceived in the former only the hateful features of the employing class. Yet the very stars in their courses fought against Chartism; the horoscope of Europe did not yet reveal a proletarian victory. A revolution, indeed, lay in store for Europe; in 1848 it swept from Berlin to Naples, from Paris to Budapest; but it was at heart a middle class revolution; and in England it was both anticipated and prevented by the fight over the Corn Laws.

III

In such a state of affairs, Peel's position was a most uncomfortable one. It was even more—it was very painful: for he had one foot in the camp of Land and one in that of Capital, and the two were drawing farther apart every day. Fame would undoubtedly be his, if he deserted his old friends the Tories; but as he nerved himself for the task, he could not help speculating, with a certain discomfort, upon the character of his new allies. The leaders of the Anti-Corn Law League were Richard Cobden and John Bright. Peel disapproved of them socially, but he *did* admire them, and history, on the whole, has admired them ever since. For they were, indeed, most admirable men. They did not attack the landed interest

18

for the sake of personal gain, nor yet in the hope of office or of honors. They were nobly stirred by the sight of poverty, filth, and ignorance. They longed for a better world. And yet, something—what could it be?—something a little drab, and more than a little uninspiring, could be discerned in their characters. They were not utilitarians, they had moved far beyond that unworkable philosophy; but the utilitarian stain had somehow or other touched them. Once, confronted on an Eastern tour with all the mystery of the Pyramids, Cobden could not restrain his vexation. One third of the labor employed there, he exclaimed, could have built a much more useful object—the Plymouth breakwater! Bright, it is true, was cast in a more poetic mold; he would not have gazed upon those singular monuments unmoved. He would have used them to adorn his speeches; and as he thundered against the regulation of working hours by Act of Parliament—a subject upon which, as a textile manufacturer, he was particularly touchy—the Pharaohs would have provided some very ornamental passages. For Bright was a most eloquent man. His images, culled sometimes from the classics, but more often from the Bible, and most sonorously uttered, filled his hearers with delight. Even in the most obstinate quarters, his powers of speech did not fail him. He was a Quaker, and for a Quaker to enter into politics was a most unusual and undesirable thing. At last he arose in meeting to explain his activity in the Anti-Corn Law League; he did not mention the League by name—that would never have done—but the tenor of his argument was unmistakable, and he brought all his extraordinary powers of persuasion to bear upon it. And then a quite unprecedented event took place. As he sat down, a faint scratching noise disturbed the customary silence of that assembly. The Friends were applauding!

For all their command of imagery, however, Bright's speeches were wanting in a most important respect. They took little or no account of two vital factors in the progress of the world—they paid scant attention to Tomorrow and almost none at all to Yesterday. Both he and Cobden believed that unrestricted competition would solve everything—that it would eliminate unemployment, warfare, poverty, gentry, collective bargaining, and anything else of which their philosophy did not dream. For theirs was a middle class philosophy, and they gloried in it: their integrity, their courage, their personal fortunes even, were freely given to its furtherance. Did it ever occur to them that they were expending these treasures on behalf of a rising and acquisitive class of far less selfless men than they? Undoubtedly it did: but the humane motive and the profit motive were so subtly blended in their intellectual chemistries that such a consideration did not disturb them in the least.

Peel, on the other hand, though he had come to agree with the arguments of the League, did not relish even a temporary alliance with its leaders. His sense of responsibility was very strong; but so, too, were his social prejudices. He liked the cause, he disliked the connection. Even his financial shrewdness might not have sufficed to urge him onward, if two of the deepest motives in his guarded character—a love of fame, a love of his fellow man—had not made his decisions for him: and of these his enemies were afterwards able to recognize only the first. Alarm, exhilaration, foreboding—he could hardly tell one from another; he could only wait for his opportunity with such outward composure as he could muster. In 1845, the opportunity presented itself in a humble and fateful shape. In the autumn of that year, there was a potato disease.

All through the preceding summer it had rained; and as it became clear that a ruined harvest was to be the consequence, Peel's strange excitement communicated itself to his Cabinet. "I know not," said Sir James Graham, the Home Secretary, "that the state of affairs is exactly sound when Ministers are driven to study the barometer with so much anxiety." Sir James believed that the weather, and all that it portended, was best left to Providence. Peel believed in Providence, too; and he could not help seeing that in this instance—regrettable, indeed horrible, though the immediate outcome might be—Providence was on his side. A ruined harvest; and then a potato sickness! The prospects for England were grim, but for Ireland—where 4,000,000 people subsisted entirely on potatoes—they were quite appalling: who, in such circumstances, would dare oppose the opening of the ports to foreign grain? Who indeed? He gazed at the stolid Tories on the benches behind him; his eyes roved over the too bland countenances of the Whig opposition: he was not reassured. Between October 31 and November 6, he held three Cabinets. "Four Cabinets in one week!" exclaimed Disraeli's Lord Roehampton, with the pardonable exaggeration of a fictional character. "The Government must be sicker than the potatoes." A brilliant strategist, Peel did not at first suggest a total repeal of the Corn Laws; what he had in mind, he said, was a gradual reduction of the duties until, in some ten years, the Trade should be free. By December 2, all the Cabinet but Lord Aberdeen, Sidney Herbert, and Sir James Graham had refused to countenance such a step. Peel, therefore, resigned: it was the first move in his campaign.

The attitude of the Whig leaders towards repeal of the Corn Laws was somewhat ambiguous. On the whole they approved of it—as a general principle; but general principles, in the world of politics, are apt to be inconvenient when one attempts to give them a practical application. The Whigs had neither the power nor the inclination to undertake repeal on their own responsibility; on the other hand, they did not dare to oppose it. They were now expected to form a Government, and their anxiety was much increased by the singular actions of their leader in the House of Commons, Lord John Russell. Lord John, a prosaic elf, had a small and sickly body, a high thin voice, and a remarkably headstrong character. Many of his political views were founded upon an enthusiastic misunderstanding of the Revolution of 1688; and when, on November 22, without consulting anyone, he wrote a letter to his constituents, advocating total repeal, he did so for two somewhat contradictory reasons: he believed that a rich and powerful aristocracy was essential to the well-being of the country; he was convinced that English aristocracy could remain rich and powerful, but only by not opposing the wishes of the people. Had anyone asked him to elaborate upon these two propositions, he would undoubtedly have taken refuge in the remote thickets of the Revolution of 1688, where it would have been a waste of time to follow him. Meanwhile, the letter of November 22 had been published; it seemed to commit the Whigs to repeal; and now that the Queen had called upon Lord John to form a Government what, exactly, did Lord John propose to do? Lord John was not abashed; he began the task of assembling a Cabinet; and almost immediately a curious and convenient difficulty arose. Earl Grey refused to serve if Lord Palmerston were to become

Foreign Secretary; Lord Palmerston maintained that no other office would suit him. It is quite possible that some plot was on foot to get rid of Palmerston—who was not loved by the Whig grandees—with the bribe of an English peerage and the leadership in the Lords; but no one who knew him could have expected him to swallow such a bait; and he did not. His misunderstanding with Earl Grey, however, still seems like a very obvious plot . . . to extract the Whigs from their dilemma. At any rate, Lord John declared that he could not form a Cabinet: with a sigh of relief, and in the words of Mr. Disraeli, he handed back "the poisoned chalice" to Sir Robert.

Yet how true it is that one man's poison is another man's meat! Sir Robert seized the bitter draught and drained it with avidity. His appointment with destiny was at hand, and, like any other man in a lesser but analogous situation, he wished to keep it in his best clothes. Declaring that the Queen's government must be carried on, he imposed upon his own schemes and ambitions the austere but attractive colors of self-sacrifice. The Duke of Wellington was not entirely taken in —he accused the Prime Minister of being "in a damned fright"; but here the conqueror of Napoleon seems, in a rather unsoldierly fashion, not to have distinguished between timidity and temerity. The time had come for Peel to break with the Tories; some of his more enlightened followers saw eye to eye with him; and a government was easily formed, with Mr. Gladstone (after an affecting interview) taking the place of Lord Stanley.

A silence had followed upon Sir Robert's action. Was it a silence of awe, or of cogitation? At any rate, the debates had been languid, and it almost seemed as if Peel's great Free

Trade measure, his Corn and Customs Bill, was to pass through the Commons with very little disturbance. And then, on January 22, 1846, up rose Benjamin Disraeli, with his odd clothes, his flat contemptuous voice, his lizard eyes, his impassive, implacable countenance. Peel knew that he need expect little kindness from that quarter although he had said that he was prepared to leave his actions to the judgment of posterity. "Sir, posterity is a most limited assembly," said Mr. Disraeli; and he went on to doubt very much that Peel would reach it. He may be said to have entertained this doubt since the year 1841, when he had written to Peel, asking for a place in the Government, and had received a glacial and negative reply. As for Disraeli's opinions upon the relative value of free trade and protection, or upon the breaking of pledges, they were not, as some supposed, entirely opportunistic; but they certainly ranked second to his desire for revenge. And when revenge might bring with it some political advancement, Disraeli was the last man to deny himself its pleasures. For months he had suspected that Peel was unsound on the Corn Laws, and now that the Prime Minister had come right out into the open, Disraeli turned upon him with a venomous brilliance which evoked, even from those who most agreed with it, an odd mixture of delight and distaste.

For indeed he was hardly the man one would have expected to find as spokesman for the landed interest. The Whigs listened with approval, they were not so fond of free trade themselves, but with relief that he was not one of them. The Tories for the most part could hardly abide the fellow. And yet—and yet—who else could deal so ruthlessly with the traitor Peel? Oh, yes, it was Disraeli's chance. He was past forty —an ageing, rococo dandy, with a distinct flair for the composition of political novels. He had succeeded, after a fashion, in London Society. He had dined in many of the best houses: kings had extended their hands to him, not perhaps the best kings, but kings none the less. Society could be won over, if the women were on your side; and women were always on Mr. Disraeli's side. But the House of Commons, alas, did not as yet contain women; and there Mr. Disraeli, for all his brilliance, was not a success.

He knew, even while they roared with laughter at what Mr. Greville called his "smart, Israelitish philippics," that the Tories were still, obscurely, on Peel's side. They despised his tormentor, he had neither birth nor wealth to recommend him; yet how much more did the strange, detached creature despise *them!* He knew that if he succeeded now, he would end as their master. He knew, too, more than any man in that assembly, what quivering nerves Peel hid behind his frigid demeanor; and even while he stung his victim, he pitied him. At once serpent and dove, charlatan and genius, the future Earl of Beaconsfield laid down in those speeches the frail foundations of his preposterous career: realizing, none better, how frail they were. And then other emotions would assert themselves. The loud Tory benches, urging him on against their own leader, were they, after all, so very stupid? Did they not represent the flower of England? And was he not playing a part that even his own novels would hardly have dared to create? To live out, to exceed one's own fictions; to pursue one's day-dreams from print into politics; to stand forth as the alien champion of an old nobility—what more could one ask? With a characteristic gesture, he drew out his handkerchief; his sentences came to their beautiful, their deadly climax; there was a great cheer behind him: and Mr.

Disraeli tasted, before he entered once again the world of reality, the ultimate pleasures of the world of illusion.

To the end of his life Disraeli maintained that Peel's offense lay, not so much in abolishing the Corn Laws, as in breaking his own party; and here the more conventional Tories were disposed to agree with him. The issues were momentous: on one side loomed starvation, on the other the protection of agriculture; surely a humane man could not hesitate in his choice. Ah, but a man had his honor to consider as well as his humanity; and the Tories salved their consciences by maintaining, over and over again, that they were pledged to protection. The excuse was a poor one; but it carried weight in those days, for in those days a party was not an obedient machine. It was a most complex entity. Some of its members voted in obedience to the commands of great landowners, some followed their ambition into the lobbies, some pursued their conscience; a personal dispute, a chance debate, could effect the most startling realignments within its ranks. Wavering, shifting, constantly on the edge of dissolution, it none the less maintained itself by a common agreement on one or two principles. Such a principle, with the Tories, was the protection of agriculture; and when Peel deserted this principle, taking the more enlightened of his followers with him, he left behind him a leaderless and discordant mob. A party, thus broken, did not easily mend: and years, indeed decades, passed before the Tories recovered from the blow that Peel had dealt them.

It was a righteous blow, dealt in the name of the common people; and Peel did not falter. He knew that the Whigs, the radicals, and his own small following among the Tories, could muster enough votes to pass repeal: but before that could come to pass, he had much to endure. His flushed face buried in his hands, he listened in agony to the meanest insults, the vilest insinuations. Once, in his exasperation, he threatened Disraeli with the production of that unfortunate letter in which "Dizzy" had asked for office in 1841; and his adversary cringed. Once he was only just restrained from challenging Lord George Bentinck to a duel. The Whigs observed all this with pleasure, for their hour of triumph was very close. One or two of them, it is true—Lord Melbourne, for instance—declared for protection; while Lord Palmerston had some hopes of forming a Whig-Tory coalition around the unworthy banner of a small fixed duty. Lord Melbourne, however, was sinking into imbecility; besides, he was in the Lords. Lord Palmerston was not in the Lords, but his schemes depended, in an odd and intricate manner, upon the goodwill of Prince Albert and of King Louis Philippe, which neither of these eminent personages was prepared to extend. The Tories, meanwhile, proposed that a Coercion Bill for Ireland should be passed before the House dealt with corn; they suggested that six months hence the House might, perhaps, go into committee on the Government's proposals. But in vain. With consummate skill and extraordinary courage, the Prime Minister held on his way.

At length, on May 15, the Corn and Customs Bill passed its third reading in the Commons with a majority of 98. Would the House of Lords dare to veto it? Their lordships were restless, but they knew that the feelings of the country were with Peel, and their experiences in the days of the Reform Bill had given them a certain distaste for running counter to the feelings of the country. Besides, the Duke of Wellington was preparing to support the Prime Minister, for the Duke had, politically speaking, one progressive virtue—he knew when to retreat. The Lords contented themselves, therefore, with hurling some of their choicest epithets at that venerable head, epithets which the Duke—his hat over his eyes—received with equanimity, since he was almost stone-deaf.

IV

The repeal of the Corn Laws, strange to say, had little or no effect upon agriculture until, in the late '60's, improvements in transportation brought with them a deluge of American wheat. Even then, the landlords who owned urban property or extracted royalties from mines were not in the least disturbed. On the other hand, it was no longer necessary, in years of bad harvests, for the people of England to go short of bread: to this extent, the landlords had been defeated. The defeat seemed, in a most curious way, to touch their consciences; it was an odd thing to see protectionists voting for factory legislation and to hear them talking about the condition of the working classes. Yet it was around factory legislation, and all that it meant, that the battle continued to rage. A cynic might, perhaps, have wondered just how tender was the protectionist conscience; might have inquired whether the erstwhile foes of cheap bread were not, after all, out for nothing more than revenge. . . .

Revenge! It was pleasant enough, as one discussed the possibility of governmental regulation of the hours of labor, or cast a sidelong smile at the infant Trade Unions, to realize that one was hurting Capital. But first of all, there was Peel to be dealt with. And so it came about that at the very time when the House of Lords was preparing to pass his Corn and Customs Bill, the House of Commons was getting ready to throw out his Coercion Bill. Peel's career, so full of contradictions, was not unfittingly sealed by this ominous coincidence. The Coercion Bill for Ireland was a most unworthy measure. The repeal of the Corn Laws, though it had been provoked by the alarming condition of the Irish, was not, after all, to do very much for those most unhappy people. Politics and economics were frequently at cross purposes in the '40's. It was one thing to open the ports to foreign grain; it was quite another to get that grain into the stomachs of the Irish. Indeed, the movement was in a reverse direction; and while Irish corn poured into the insatiable harbors of England, all that came back in return was maize—Peel's brimstone, the Irish called it—a not very satisfying diet. The Irish dragged their fainting bodies up and down the grim length of a number of remarkably pointless relief projects; others allowed themselves to be herded into plague-ridden emigrant ships, and fled the starving land; others still, even less fortunate, leaned upon the railings outside the poor-houses, and died. Yet the spirit of Ireland is hard to break; and even in the very beginning of this horrible process, the country was in rebellion. And all that Peel could do was to reply to violence with worse violence, and answer despair with repression.

Oh, yes, the Coercion Bill was an unworthy measure. It was one of the most singular of Peel's limitations that his sympathies did not seem to extend beyond the borders of England. In his attitude towards Ireland he seemed instinctively to side with the Anglo-Irish, the Protestant Ascendancy, the absentee landlords—an unlovely crew. But if the measure was unworthy, how much more so was the opposition to it!

The Whigs and the radicals had no choice; but why were the Tory protectionists, who cared not a fig for Ireland, voting against the Bill? Why, indeed? On June 25, the most desperate of them [1] swept in triumph into the hostile lobby; the Bill was thrown out by a majority of 73; and Peel's downfall was accomplished.

It was his great moment, and he lived up to it. On June 29, he made his speech of resignation. Reviewing once again all the circumstances and motives that had brought about the repeal of the Corn Laws, he said that the name chiefly to be associated with that event was the name of Richard Cobden. It was at once apparent that he had given up all thought of ever again leading the Tory party; those two words—"Richard Cobden"—had sealed his decision in the most public, the most irrevocable fashion. And something else was apparent, too—something very much less to the protectionists' taste. For behind Richard Cobden there crouched, in mysterious, extra-parliamentary shadow, a menacing host—the manufacturers, the radicals, the middle class. Step by step they had advanced; and now they ringed Parliament about, half-seen, but soon to emerge in all the plenitude of their power. Theirs was the victory; it was with *them* that Peel had allied himself!

And so at last, after many a preliminary fanfare, many a stop and start, the curtain had been drawn up upon the drama of Victorian England. Peel himself spoke the prologue in that speech of resignation; and these were its last words. "In relinquishing power, I shall leave a name severely censured by many who, on public grounds, deeply regret the severance of party ties . . . I shall leave a name execrated by every mo-

---

[1] One hundred, under Lord Chandos, voted for Peel, much as it hurt them; eighty others abstained from voting at all.

nopolist. . . . But it may be that I shall leave a name sometimes remembered with expressions of goodwill in the abodes
of those whose lot it is to labour, and to earn their bread by
the sweat of their brow, when they shall recruit their exhausted strength with abundant and untaxed food, the sweeter
because it is no longer leavened by a sense of injustice."

These words created a most unfavorable impression even
in friendly quarters. The Queen was upset, Prince Albert
raised his eyebrows, and even Mr. Gladstone could only
react with a sentence that was, for him, the verbal equivalent
of a low whistle. His leader, he said, "like some smaller men"
was "very sensible of the sweetness of the cheers of opponents." Sir Robert's peroration does not seem, today, to be
very excessive. It is what one might expect from a Tory who
was also a great exponent of bourgeois finance, a paternalist
who had allied himself with the champions of *laisser-faire*—
in short, from a man who was simply the instrument whereby
was effected a quite inevitable change in economic power.
And yet, perhaps—considering the character of the man and
the character of the times—there is something in it from which
the Queen and Prince Albert and Mr. Gladstone might well
have recoiled. As one examines once again those ponderous
and formal phrases, it almost seems as if—indistinctly and only
for a moment—Sir Robert was looking into a distant future
where neither his late friends nor even his new allies would
have any place at all.

V

The followers of Peel remained for years in a high-minded
indecision until, after the death of Palmerston and the end of

Whig domination, their survivors were absorbed into the Liberals. Peel himself was soon to disappear. On June 29, 1850, he was thrown from his horse, and, after lingering for two days in agony, died. It is said that a gentleman who was also riding in the park on that fatal morning, and who recognized Peel's hireling for a dangerous beast, almost rode up to warn him, but could not bring himself to face that icy hauteur.

There was much perturbation in many quarters. Lord Londonderry left a morning fête at Rosebank, where his friends were sipping ices and his wife was making tea from a suite of golden pots and kettles, and galloped off to London. The Duke of Wellington, in great distress, remarked that Peel had never told a deliberate lie. The Queen, the Prince, the begging-letter writers, even his enemies in the Commons—they all gave vent to suitable expressions of grief. But there was one tribute which even the recipient himself, it may be, would not have expected. When the news of his death was made known, poor men wept aloud for him in the streets of London.

Chapter One

THE RESPECTABLE MONARCHY

TO HAVE been born in the year 1841, before the events narrated in the previous chapter had taken place, was to have been born into a world that still hovered indecisively between the eighteenth and the nineteenth centuries; a world that possessed, as its portraits and its literature bear witness, a pleasant opulence of outline. It was an upper class world. The strong language of the elder generation, to whom the Almighty was little more than an expletive, recalled those days, before the Reform Bill, when the nobility and gentry of England had seemed to possess both the earth and the heavens above it. Nor had those days altogether departed.

The speed of life, it is true, was already beginning to increase as it had not increased since the days of the Caesars: the railway and the machine were responsible for that, and the upper classes for the most part regarded these innovations with alarm. An instinct, deeper than reason, warned them that innovations of any sort boded them no good. Dr. Arnold might contend that the rural landscapes through which the railway passed would have a salutary moral effect upon the traveler; such considerations, though weighty, did not reassure the owners of the rural landscapes who, seeing visions

33

of "the loco-motive Monster, navigated by a tail of smoke and sulphur, coming thro' every man's grounds," had for years done their best to cripple the Monster in Parliament. As for machinery, no doubt a certain class of persons did well out of it, while yet another class of persons, more numerous and even more obscure, were plunged by it into an existence so horrible to contemplate that (unless one were a Lord Ashley—and was he not, perhaps, a *little* unbalanced?) one simply did not contemplate it at all.

In an aristocratic society, however, the ruling class lives very close to the people. In 1841 the intervening walls were high, but they were thin; could they resist the pressure of what, in those days, was still called the Mob? The Mob, indeed, ever since the Reform Bill riots of 1831-2, in fact ever since the French Revolution, had haunted the imagination of the upper classes of England. No politically powerful middle class, no intricate administrative system came between; and though there was evidence enough that the former would soon arrive and bring the latter with it, the question remained whether these undesirable allies would arrive in time. It was, therefore, an indecisive world; nor did its indecisions remain merely in the realm of social behavior; they were deeply rooted in the realm of thought and of conscience. The rationalists and the utilitarians had not been difficult to dismiss; they were just ill-bred people with notions. But what of the Anti-Corn Law League; and what of Chartism? However pertinaciously they might chatter and laugh and pray, the upper classes of England were uneasily aware of the discontent and misery upon which their world was founded. The contagion reached them, often enough, in the most significant, the humblest forms—and in the highest places. The young Queen's apartments in Buckingham Palace, for instance, were ventilated from the common sewer. In these apartments, into such a world, was born, on November 9, 1841, a new Prince of Wales.

II

Good Archbishop Howley, hastening up from Lambeth, an impressive if anxious figure in his wig and his lawn sleeves, heard the joy-bells pealing and knew that he had arrived too late. The little prince had entered life with an excessive punctuality that was to remain in after life one of his besetting virtues; even Sir Robert Peel, the new Prime Minister, had arrived only just in time to be present at the birth.

It was a gray morning. London, whose inhabitants were rarely quite well in those days, brooded over its poisonous river. But the bells made a cheerful sound, and as they called from belfry to belfry, they had a cheerful effect. It was hard not to rejoice in the news of a birth, and the birth of a prince had a symbolic significance; it evoked the most archaic and irrational response from the poor; it suggested that England herself was fruitful. In a year of wretched crops, dear bread, and imminent starvation, a suggestion of this sort, though illusory, was not inopportune. As the news passed upwards it produced, naturally enough, reactions of a more civilized description. The Mayor of Chester, for example, was entitled to a baronetcy on the birth of a Prince of Wales, who was also Earl of Chester; but there had been a change of mayors on the 9th, and in consequence there were two potential baronets, who disputed their claims with the utmost bitterness. There had also been a change of guard at St. James's Palace just three minutes before the birth; and the question whether the officer of the old guard or the officer of the new guard should receive the customary promotion provoked an obscure and intricate military debate. Higher still, in the inmost recesses of the palace itself, the Baroness Lehzen, the Queen's old governess, was sorely perplexed. She was a loyal subject—a devoted, an adoring companion—an adviser even, the extent of whose powers has never been gauged. She had not kept her place about the Queen unchallenged: many a battle, full of whispers and lifted eyebrows and deadly silences and the secretive pulling of strings, had been fought in the past against those who sought to dislodge her. Sir John Conroy—Lady Flora Hastings—the Queen's own mother, the Duchess of Kent—all these enemies had been routed; but against a cradle she could not contend. The birth of a Princess Royal in 1840 had shaken her strange authority; and now the birth of a Prince of Wales had quite undermined it. She was a shrewd woman: she knew that forces more powerful than any she had encountered before were moving against her.

The arrival of an heir had, in fact, done much to strengthen the ambiguous position of a singular personage—the infant's father, Prince Albert of Saxe-Coburg-Gotha. The early circumstances of his marriage are all too familiar—the handsome, awkward stripling, younger son of an unimportant German duke, with a loving wife who did not confide in him, and an adopted country that he could not understand. The appalling tedium of Victoria's court bored him to distraction —he longed for warmth, for long happy conversations on erudite topics, for understanding: the prickly manners of a German princeling restrained him from finding such warmth as, even in those cold surroundings, might have been his had he gone a little out of his way to seek it. He was not disturbed by the fact, the ill-concealed fact, that fine ladies and great gentlemen looked at him askance: this was merely the insignificant manifestation of a far, far deeper maladjustment. What could it be? In spite of his chilly manners, he was eager, he was enthusiastic; and eagerness and enthusiasm had now, after a century of subtle repression, once more come into their own. The up-to-date early Victorian young gentleman —with his scented hair, his resplendent waistcoats and flashing jewelry, his arrogance, his sensitivity, his readiness at any moment to point a moral or to preach a sermon—did not, it is true, find his way into the English court. Along with scholars and scientists, Victoria had "no fancy to encourage such people"; but even had they been privileged to meet him, it is doubtful if they would have understood Albert or he them. In a somewhat excessive period, he was excessively German. The floods of tears which he shed at his father's death gave his secretary Anson a sick headache; his sudden high spirits, his loud jokes, his unrestrained appetite astonished rather than pleased the royal governess, Lady Lyttleton. And Anson and Lady Lyttleton were very fond of him.

And yet to be excessively German, though a formidable handicap, was not in itself enough to account for the strange solitude of the Queen's young husband. It seemed as though his German blood and training merely served to accentuate some more fundamental and more individual complex. Those who had most to do with him, with whom he was most at ease, confessed themselves baffled. "Nobody but the organ," wrote one affectionate and exasperated observer, "knows what is *in him*." He was able, intelligent, versatile; though he lacked humor, he did not want for imagination: yet—it was difficult to say just how it happened—at the very moment when one seemed to be closest to him, joking or laughing, his essential being, cool and melancholy, would glide away. Only at the organ perhaps—he called it the noblest of instruments and played it with skill—lonely and absorbed, did he express his inmost aspirations. To be good—to do good! It was a princely ambition, no doubt—but was it human? and, even if human, was it the sort of ambition to cherish in England, of all places? Those who caught a glimpse of him at his music, the heavy body stooping in strange ecstasy over the keys, may well have asked themselves whether this odd youth would not have been happier among the trivialities of a provincial German court. They would never have guessed that the man at whom they were looking was eventually to become one of the leading statesmen of Europe.

In 1841, all this began to change. It was not that the Prince grew more accessible: if anything, his stiffness increased. It was rather that his inmost cravings had found, at last, some food with which to satisfy themselves. His wife was now prepared to give him, not merely her love—he had always had that—but her confidence. Those influences which had softly counteracted his own were on the wane. Lehzen was soon to go—Lord Melbourne had already gone, and in his place, as Prime Minister, was Sir Robert Peel, whom the Queen could scarcely abide, and with whom the Prince had much in common. Melbourne, who had once been almost a second father to Victoria, could not refrain during his first few months out of office, from corresponding with her on matters of an official kind; but this unconstitutional behavior did not last very long; and in the course of time his communications assumed a wistful, harmless character. "As Lord Melbourne drove down from the Park on Saturday evening last to dine with his sister, he could see clearly into your Majesty's room, so as to be able to distinguish the pictures, tables, etc., the candles being brightly lit and the curtains not drawn. Your Majesty was just setting off for the Opera." The Prince may be forgiven if, when Victoria handed him this to read, he permitted himself a faint smile of satisfaction. The symbolism, if unconsciously selected, was very appropriate; Lord Melbourne could see into her Majesty's room, but only from the outside; and as he drove by in his carriage, he was even then driving further and further out of her life.

And so the long conversations, the innumerable letters, the solemn memoranda of Baron Stockmar were, in the end, to take effect. The dyspeptic baron, like a portable conscience, had been handed on from King Leopold of the Belgians to Queen Victoria. He had then attached himself to Leopold's nephew: for many months he had not strayed far from Albert's side. He touched consistently upon one theme—the theme of Duty; he played upon it an infinitude of variations: and Albert, though he listened and agreed, though he began to take an interest in politics and to compose long memoranda on foreign affairs, could not but ask himself what point there was in having a Duty to perform if no one—not even his own wife—wished him to perform it. Surely the baron was agitating himself in vain. But the baron's agitations resembled those of a divining rod. He had sensed, hidden deep in the young soil, the springs of a boundless ambition. Albert was persistent, Victoria was passionately in love: the baron knew how it would end. And he was right. When Melbourne went out of office, it was not the Queen—it was the Prince—who conducted, with triumphant tact, certain delicate and intricate conversations with Melbourne's successor. Power was his; he tasted it with relish; he began to demand, and to obtain, more and more.

Encouraged by Stockmar, he had for some time occupied his mind with hopes and speculations of a high but peculiar description. From the infinite gradations of mankind, two distinct classes, it would appear, emerged—the human and the royal. Of the former not too much was to be hoped; and the little hope there was depended, to a great extent, upon the exertions of the latter. Not that the Prince was so optimistic—indeed, he was nothing of the sort—as to derive any comfort from the state of contemporary royalty. In Russia, at Naples, in the scandals of Bavaria, in the fearful mismanagement of the Papal States, there was much to dissatisfy an upholder of the monarchical system. The Prince was no materialist; he believed that all this sort of thing could be swept away, not by the forces of history, manifesting themselves in the irrational impulses of human beings and the blind precision of economic law, but by the force of an idea. Let royal personages be truthful, courageous, industrious, intelligent, indifferent alike to popular acclaim and personal interest, and the world would proceed to get better. His uncle had already set an example in Belgium; his wife and himself would ignite, in England, a similar candle; and slowly but surely the light would spread. It would of course be a modern illumination; Albert believed in constitutional government; but no constitution had yet been able to define exactly the nature and extent of the royal prerogative. It only remained for royalty to become, as far as was possible, perfect. To this task Albert proposed to apply himself for the rest of his life; and he was determined that his infant son should follow in his footsteps.

Victoria endorsed this program with an emphasis, a lack of reticence, that were among her most endearing characteristics. She prayed that the Prince of Wales might resemble his "angelic, dearest father in *every, every* respect, both in body and mind"; and submitted this prayer to Lord Melbourne. Melbourne's reply was equally typical. Mingling the complaisance of a courtier with the freedom of an old friend, who was also a Whig grandee, he replied that "the character depends much upon the race, and on both sides he has a good chance." A good chance! Perhaps that was just Lord Melbourne's casual way of putting things. And yet around the infant's cradle there hovered, unbidden but inexorable, the thought of those appalling old men, his great-uncles, the scandalous sons of George III. How dreadful if he should come to resemble *them!* Once more, she scanned her son's features. The nose, perhaps, was a little too large; but what lovely blue eyes he had, what a pretty little mouth! No, "Albert Junior," as she sometimes called the little Albert Edward, was no Hanoverian. Stockmar, her ladies, everybody, could detect in the little creature's countenance a striking resemblance to that of his father.

In this, as it turned out, they were incorrect.

The royal family, increased every year by yet another child, led a retired existence. Fashion and frivolity whirled away into remoter and remoter distances, never to return. The Queen and Prince Albert, like two figurines in those diminishing perspectives, seem to have ascended to a shelf beyond the reach of the society of their time and the historian of ours.

State business, domestic cares absorbed them; and though an unrelaxed etiquette defended them from the outer world, the simplicity of their private lives might almost have been called middle class.

Almost, but not quite. That exceedingly gifted artist, Winterhalter, who traveled the courts of Europe endowing royal personages with a beauty that they did not always possess, has made the growing family bloom with majesty, in a rich setting of fat fruits and heavy draperies. And there were times when the domestic scene was invaded by large figures from a vanishing epoch and Windsor put on its glories for a visiting king or emperor. "The children are much admired by the *Sovereigns*," Victoria wrote to her uncle Leopold "(how *grand* this sounds!)." Little Bertie was not too young to share his parents' alarm at the presence of the Czar Nicholas, who showed the whites of his eyes in a most terrifying manner. To be sure, his visit was most complimentary, he bestowed the Grand Cross of St. Andrew on the little prince, he discovered in Albert's features "tant de noblesse et de bonté réunies": but one was not sorry to see him go. Others were more congenial: the elderly King of Holland, who had lost all his front teeth; the kind King of Saxony; and the good King of the French, with his funny pear-shaped head, his unpretentious manners, and all the odd instructions one had to follow about his food and his bed-time! The children loved him, and when he left he sent little Bertie a gun, "un très modeste fusil de munition adopté à sa taille et d'un genre à supporter tous les accidents que l'enfance aime à infliger à ses joujoux." What a dear, dear old man!

The visitors departed, the splendors were put away, and life flowed easily back into the accustomed channel—a quiet stream, murmuring and chattering between its stiff, steep banks. The royal family moved from London to Windsor, from Windsor to the new home at Osborne, from Osborne to London. In the early years there were not many divergences from this course—a visit to the Royal Pavilion at Brighton, of which the Queen disapproved, for its riotous interiors reminded her dimly of her gross uncle George; a journey by way of Wales to Scotland; a day or two with the Duke of Wellington at Walmer Castle, where the November winds, shrieking at the ramshackle doors and windows, seemed to mock the stately mummeries that the Duke maintained within. On such occasions, they would sometimes be almost mobbed by the Queen's subjects before they reached their destination. Strange people crowded about the carriages, people not otherwise encountered, those exuberant outcasts—the early Victorian poor. The royal party gazed at these apparitions with affection, astonishment, and fear, as though they were a parcel of innocent savages, who had somehow or other acquired the English tongue. "Well done! That's right, old girl!" they shouted, when Lady Lyttleton, the royal governess, ordered the Prince of Wales to be held up. It was a most unusual experience. But the voices receded, the outer world, social or unsocial, fell away; and in the evenings, in the blessed interval before dinner, the Prince would read aloud from Hallam's *Constitutional History* or, in a lighter mood, from the *Memoirs* of St. Simon; and the little Queen at her cross-stitch, straining her ears so as not to miss a word, would forget that she had once found the novels of George Sand *"dreadfully* interesting."

The children, naturally enough, assumed the coloration of their surroundings. They were obedient and plainly dressed.

Mrs. Gladstone, a relative of Lady Lyttleton's, visited the royal nurseries from time to time, and was very favorably impressed. The Princess Royal was not exactly pretty, but very engaging; and though the Prince of Wales was small for his years, and his head not well-shaped, he had the nicest manners. The Queen, Mrs. Gladstone observed, was a little touchy about his size. "The Prince is the tallest of the two," she exclaimed, in her most peremptory and ungrammatical manner, when little Agnes Gladstone, standing beside the heir to the throne, seemed to be measuring her height against his.

Height, alas, was not the only subject upon which the Queen was inclined to criticize her son. He was backward. He could not acquire a good English accent—he never *did* acquire a good English accent; his mind was not, like his elder sister's, quick; even when he was six years old and should have known better, he expressed himself in a babyish fashion. "Pray, Mamma," he said, one day out driving, "is not a pink the female of a carnation?" and the shouts of laughter—and it was not indulgent laughter—that greeted this artless question made him hang his head in shame. Yet, even if he had been brilliantly endowed with intellect, it is doubtful, it is even improbable, that his parents would have been satisfied. A harsh but inevitable shadow obscured their affection for him. Prince Albert had already become, in everything but name, the King of England: and with tireless persistence he strove to realize, in his own person, his remarkable ideal of monarchy. To combine the irresponsibility of the Crown with the powers of a responsible minister, to have one's cake and to eat it too! Such were Albert's dreams. Yet he could never be King: should the Queen die first, his son would supplant him, and *then*, he told his brother Ernest, he would give everything up and retire from public life. The ambitious husband, the adoring wife would have been something more than human if, under these circumstances, they had not regarded their first-born son with a certain animosity. And they were both human, very human indeed. Besides, if the boy were to grow up into an idle or careless fellow, the whole wonderful concept of royalty that Albert and Stockmar had labored to incarnate, would melt into thin air. Forced, as he was, to bear the double burden of his father's jealousy and his father's ambitions, there was not much chance of a peaceful existence for the young Prince of Wales. When the other children acted Thomson's *Seasons* for their parents with great enjoyment, little Bertie, in his white beard and his cloak with imitation icicles, went through his paces with a discomfort not entirely due to his costume: he knew perfectly well that of all the performances, *his* alone was certain to be criticized. There was no escape . . . unless, in some way, Europe itself should decide that it could manage very well without the assistance of royalty.

In the year 1848 a series of remarkable events seemed, for a very brief while, to be pointing to just such a decision.

III

The Queen could only hope, she told her uncle Leopold, early in 1848, that her children would grow up, "fit for whatever *station* they may be placed in—*high or low*. This," she added, "I never thought of before, but I *do* always now." The cause of these alarming speculations was something that could

45

be characterized as miraculous or monstrous, according to one's point of view. For suddenly, like a rain-storm in a fountainless desert, like the infusion of springtime into some remote Arctic, public opinion—exuberant and riotous—was loose in Europe. It shouted around the palaces of that abused continent until their inhabitants shuddered and fled. Europe had known other revolutions since the time when, at the Congress of Vienna in 1815, a complicated system of treaties had condemned its peoples to meditate, in cheerless stagnation, upon the sin of having had a past: but no revolution had been so general and vigorous as this.

The fierce antagonisms that had arisen around the repeal of the Corn Laws in 1846; the angry murmurs of the French press in that year; the victory which—owing to the masterful tactics of Lord Palmerston—the twelve liberal cantons of Switzerland won over the seven conservative cantons and their allies in the courts of Europe—these were signs, for those who cared to read them, of the approaching storm. More significant still was the election, in 1846, of a liberal Pope—for such, during the first two years of his reign, Pius IX appeared to be. The reforms that he instituted in the Papal States were of the mildest kind; but that he should have instituted reforms of any kind at all was astonishing; and very soon his name was upon everybody's lips. Pius was at first extremely delighted; he was at last extremely alarmed. A little something, he had thought—an amnesty for the offenders who rotted in the papal dungeons, a slight modification in the censorship of the press and in the ecclesiastical nature of his government, the release of the Jews from the ghetto in Rome—would show that he was not entirely unaware of the temporal needs of his subjects. More he had never intended. He had hoped, in short, to light a bonfire—a gay, small illumination; he discovered, too late, that he had ignited a forest. By 1848, the whole land had caught fire. In January, the citizens of Palermo arose against the hideous misrule of King Ferdinand of the Two Sicilies. In early February, the Grand Duke of Tuscany signed a constitution which, for a time at least, appeased his subjects in Florence and Leghorn; and Charles Albert of Sardinia prepared to follow his example. Milan revolted in March; the Austrians were driven from Venice; the rulers of Parma and Modena vanished. This was more than the Holy Father had bargained for; and when, in November, the exhilarated citizens of Rome first murdered his chief minister and then advanced upon his own palace, Pius IX decided that he had had enough of reform. He fled to Gaeta across the border, and there consoled himself as best he could with the ambiguous companionship of King Ferdinand, who had temporarily gone to ground in this far corner of his kingdom.

The governments of Europe were, it seems, taken by surprise. Even King Leopold of the Belgians, who prided himself upon being exceptionally well informed, could hardly believe his eyes when, in February, he read the news about the signing of the constitution in Tuscany. Oddly enough, he was horrified. He was a constitutional monarch; for seventeen years he had devoted himself to the task of becoming more and more constitutional every day; but constitutions, he felt, were designed, perhaps by providence itself, for the display of royal virtue. They were not to be construed as expressions of the popular will. "The human race is a *sad* creation," he wrote to Victoria, "and I trust the other planets are better organised." But worse was to follow. By the end of February, there had arisen in Paris a united opposition to the government of his venerable father-in-law, King Louis Philippe. That the French king and his ministers had come to resemble, more and more, the directing board of a rather dubious concern was a fact which, though true, counted less with Leopold than the consideration that they had kept the peace in Europe for nearly eighteen years. But now, suddenly, like a landslide that starts with a trickle of soil and ends in uproar and catastrophe, the work of those eighteen years melted away; and the accumulated resentments of France drove Louis Philippe out of his palace, by a side door, and away to England. The Queen of the Belgians, in great distress, decided to commit to Victoria's keeping "what we have of precious"; and several boxes duly arrived, containing, the poor lady explained, "your Uncle's letters . . ." Though she flitted through the gloomy apartments at Brussels like a mute shadow—for Leopold seemed to be of the opinion that gaiety and small-talk were unconstitutional—she was a loving wife.

She was also a loving daughter. "Alas!" she wrote. "I fear my dear beloved father was led away by his *extreme courage*." This interpretation of the actions of Louis Philippe, who had fled from Paris with alacrity, leaving a daughter-in-law to face the music, might perhaps have made some impression upon Victoria; but a dispatch, forwarded by the delighted Lord Palmerston, was very disillusioning. King Louis Philippe, it seemed, his whiskers shaved off, wearing a coarse overcoat, with a sort of casquette on his head, and immense goggles over his eyes, and answering to the name of Smith, had appeared in Le Havre to be greeted by Mr. Fetherstonehaugh, the British consul. "Ah, my dear uncle, I am delighted to see you," cried Mr. Fetherstonehaugh, who had received his instructions. "My dear George," was the reply, no doubt a

48

truthful one, "I am glad you are here." The subsequent interview, related with irreverent relish by Mr. Fetherstone-haugh, was even less edifying.

Victoria received the exiled king and queen with mingled feelings. On the one hand, she could not but feel that their unhappy fate was a judgment upon them for having unpardonably deceived her in the matter of the Spanish marriages; and, indeed, if Louis Philippe had not lost the goodwill of England by marrying his son Montpensier to the Infanta Fernanda in 1846, he might still have been on his throne. On the other hand, she deplored the Paris revolution. The fugitive sovereigns, destitute, hysterical, hiding away at Claremont, were "humbled, poor people." Surely that was enough.

But the revolution moved eastward into Germany. All through the wonderful month of March, the kings and princelings of the German Confederation bowed one by one to the popular will, and constitutional governments sprang up like mushrooms. The German Confederation was an ingenious affair. Founded at the Congress of Vienna in 1815, it was a loose confederation of thirty-nine states, and its only effective institution was the Federal Diet. The Diet was no parliament, but a congress of diplomatic representatives, in which the vote of any one government (however small) could nullify the wishes of all the others; and from which, in consequence, anything resembling a progressive thought had always been banished: for the governments were all reactionary, and the president of the Diet was the Austrian representative. The various German sovereigns, in fact, were like the decorations upon an elaborate clock, designed to run backwards; and that something should have interfered with its mechanism was inevitable. The question really was whether this interference would be of an international or a domestic nature. Since many of the thirty-nine had dynastic connections with foreign rulers, the former eventuality was never very remote; with economic distress in Württemberg, industrial innovations in Saxony, political agitations in Baden, Lola Montez in Bavaria, and discontent everywhere, a domestic upheaval was also indicated. The collapse of Louis Philippe settled the issue. By the 19th of March, the domestic revolution had spread to Berlin. The city was abandoned by the royal troops; the royal palace was left unprotected; the arsenals were opened and the people supplied with arms; and the King's younger brother, Prince William of Prussia, the "cartridge prince," was smuggled from the country. "On both knees I adjure you," wrote King Frederick William IV to Queen Victoria, "use, for the welfare of Europe, *Engellands England*. With these words, I fall at your Majesty's feet." "Who would not recognise," he added in a postscript, "the avenging hand of the King of Kings in all this?"

Frederick William IV was a pious man. Resigned and romantic, muddle-headed and mystical, he saluted a procession that carried past him the corpses of civilians slain by his own soldiers. Prompted partly by fear, partly by an innate generosity, his royal rigidity began to liquefy. He exuded tears and concessions. He granted a representative constitution, he granted freedom of the press, he appointed a liberal ministry, he declared that Prussia was merged into Germany. And at length, under the black, red and gold standard of Pan-Germanism, he rode around his capital, bowing with humility to all whom he met, and scattering handbills of a revolutionary nature.

Queen Victoria responded to these events with a stream of

shocked communications to her ministers and her uncle Leopold. Germany—her "dear little Germany" as she had once called it—was behaving in a "frightful and shameful way." She seemed to think of it as a small but picturesque bottle from which there had just emerged, unasked, a hideous genie. The Prince's reactions were more restrained. He composed a model constitution and sent it round—also unasked—to the rulers of Germany. It was not received with any noticeable *empressement*; but since its recipients had already been forced, under humiliating circumstances, to append their signatures to constitutions drawn up by their own subjects, they can hardly be blamed for paying little attention to that of Prince Albert. Virtual prisoners, they gazed from their windows at the convulsive crowds below, and shook their heads in bewilderment. Obviously these people wanted something more than a constitution; but what could it be?

There were any number of answers to this question, but not one of them was entirely satisfactory; for within the minds of the revolutionaries themselves there existed a deep and potent confusion. The middle classes were responsible for the whole movement, and the middle classes owed many of their ideas to France and the principles of 1789. Yet an intellectual renaissance, the result of the conquests of Napoleon I, maintained that ever since the Treaty of Verdun—that is, ever since the ninth century—France had always arrayed herself against Germany; and supported this proposition with a number of theories, all the more persuasive because most of them were false. The revolution in Germany, therefore, in spite of its innumerable shades of opinion, its innumerable divergences of direction, had but one visible objective—a strong, united German people, at once liberal and nationalistic, dedicated simultaneously to two incompatible causes—political freedom and racial dominance. With these aims, it is hardly surprising that the German people should have turned towards Prussia for their salvation. Let Prussia become the cornerstone of a new, democratic German Empire; then, surely, Austria would see the light; and Europe, indeed the whole world, would be blessed with the ensuing demonstration of superior freedom. A powerful Prussia! Undoubtedly, it must all begin there, and the German liberals regarded such a beginning without uneasiness. The educational system, the civil administration, the Customs Union—who could regard these features of the Prussian state without pride and hope? Destiny, it was true, had placed at the head of this state a dynasty that was anything but liberal: but all that could be changed now. Drastic political reforms in Prussia must be accompanied by the formation of a National Parliament in Frankfurt; and, meanwhile, amidst this swirl of high aims and incoherent visions, all eyes were turned to the dubious figure of Frederick William IV, as he draped himself in the Pan-German colors and crawled around the streets of his capital.

For a moment it did, indeed, seem as if Austria had seen the light. Vienna did not avoid the fate of Paris and Berlin, and among the March refugees was no less a personage than Prince Metternich. When the crowds first gathered in the Austrian capital, Metternich called them "a hubbub of bakers." It was pointed out to him that they were composed of most respectable people. He replied that even if his own son had been among them, they would still be a hubbub of bakers, and maintained this opinion, more from contempt than conviction, until he was unfortunately obliged to leave Vienna, hidden in a laundry cart.

Metternich alone, it may be, among all those self-pitying exiles in London, faced the issue with a certain insouciance. His only error had been a chronological one. He had thought that the Europe which had been constructed, so materially through his efforts, at the Congress of Vienna, would outlive him; and it had not done so. He had attempted to stop time in its tracks, and for many years time had merely crawled; all efforts to hasten it had been visited with whips and scorpions. Now, as the revolutions spread from Berlin to Vienna, to Prague, Budapest, Lombardy, Venice, it was clear that time had caught up with Metternich. The old Austrian Chancellor shrugged his shoulders and prepared to make himself agreeable to those visitors who came, like pilgrims, to shake his hand. Liberalism, nationalism—he did not know which he disliked the more; but any reasonable man—and Metternich considered himself a very reasonable man—knew that they could not be repressed forever.

IV

Many years later, the nationalism of Bismarck destroyed what was left of the system of Metternich. The revolutions of 1848 merely questioned this system; they had neither the unity nor the means nor yet the desire to do more. They were not wasted, since no question is ever wasted; but once the question had been asked, they collapsed. One of the clues to this collapse revealed itself in London—where, on April 10, 1848, a melancholy and tragic fate at length overtook one of the greatest workers' movements in English history.

53

On that day, the Chartists gathered upon Kennington Common, ready to march to Westminster with their third Petition—which demanded, among other things, annual parliaments and universal male suffrage. An old law had been resuscitated, forbidding the presentation of a petition by more than ten persons, and troops had been concentrated in London under the command of the Duke of Wellington. The Duke himself expressed the belief that nothing much would happen; and a number of polite personages—among whom were Prince Louis Napoleon and Mr. Gladstone—gave body to this belief in the most condescending manner by patrolling the streets as special constables. These considerations, however, did not hearten the respectable public, which—maintaining not incorrectly that the Chartists threatened the very foundations of its society—had been for some weeks in a state of deep alarm. Chartism, however, with its mixture of the solid and the fantastic, of sound thinking and utopian speculation, came to grief that day on Kennington Common. Ten years of death, transportation, courage, self-sacrifice, of the misery of hope deferred and prophecy annulled—ten years which revealed, if nothing else, the essential grandeur of the human spirit—had only this issue, that the crowd dispersed and that the Petition, in three cabs, was driven all by itself across the river to the Houses of Parliament. On examination, it was found to contain such signatures as "Victoria Rex," "Sir Robert Peel," and "Mr. Punch"; while an improbable warrior called "Cheeks the Marine" had subscribed his name over and over again. Laughter succeeded alarm and the laughter served to emphasize the tragedy of the People's Charter—a great document, but historically premature, and therefore condemned to rattle across the Thames and out of the realm of immediate affairs.

Yet the rattle of those disappearing cabs was repeated, in a more terrible way, in Paris some two months later, when the workers of that city died before the muskets of General Cavaignac. They had joined in the revolution against Louis Philippe because they had been promised that the *ateliers sociaux* of Louis Blanc would be established as a result of it. But the *ateliers sociaux* were soon turned into *ateliers nationaux*—a meager and mocking charity—and the workers, cheated and furious, were slaughtered on the barricades. In the end of Chartism and the end of the proletarian movement in Paris there was a certain similarity; for both had been useful, and both were abandoned once their usefulness was over. At the time of the Corn Law agitation, when the middle classes of England were expressing themselves in a menacing way, Chartism had been a hateful bogey with which to threaten Parliament; once the Corn Laws were repealed, Chartism was categorically denounced, and its supporters had neither the organization nor the economic power with which to put it into effect unaided. The repeal of the Corn Laws was, in fact, the first of the European revolutions; and those that followed, in Paris, in Germany, in Vienna, in Italy— though they differed in many important respects—had at any rate the same middle class impulse, and the same distaste for proletarian backing. The success of these revolutions might almost be expressed in a paradox—they succeeded because they did not succeed. Their intention had been, not to overthrow, but to modify; to find within the complex rigidity of society some place for the rising and as yet excluded middle classes. It was not freedom they sought; it was opportunity:

55

they were the last reverberations of the French Revolution.

And so it came about that when the Italians tried to expel Austria and the rulers who were allied with her, they did not turn to Garibaldi, though Garibaldi proved useful and inspiring. A somewhat improbable person emerged as the only man who could unite their interests and reconcile their animosities. Charles Albert, King of Sardinia, was not, it is true, altogether Italian. His dynasty was half French; he himself preferred to speak that language: and his Piedmontese subjects had very imperfect affinities with the expansive peoples of the south. Moreover, he cared little for democracy; but then he cared less for the Austrians. In order to be rid of the latter, he must accept the former—a difficult choice, particularly for one who was already known as *il re tentenna*, the hesitant king. But at last the horrid decision was made; he agreed to the institution of a limited and parliamentary monarchy, unfurled his banner, and advanced across the Ticino. Ahead of him lay defeat, the execration of his subjects, exile, a broken heart; but even had he known this, it is doubtful if he would have drawn back. Amidst all his indecisions, he was a very high-minded man; he was also a very brave one. A doubting leader, however, is rarely successful; and when, after some preliminary skirmishes, the Austrians retired within the famous Quadrilateral, Charles Albert had enjoyed his last success. Radetzky, the Austrian commander, was old, but he was skillful; he bided his time, he struck with all his energy. On July 25, the Piedmontese army was defeated at Custozza, and Charles Albert led his broken troops back by the way they had come, back through the snarling streets of Milan, and across the frontier into his own kingdom.

Both his pride and his parliament demanded a renewal of the war; and in March of the next year, he led out his troops again. At Novara, where the Austrians met him, he sought death all day on the battlefield; he did not hope for victory. That night, amidst the wreck of his army, he abdicated, and two months later, in Portugal, he died. His heart had been broken. So, too, it appeared, had the cause of the nationalists and the liberals. The prolonged and valiant resistance of Garibaldi and Mazzini, who had proclaimed a republic in Rome, yielded at last to the guns of Oudinot and the French. In Parma, in Modena, in Tuscany, Lombardy, Venice, throughout the Papal States, and in the domains of King Ferdinand, the reaction set in. King Ferdinand, to be sure, was restrained by the presence of an English fleet from visiting upon the inhabitants of Messina all the horrors that his inventive mind had prepared for them; but such instances were rare.

Elsewhere, all over Europe, the tide of revolution was receding, and with diligent brutality the debris was being swept from the shore. The democrats of Vienna had set up a Constituent Assembly in July, 1848, but their disgust at the predominance of the Slavs (the proceedings had to be conducted in six languages) was a bad omen. So, too, was the return of the Emperor Ferdinand, who had been plotting reaction at Innsbruck. In October, a second upheaval, of a more proletarian character, sent him off again into Moravia, abdication, imbecility; while the corpse of his Minister of War, Latour, dangled from a lamp-post. But the proletariat of Vienna bestirred itself in vain; it was defeated by Windischgraetz, fresh from his conquest of the insurgents of Prague, and the revolution came to an end. In Hungary, Kossuth and Gorgei fought on, far into 1849, against a triple invasion of Haynau, the Russians, and the Croats; for nationalism can be very ignoble, and the Croats sacrificed their own chances of independence to the dearer cause of humbling the Magyars. At last, in August, 1849, after burying the Hungarian crown near the border, Kossuth fled to Turkey; and the Hapsburg, restored in the person of young Franz Josef, reigned once more over chaos and old night.

In Germany, too, the lamps were dimmed. There had been a sort of race between the new National Parliament at Frankfurt, dedicated to the unification of Germany; the National Assembly in Berlin, dedicated to the reform of Prussia; and the possible recovery of the old Austrian government. The Austrians won, with the assistance of the Croats and Czar Nicholas of Russia. Set free to meddle once again in the affairs of Prussia, the Viennese government soon achieved the dissolution of the Berlin Assembly; it was then only a question of time before the Frankfurt Parliament went the same way. Vainly but pertinaciously, the lawmakers of Frankfurt talked on; they could do nothing else; they had neither an army nor an executive. At length, in April, 1849, they offered the imperial crown of a constitutional German Empire to Frederick William IV. But much had happened to Frederick William since the days when he had scattered liberal handbills around Berlin; he had been listening to the particularists, to the Austrian party, and above all to that inner voice which spoke with the peculiar distinctness of fantasy about the restoration of a Holy Roman Empire. He turned down the offer of the crown, and all hopes of a liberal German Empire were killed, then and forever. The Frankfurt Parliament thereupon broke up in disorder; and in every step that followed, a humiliated Prussia shrank more and more beneath the shadow of Austria. It was, perhaps, inevitable: for amidst the fears and jealousies that surrounded and interpenetrated her, Prussia had only one ally—liberalism; and rather than be liberal the rulers of Prussia preferred, for the time being, to be lowly.

v

Insufficient industrialization, lack of arms, lack of organization, the fatal incompatability of liberalism and nationalism—these were sufficient reasons for the swift collapse of the revolutions. But there was another reason. To shame a few backward princes, to create a world in which a man of property could have some say in the running of his own affairs—such were their aims, and such eventually were their achievements. The loftier cries for a more selfless and more difficult liberty fled down the wind and died away. In France, Louis Philippe was succeeded by Louis Napoleon, whose regime was soon to represent all that was adventurous, all that was glittering, and all that was shoddy in nineteenth century capitalism. In Germany the way had been cleared for the rise of Bismarck; in Italy for the efficient dispensation of Cavour. But Metternichian Europe, at any rate, in spite of its apparent recovery in 1849, was doomed. Its venerable anomalies, its intertwined abuses, had barred the way to enterprise: that is why the revolutions of 1848-9 might, perhaps, be called the revolutions of the *entrepreneurs*. Many of the leading actors were men of high vision and disinterested purpose; but the central impulse was a businesslike one, and it received a businesslike reward. It is doubtful if European liberalism ever recovered, either from its efforts in 1848-9, or from their outcome.

England settled down to a period of complacency. There was no more talk of revolution; no longer did Victoria mention—not even to Albert, not even to herself—the possibility of her children's being, not royal children, but just—well, just like anybody else. She did not realize that the balance of power had now shifted towards the middle classes, nor would she have approved of such a shift if it had been brought to her attention. She merely observed that much of the profligacy, the nastiness of the upper classes was, somehow or other, disappearing. It was enough. She gave all her intensity, all her abundant vigor, to the furthering of Albert's schemes—to the creation of the perfect monarchy.

Albert, too, was more at ease. He did not understand England, but he could appreciate primness and respectability; in such an atmosphere his painstaking genius was most at home; and such an atmosphere now prevailed in the enigmatic island of his adoption. Beyond, there was much to cause uneasiness. The revolutions had left behind them many problems of great complexity; and the Prince, whose approach to a complex problem was distinctly reverent, was profoundly upset by the behavior of Lord Palmerston, in whom there was no reverence at all. Yet even Lord Palmerston could not prevent a diligent, respectable monarchy from inserting itself more and more into the very heart of English affairs. The Prince perceived that he and his family were safely intrenched; that, although one must never stop digging, never stop reinforcing the entrenchment, the future was reasonably secure. His family! His glance, when it rested upon the young Prince of Wales, was severe and speculative. Upon that small, that trembling object so much depended.

Chapter Two

THE CONSERVATORY AND THE FORT

THE procession moved down the West Nave between six shrill rows of ladies in their bright dresses, with a somber bass background of enthusiastic gentlemen. It moved very slowly along the red carpet. Towards the middle, just behind the Corps Diplomatique, walked two Waterloo heroes of great antiquity—the Duke of Wellington and the Marquis of Anglesey, who had just made up a long-standing quarrel. They would pause every so often, arm in arm, to admire such objects as were tall enough to be visible above the crowd; and their comments, spiced with Regency oaths and shouted at the top of their voices, for both were exceedingly deaf, filled the onlookers with affectionate admiration. Further back, behind the Cabinet, wandered the Archbishop of Canterbury. He, too, would pause from time to time and stare about him; and this had an unfortunate effect upon the gentlemen of the Household, who were walking backwards, and whose heels were bruised from a series of collisions with the Archbishop's chaplains. Then came Queen Victoria, in pink and silver, leading the Prince of Wales, who wore kilts; and Prince Albert, dressed as a Field Marshal, leading the Princess Royal.

Behind them were four insignificant foreign royalties—the

only ones who had dared assassination on this momentous day—May 1, 1851—the day of the opening of the Crystal Palace.

Of the triumphs of that day, Victoria's journal was full. She knew who was responsible. It was all Albert's doing, and she filled page after page with her italics and her adoration. In this she was not entirely correct. The original idea had sprung from the brain of Mr. Henry Cole, a gentleman to whom history has been insufficiently grateful. There had been exhibitions before: but an international exhibition—that was without a precedent: and when the notion occurred to Mr. Cole, at the Paris Exposition of 1849, he had not wasted any time. He hastened to England, obtained an audience of Prince Albert, and poured forth his plans into those august ears. Nor were they unreceptive ears. As President of the Royal Society of Arts, Albert was not averse to exhibitions; as a Free-Trader, as a consistent promoter of Peace and Progress, he could hardly fail to be impressed by the moral lessons inherent in Mr. Cole's scheme. But to be impressed is one thing; to be actively impressed is quite another: and if Mr. Cole had not enjoyed, from the beginning, the close support of the Prince, it is more than probable that his international exhibition would have died a-borning.

A Royal Commission met in January of the next year, with the Prince presiding. In the interval, Mr. Cole had been doing the work of several men; he had whirled up and down England from south to north; he had visited Ireland and Scotland; manufacturers, mayors, editors had been converted to the idea in hundreds. After that, the Royal Commission took over; and Mr. Cole, as is often the case, though he worked as hard as ever, retired into obscurity. The Great Exhibition, thenceforward, came to be connected more and more with the name of Prince Albert.

The Prince was far from popular; the exhibition was unprecedented: this combination was enough to arouse a deep and determined opposition. An Exhibition in Hyde Park! Would it not, inevitably, attract ruffians, vagrants, and international revolutionaries? Would it not entail the destruction of valuable trees? Some quoted an act of the time of George IV which seemed to forbid the erection of buildings in Royal Parks; others, opening their Old Testaments, pointed with a trembling finger to certain passages in the Book of Chronicles about royal personages who did evil in the sight of the Lord. The opposition was a very odd one; it was also very English. It included Protectionists and radicals, pious clerics and the scurrilous Brougham: but, however diverse and contradictory its various parts may have seemed, as a whole it gave expression to a deeply rooted prejudice—a prejudice against anything foreign and anything new. The Prince was disgusted, though not surprised; the Government, having to a certain extent committed itself, grew more and more anxious: but what could one do? It was all very well to talk about the good sense of the English people; but the fact remained that when Colonel Sibthorpe declared in Parliament that the Exhibition would bring, among other disasters of a more economic character, an invasion of papists in its train, it almost seemed as if, in the muddiness and obstinacy of his rhetoric, the fens of his native Lincolnshire had uttered their voice. And it is hard to fight against England when England is in an obstructive mood.

Then, as if to provide all this criticism with a precise objective, the Building Committee published its plan for an Exhibition Building. The Committee had some eminent members, including Barry and Brunel, so that the plan can only be ascribed to the intervention of some crossing star. For the building resembled—with a horrid air of permanence, since it was to be composed of brick and iron—something between a railway station and a penal establishment. At this, the opposition redoubled its fury. *The Times* began to thunder. The Prince, the Committee, the Commissioners, were in despair. And Joseph Paxton intervened.

Joseph Paxton represented, in an almost explosive manner, the expanding energies of the early Victorian age. He had begun as a gardener in the employment of the Duke of Devonshire, and had risen to the management of the ducal affairs and to a seat in Parliament—a position equal, if not superior, to that of Minister to some small German sovereign. Railway director, publisher, engineer—there was no end to Mr. Paxton's activities. Yet he possessed, for all his triumphs in the outer world, a saving simplicity: to the end of his life he remained, at heart, a gardener. He would hurry back from a speaking tour, a board meeting, a debate, to watch with tender solicitude the growth of some new plant or tree in the gardens at Chatsworth. It is not surprising that the Crystal Palace, which in some ways resembled a great conservatory, should have been of his design. Besides, had he not already built a Lily-House of glass, to contain the Duke's fabulous water-lily from British Guiana? People who came to visit Chatsworth never knew which they admired more—the enormous lily, with its elaboration of spreading leaves, or the delicate structure that housed it. And now, at the very last minute, when it seemed as if the grim plans of the Committee

65

would have to be accepted for lack of anything better; when everything, the Prince's reputation, the Government's majority, the future of the Exhibition, seemed to be hanging in the balance; Paxton came forward with a set of plans for a great glass edifice. The members of the Committee, it was only natural, hung back: it was too late to change, they said, and besides, though they admired Paxton's design, it was very startling. It is also difficult for any group of human beings to discard a project, however defective, upon which they have spent a good deal of time and thought. Paxton, however, at this critical moment, indulged in a judicious indiscretion—an indiscretion very like blackmail. He persuaded the *Illustrated London News* to reproduce his design.

The effect was instantaneous. The Victorian public may have been lacking in taste, but it had retained a capacity for delighting in the magnificent and the fantastic. Expressions of admiration and joy poured in from every side. The Committee accepted Mr. Paxton's design. *Punch* christened it, in a happy moment, "The Crystal Palace." The Exhibition was saved.

As the building rose, with extraordinary rapidity, on its site in Hyde Park, to visit it took on the nature of a pilgrimage. The light, bright, delicate thing was an intoxicating vision in the surrounding drabness; and thousands came to watch it every day. At this, the opposition increased its activity. It called the building an ice-house, a fire-trap, a papistical idol; it issued warnings about the weight of snow and the force of wind; it prophesied disaster from the droppings of birds. It prayed that God's lightning would blast the building, or hinted that the salvo of guns which was to greet the Queen's arrival on opening day would inevitably shatter the glass into flying fragments and cut to pieces the ladies who were gathered within. But in vain. Nobody paid any attention. For another influence was now at work. The spirit of the times, with its adoration of industrial adventure, had found in the Crystal Palace an appropriate habitation; and the imagination of the people of England, already quickened by railways and bridges as they sprang across the land, seemed to see, reflected in Paxton's innumerable glass, the idealized image of the age of steam.

It was a great moment for Joseph Paxton. He was everything that was admired in those days. He had risen from poverty to comparative wealth and vast responsibility; and now he had crowned it all by achieving, in practically no time at all, a stupendous feat of empirical engineering. But for Prince Albert—who had staked his whole reputation on this one throw—it was an even greater moment. At last, in spite of everything, he had come into his own.

Outwardly, however, the Prince did not share his wife's ecstasies at the stupendous success of the opening day. He contented himself with remarking that it had all been "quite satisfactory." But one may be permitted to guess at the inner tumult that possessed him. Here, embodied in the Great Exhibition, many of his deepest longings had been visibly fulfilled. Like the Exhibition, he was useful, he was respected, he was even much admired. One of the Exhibition's characteristics, it is true, and that a most important one, was not shared by the Prince: the Exhibition was popular. But what did popularity signify? Had it any part in the composition of the ideal Crown? On the whole, the Prince was inclined to think not. It was all very well to get on with people, to know the value of a jest or a compliment, to be affable as well as industrious: but did not one admit, by such behavior, that one was fallible? Albert himself was extremely grudging in social intercourse; he handed himself around, like a miser, in small cold pieces: and now that the Exhibition had brought him an almost undreamed-of success, now that his mind was filled with delicious intimations of future power, his frigidity, instead of thawing, became more and more frigid.

His family suffered, as was only to be expected. The ponderous jokes, the tremendous puns continued—they were part of the Prince's routine: but his children were very much in awe of him, and none more so than Bertie. That unfortunate little boy was now subjected to the full impact of the Prince's program, for around him, as heir, the tremendous future revolved. Two years before, he had left the protecting orbit of Lady Lyttleton; a tutor had been selected, and the serious business of education had begun. The Prince considered that the position of tutor to the future King of England was one of the greatest importance; anybody, he thought, would be flattered at being selected for such a post. He had therefore asked Dr. Liddell, the Headmaster of Westminster, to become his son's tutor. Dr. Liddell, however, with the deepest respect, let it be known that the compilation of a lexicon and the management of a great school would prevent him from complying with the Prince's wishes. Albert was disappointed. He had thought better of Dr. Liddell. But he realized that he would have to look in less exalted circles for what he wanted, and at last he chose the Reverend Henry Birch, a junior Eton master.

Mr. Birch was a kindly man, and the little prince grew very fond of him. It was this consideration, no doubt, that prompted the Prince to get rid of Mr. Birch. He wished his son's education to be conducted in the atmosphere of a Jesuit seminary, where affection is frowned upon. That the young prince should have been subjected to a course of training that only a very bookish child could digest was, perhaps, under-standable: Albert had been bookish himself. But had he for-gotten his own childhood—how he had rambled in the hills with his brother Ernest, and shot rabbits, and whistled to the nightingales? Apparently he had; or perhaps he thought that what was suitable for the son of a German princeling was al-together out of place where a Prince of Wales was concerned. And even if he had relented—even if he had thought of allow-ing a little warmth, a little gaiety to creep into his eldest son's life—there were two colossal memoranda from Stockmar to remind him that the education of a model prince must be one of unremitting application to his studies. A model prince! Yes, Bertie must be forced into that terrible mold, all the more terrible because it was quite illusory. It would never do for him and Mr. Birch to be *friends!* And so it was discovered that Mr. Birch paid too much attention to the catechism; and on this disingenuous excuse the kindly tutor was sent away.

Lady Canning said that the little boy "did no end of touch-ing things" when he heard that Birch was to leave him. He was an affectionate child. But at last the dreadful day came, and in Mr. Birch's place there was Frederick Waymouth Gibbs, who was not only a Fellow of Trinity but "a firm believer in decorum." At first Mr. Gibbs seemed inclined to object to the number of books that his pupil was expected to peruse; but the Prince very soon put a stop to such English notions. If the boy did not care for books, the answer was more books. It was very simple, and he was surprised that

Mr. Gibbs should have other ideas. Mr. Gibbs yielded. He discovered that he was not only a tutor but also, in a very minor way, a courtier. And then, in his capacity of courtier, he made another discovery. Favorable reports upon his pupil were frowned at: he was to look for faults—and, alas, they were not difficult to find. Like many another child in similar circumstances, the prince was at the mercy of an inner rebellion, altogether beyond his control; and the more severe his course of studies, the more stupid he became. Between the decorous Mr. Gibbs and the menacing father there was a daily interchange of notes; each was filed away for future reference: but the situation grew steadily worse. Between Prince Albert and his elder daughter, on the other hand, there was already a companionship; they would hold long talks together on serious topics; and the Prince watched, with a peculiar delight, as Vicky grew into a formidable but inferior copy of himself. Yet the delight was tinged with bitterness. Nature, it seemed, that enemy of the categorical and the ideal, had risen to thwart him. If only Vicky had been a boy, and Bertie a girl! Upon such biological chances as this even royal ambitions, it seemed, might come to grief.

It was about the time of the change from Mr. Birch to Mr. Gibbs that the Great Exhibition was opened. The royal procession, which Canon Stanley likened in some respects, if not all, "to the entrance of the Pope into St. Peter's on Easter Sunday," must have made no light impression. The shining glass walls—the tremendous cheering—the ladies bowing like flowers in their bright velvets—the sudden organ—that extraordinary Chinese "mandarin" who appeared from nowhere and was asked to join the Corps Diplomatique (and

who, it subsequently transpired, was the ingenious proprietor
of a pleasure junk) . . . all these were lovely memories
but how soon obscured! How soon the Crystal Palace itself
became just another item in Bertie's schedule of studies! He
was dragged from one exhibit to another—for surely much
could be learned from the displays of Antigua and Canada,
of Jamaica and St. Kitts. There were many objects which,
had he been permitted to linger over them, might have given
him pleasure. But no—it was among the geographical exhibits
that the prince was expected to spend his time; and then he
had to commit his thoughts to a diary which was inspected
by Mr. Gibbs, by Prince Albert, and sometimes by Stockmar.
Its arid pages filled both the diarist and the inspectors with
mortification; the sentences, written out with such painful
care (for Stockmar placed a legible handwriting very high
among royal virtues), revealed not the dimmest trace of an
original mind. And then, one day, wandering through the
tedious immensity of the East India Company's exhibit, he
discovered among the bamboos and the brasses and the models
of Indian village life, a lively group representing the murderous Thugs at their work. He was enchanted. His diary
.for that day was filled with the most exuberant and detailed
descriptions of the Thugs; never before had it shown such
life: and it was sent to Stockmar. The implacable baron was
far from gratified. Perhaps, if imperialism had been in fashion,
he might have expatiated in his reply upon the blessing that
British rule might bring to India by putting down the Thugs.
As it was, he limited himself to a severe expostulation. He
was disgusted, he said, that a Christian prince should interest
himself in such matters. His little victim hung his head; and

the diary subsided once more into a flatness that was to be its distinguishing, indeed its only, characteristic during the next seven years.

Prince Albert continued to hope that the public, unlike his son, would derive substantial benefits of an educational nature from the Crystal Palace. He was strongly against any proposal that the Exhibition should remain open beyond October 11; he had no wish, he said, for it to become a show. The ignorant and the illiterate, whom the Prince mistrusted, were, it is true, largely precluded from entering because of the admission price, which was steep. But once inside—amidst that astonishing profusion of sounds and sights, with the three organs booming in succession or simultaneously; with the palm trees swaying beneath the chandeliers, and the Crystal Fountain flinging up its spray between two equestrian statues of the Queen, one colored and one plain; with the heaped-up wealth of nations piled along the avenues: once inside, in a glimmer of glass and a rattle of machinery, what *did* the visitors encounter but a show? Variety is a great leveler. In that kaleidoscopic confusion size and quality, importance and absurdity were all one. They found an equal delight in Kiss's great Amazon, a water-closet, a bronze Andromeda, a pair of stays embroidered with the Royal Arms. Their eyes passed without a shock from the glowing Axminsters that hung from the galleries to an armchair made of coal. At length, since they were early Victorian, their happy bewilderment resolved itself into a desire for the ponderous and the elaborate; and objects which exemplified these qualities surrounded them on every side. The furniture, especially, seemed to mirror with gargantuan fidelity their intimate

72

tastes and ambitions. It was expensive and solid and writhing with useless decoration. It was just what they wanted. It was quite appalling. And yet there was a demiurgic fantasy everywhere apparent in it—a willingness to experiment, however indiscriminately, a love of variety, however grotesque The same energy manifested itself in the hardware and glassware and silverware, in the textiles, in the statues. It was the energy of the times, a blind force. It seethed and rumbled through the whole assemblage of curious objects—and swept them away. Nothing remains of them but a few catalogues and some commemorative verses. Nothing remains of the visitors, either, but dust; and the fact that they consumed 934,691 Bath buns, 870,027 plain buns, and 1,092,337 bottles of non-alcoholic beverage. It is only if you put them together, the visited and the visitors, the evocation and the answer, that they still defy Prince Albert's wishes and make a wonderful show.

In one respect, however, the Exhibition might have been called instructive. It was noticed that the section devoted to Machinery was the most popular; those early Victorians would stand for hours before the railway engines, the model bridges, the looms, the huge hydraulic press. Subsequent commentators, however, have remarked with regret that their attitude to these exhibits was purely materialistic. No considerations of a philosophical or an ethical nature seem to have marred their satisfaction or intensified their vision: they saw before them, not a future which demanded the utmost in human endeavor, but a fairyland of accumulating wealth and comfort. This may have been so: but in such materialism there is a certain innocence; and as they linger, wide-eyed and childlike, in that mechanistic dawn, it would be an ungenerous mind that could not salute them.

The Great Exhibition did not create any lasting impression. It was fascinating, it was immensely popular, it was a financial success. Its memory faded more slowly than do most memories. That was all. Only a few men perceived what was, after all, its lasting significance—namely, that it was a symbol. To the Free Trade leaders, to such men as Richard Cobden and John Bright, it seemed the embodiment of all their dreams, the trophy of all their hard-won victories. Had not foreign manufacturers and inventors and artists hastened to send in their exhibits? Had they not thus entered into open and friendly competition with each other and with their English hosts? A further satisfaction, to these liberal thinkers, lay in the memory that the reactionary sovereigns of Europe had viewed the Exhibition with grave distrust. They had refused to attend the opening, and through the weeks that followed they had waited for the revolutionary disturbance that such an innovation was bound to produce. And when the Exhibition closed, it was discovered that but one disturbance, and that not really of a revolutionary nature, had been created during the whole course of it . . . some ladies had been violently assaulted by a party of Welsh teetotalers. Otherwise, all had been peace. Peace! That was the mystery of the great glass temple. It symbolized the beginning of a new era, when unrestricted competition would render all wars unnecessary. In spite of its commercial nature, the vision was a lovely vision; and it is indeed a pity that the greed of men and of nations made it impossible of fulfillment. The vision has fled; but the Crystal Palace has its place in history, hanging like a toy or a jewel between the confusion of the years that preceded it and the confusion of the years that came after.

II

For indeed, very soon after the closing of the Crystal Palace, within less than three years, confusion returned. Mr. Cobden and Mr. Bright wrung their hands in vain; in vain they thundered. England was at war. Uniforms, parades, reviews now filled those hours that Bertie was allowed to spend away from the schoolroom. He stood by his mother's side on the *Fairy* as it led out Napier's warships—"those murderous queens"—on their expedition to the Baltic. He contributed a signed drawing to a bazaar for the wounded, and it sold for fifty guineas. And since, in this way, the habitual gloom in which his days were spent was sometimes invaded by cannons and brass and bunting, the boy must sometimes almost have been happy. The greatest contrast of all, however, was provided by the city of Paris, which he visited with his parents in August, 1855—the first time that an acknowledged English sovereign had set foot in its streets since the coronation of Henry VI. The magical atmosphere was as responsive as ever. When Bertie knelt, in kilts, before the tomb of Napoleon I, the Parisian sky produced an authentic clap of thunder, and all the French generals burst into tears. At court, too, he acquitted himself with grace and distinction.

The reign of Napoleon III was still young: Eugénie was at the height of her beauty, and Napoleon of his peculiar prestige. Theirs was a spectacular court. The extravagantly ordered mummeries of the Court of Napoleon I had been revived with care and displayed with discernment. A rare zest, a rarer gaiety pervaded the whole. Yet there was a certain embarrassment about it all as it moved in splendor through the dull interior of the Tuileries; and in the behavior of everyone—from the loftiest official to the officer of the Cent Gardes who slept all night outside the Emperor's bedroom— there was, so slight but, oh, so puzzling, an air of make-believe. The wealth, the power of Napoleon III—ah, yes, they were there, they were quite apparent; but his court was a *parvenu* court, its social position in Europe was, to say the least, ambiguous; and, figuratively speaking, it was haunted by the ghost of Napoleon I, a necessary but disparaging spirit. Victoria, however, declared herself delighted. She even went further—she said that Napoleon held a more agreeable state than did Louis Philippe. This was true; but that Victoria should have admitted it showed what an astonishing reversal had taken place in her attitude towards the Emperor of the French. Was he not a usurper, an adventurer? Could not his sojourn in England, when he was still just Prince Louis Napoleon, be summed up as a tale of debts and of Miss Howard? It was very odd indeed that Victoria should have taken a liking to such a man; a man whose whole career was a perfect compendium of her husband's opinion of the French—namely, that they were an untrustworthy and immoral people. Napoleon III, of course, was not exactly French: and Prince Albert's opinions were not exactly opinions—they were prejudices, acquired, one is tempted to think, while he was still a student at Bonn. But his prejudices were Victoria's law. Yet, in spite of this, Napoleon had won his way into the Queen's affections. He had come to Windsor in 1854 with precisely that object in view, and from the first he had imported into his dealings with her some of those methods that had proved so successful with frailer and less formidable ladies; amidst all his politenesses, all his deference, he never let her forget that she was a woman. She noted with surprise that he was gentle, dignified, modest; she liked his face and his soft voice; and then, looking it may be into his eyes, those cloudy eyes (rather like a goat's, some less friendly observer might have thought), she found "something fascinating, melancholy, engaging, which draws you to him." And, indeed, her heart had been softened by precisely those elements in his personality which had hardened that of Albert. He was mysterious; he was even a little bit of a mountebank: it was one of Victoria's strangest idiosyncrasies to be fascinated by such men.

The favorable impression created at Windsor was intensified by the visit to Paris. In spite of their deficiencies as crowned heads, or perhaps because of them, Napoleon and Eugénie were charming hosts. When the time came to leave, Victoria felt quite sad. But her sadness was as nothing when compared with her son's; Paris and its Empress had had their effect upon an already susceptible nature. Ahead of him, once more, his education beckoned from the gloom of England: and, on the evening before their departure, he begged Eugénie to let him stay a few days longer. There were other children at home, he said, and he would not be missed.

The circumstance which brought about these agreeable encounters was the Crimean War. It has often been said that the Crimean War was an unnecessary and wasteful war, and this proposition can be maintained with a formidable array of facts. It is certainly true that the principal belligerents, as the crisis approached, would have been glad to avoid it altogether. But history illustrates, among other things, the eternal

77

attempt of individual human beings to hasten or retard, to obscure or illuminate the inevitable; and it would be a mistake to call any event wasted because it was wasteful, or unnecessary because it was not wanted.

The war of 1854-5 might have been postponed, it might not have taken place in the Crimea; but, considering the condition of Europe in the mid-nineteenth century, it was more than probable that, sooner or later, it would have to be fought. Forty years of what might charitably be called an intermittent peace had fouled the eastern margins of the Mediterranean Sea with blood and strewn its floor with the wreck of ships. From these catastrophes, from the intervention of the Czar in the revolutions of 1848, from the greeds and idealisms of the Western powers, from a thousand and one different circumstances, a Near Eastern Question was bound to emerge. Only a good deal of resolution on one side and of mildness on the other could have prevented such a question from passing out of the realm of words; and there was little resolution in the characters of Lord Aberdeen and Napoleon III, and no mildness at all in that of Czar Nicholas I. As a result, a number of innocent human beings perished miserably of frost, bullets, pestilence, and gangrene, and Europe as a whole took another faltering step forward.

Napoleon III was an opportunist; if he had not been, he would hardly have dared, while still Prince-President, to re-open an old quarrel about the Holy Places in Palestine. The dispute between the Latin and Greek Christians had slumbered, fitfully, for many years; and when Napoleon, in 1852, demanded of the Sublime Porte that the keys to the Holy Places should be handed over to the Catholics, his motives were frankly political. He needed the Catholic vote in France. Wisdom and experience would have informed him, had he possessed them, that old quarrels are like old tombs; if you open them you are apt to release, among other objects of a more substantial nature, a cloud of curses or a swarm of bacteria. And so it was in 1852. The Czar, as protector of the Orthodox Christians, lodged a protest; and from these beginnings a complex and sinister situation proceeded to develop with an appalling rapidity.

The preliminary maneuvers, it is true, were harmless enough. The Sultan and his ministers at first leaned towards the French, who quoted the Capitulations of 1742; then seemed to favor the Russians, who founded their view of the case on the Treaty of Kuchuk Kainardji. The Treaty and the Capitulations had this in common—beside the fact that they were both out of date: they were susceptible of whatever interpretation one chose to put upon them. Could he have had his way, therefore, the Sultan would have lingered for years and years in a delicious indecision, making concessions and withdrawing them. Nor would Napoleon have been displeased with such an outcome. He had gained his point; a silver star, embossed with the arms of France, hung in the Holy Grotto, and a most desirable accretion of Catholic votes had been the result. As to the subsequent fate of the Catholic pilgrims who came to pay their vows at the Holy Sepulcher in Jerusalem or the Church of the Nativity in Bethlehem— there was nothing in his character to indicate that he would bother about them. He was perfectly content to let things slide. But he had reckoned without the Czar.

Nicholas I, there is no doubt of it, was a godly man. How else could one characterize a prince who believed that the

burning of the Houses of Parliament in London was due to
the wrath of the Almighty at the passing of the Reform Bill?
Even the English Tories, whose gifts in this direction were
far from inconsiderable, had never advanced such a claim.
In other respects, the Czar's attitude towards the Deity was
equally decisive. He was convinced that he ruled by divine
right; and if any of his subjects, taking a more mundane
view, murmured, however inaudibly, about human rights,
they were visited with whips and prison and exile and death.
A Europe which had lost America and not yet acquired
Africa was naturally inclined to regard Russia and its sovereign with an exaggerated awe; and Nicholas, so upright
and so horrible, was just the man to keep this feeling properly alive. Those who were privileged to meet him never
could decide which was the more terrifying—his politeness
or his power. A man of a gloomy temperament and a character so rigid that he was never happy out of military uniform, he none the less knew how to be affable. Yet even as
one felt his charm, one was conscious of the ruthless and
almost mythical background from which he had emerged
and into which he would presently retire. He was a living
contradiction—a civilized savage, a barbarous gentleman.
And so when, as a consequence of Napoleon's original
maneuver, he suddenly demanded the right to protect, not
the Greek Christians in Palestine, but *all* the Greek Christians within the borders of the Turkish Empire, a justifiable
shudder ran up and down the rather plastic backbones of the
leading statesmen of Europe.

In Constantinople, Nicholas' spokesman was Prince Mensch-
ikoff, a nobleman whose speech betrayed an innate inability
to distinguish between what was firm and what was foul.

The Czar's language, though more delicate, was just as deadly. He began to talk, once again, about partitioning Turkey. There had been a time when it had seemed to him that it would be more politic to pose as the friend of Turkey; but he had never been able to obtain the closing of the Dardanelles to foreign navies in time of war, and though he had tried to console himself by building a naval fortress at Sebastopol, the consolation had proved insufficient. He now confided to the English Ambassador his belief that the Turkish Empire was "a sick bear." The English Government subsequently diluted this phrase into "a sick man," but they did not become any easier. And when he began to talk, in his pleasant way, about "protecting" the Danubian principalities and occupying Constantinople, while England seized Egypt and Crete, their uneasiness became acute.

They wished, indeed, that the Turk would resist the Czar's pretensions by reforming himself. And of late, as it happened, certain quiverings, which might almost have been called progressive, could be discerned in that mass of Byzantine fungus known as the Turkish Empire. Tax-farming and slave-markets were prohibited, education was to be secularized, and the army shaken up. Perhaps, they thought, something would come of all this; but the wish was father to the thought, and the thought was still-born. The changes were proclaimed, they were not put into effect. As for the Czar, his autocratic mind was bewildered by these feeble gestures of reform. He took them to be the delirium of approaching death, and pressed his demands more insistently than ever.

Yet, oddly enough, he had no liking for a war. A firm opposition would certainly have persuaded him to make some compromise with the Turks. His motives were sufficiently mixed. He did not believe that England would fight, she was too interested in making money . . . unless he went too far; and he wanted to see how far he could go. Even he realized, of course, that England would never, so long as she held India, permit him to occupy Constantinople; but Constantinople was a useful threat. In this respect, his state of mind somewhat resembled that of a bandit who holds up a rich tradesman at the point of an empty pistol. He was also a crusader, who sincerely believed in the cause of Orthodox Christianity, and who—like other crusaders before him—would have thought it rude to turn his back upon the opportunity of extracting some material profit from it. Then again, as Protector of the Orthodox Christians, he was playing a rôle of which his unfortunate subjects approved—and he needed their approval: for even the most cold-blooded of tyrants is often lonely and frightened at heart. Such were his conscious motives: but how much stronger was the unconscious compulsion, the prompting of that strange destiny which, every now and again, prodded the ungainly Russia into a shambling move against the Near East, and of which he was the puppet not the master!

A firm opposition—but where was it to be found? It was once the fashion to blame Napoleon III for helping, rather than hindering, the cause of war. Would not a successful military exploit do much to revive those neo-Caesarean cravings that still clustered rather sluggishly around his name? Would not an alliance with England, and a friendship with England's Queen, much improve his very dubious position among the crowned heads of Europe? These considerations undoubtedly carried some weight with Napoleon. He also had a very new bone to pick with the Czar, whose first communication to him as Emperor had begun with the words "Cher Ami" instead of "Sire, Mon Frère"—an insult which Napoleon, though a checkered career had made him somewhat impervious to slights, found it hard to forgive.

Yet those who were close to him in this crisis—Lord Cowley, for example—have testified to the extreme reluctance with which he faced a war. He was a clever man, in some respects he was one of the cleverest men in Europe; but he was not a wise man and he was not a statesman. A sad indecision crippled his every move. The divided heart of his regime lay in two opposite receptacles—the tomb of Napoleon I and the Paris Bourse; and this enigmatic state of affairs, which puzzled and alarmed Europe for many years, was also a source of bewilderment to Napoleon himself. He might almost be said to have spent the whole of his reign trying to find out what it meant; and at the end, in the wreckage of Sedan, he was even farther from a solution than he had been at the beginning. He had risen to power because the French bourgeoisie and peasantry, terrified by the proletarian uprisings of 1848, had seen in him the representative of order. His coup d'état, his subsequent assumption of the imperial crown, were due, not to the French bourgeoisie, nor to the French peasantry, but to his belief in a star that had set with Napoleon I. He also fancied himself as a revolutionary. It was impossible to reconcile these conflicting rôles. As the representative of order, he had suppressed the republic of Mazzini and Garibaldi and restored the Pope to Rome. As a revolutionary, he dreamed of Italian freedom, though an Italian freedom that included the temporal sovereignty of the Pope was, to say the least, a perplexing concept. As an Emperor . . . there his thoughts became incoherent: the glory of France, the resettlement of Europe—they swirled in his brain. It is hardly

83

surprising that such a man, so constituted and so situated, should have confronted a Russian war with something less than a clear mind. Or that, for all his airs of inscrutable authority, he should have leaned in this crisis upon two frail supports—an hysterical French ambassador in Constantinople, and a hesitant English government.

The English Cabinet at this time was a most distinguished gathering. Three of its members had held the office of Foreign Secretary, and one of these three was the formidable Palmerston. But Palmerston was now Home Secretary, and the Cabinet as a whole was more than usually divided. Like an expensive barometer that has suddenly broken down, it pointed to "Calm" when it meant "Stormy," and to "Stormy" when it wished to signify "Calm." In all the negotiations that led up to the Crimean War, throughout the effort of the Russians to withdraw from their predicament and that of the Turks to plunge themselves deeper into it, amidst the agitations of diplomats and the resounding oratory of politicians, its hesitations can be discerned, a wayward needle in the gathering storm.

The effect of these hesitations upon the English Ambassador in Constantinople was considerably increased by the fact that the electric telegraph now reached as far east as Belgrade. Lord Stratford de Redcliffe was not, like his French colleague, an hysterical man; but he was an independent one. A long career had taught him, through the interactions of circumstance and character, the pleasure of making his own decisions. The telegraph, sputtering forth the indecisions of the home government, was a constant source of irritation. If only dispatches could have arrived in the old manner, at decent and protracted intervals! But it was not to be.

84

There was a time when Lord Stratford was accused by quite responsible thinkers of having deliberately hastened, if not actually contrived, the Crimean War. His personality, no doubt, had something to do with this accusation. He was a cousin of George Canning; and if he lacked "The Pope's" ability to make a life-long enemy with a single witticism, he retained, long after his death, an almost unrivaled gift for exacerbating historians. There was something about him which provoked admiration or animosity, but not surmise; people were inclined to see him either as all black or all white. He was a tall, spare man, with expressive gray eyes and extraordinarily handsome features. When he chose to unbend, he could be very courteous, but his courtesies were not always well received—Lady Hester Stanhope, for instance, declared that he reminded her of the permanent head of a society for the suppression of vice. He was easily and often enraged; but if his temper was bad, his taste in poetry was worse; and he inflicted both upon his subordinates. At last, even in that awed circle, there was a revolt. One day he read aloud to his staff some allegorical verses about a train in a tunnel, which he declared to be the work of his children's governess, although everybody knew that they were of his own composition; and a Mr. Layard (whose subsequent diplomatic career was most distinguished), being asked his opinion of them, and realizing that for once he had the tyrant at his mercy, roundly declared that he had never listened to such nonsense. After this, Lord Stratford read no more of his poems aloud; but his temper did not improve.

Such a man, with his overwhelming presence, was well calculated to make an impression at Constantinople. A more subtle, a less experienced diplomat might have been lost in the endless labyrinth of Turkish duplicity; Lord Stratford, however, never made the mistake of attempting to fathom the Oriental mind. His attitude was magnificently paternal. He held before the Sultan's ministers the image of the Reformed Turk; and though nobody, not even Stratford himself, really believed that such a paragon could ever exist, all were carried away. The effect, of course, was enormously to increase the prestige of the Ambassador; while the cause of Turkish reform suffered, if anything, a corresponding diminishment. Reschid Pasha might struggle to bring about, here or there in that waste of corruption, some minor improvement: but it was in vain; he was too much a part of it himself. And meanwhile, as one blandly continued on one's fatal way, there was Lord Stratford—to scold, to admonish, to give advice about repairing the roof of the Holy Sepulcher, or to demand with threats the abandonment of a new palace. He told Lord Palmerston that in Turkey he was a radical, and he may actually have seen himself in that light; yet it was a revivalist—an Olympian revivalist—that he most resembled; and his unusual exhortations, as they passed in at one pasha's ear and out at another's, filled his alarmed, his repentant, his admiring hearers with an added zest for committing the same sins over and over again.

In the year 1853, in the face of war and disaster, the Turks turned naturally to him. And now it seemed as if, after all, he and they had something in common. Lord Stratford was, at heart, a Tory of the most rigid type. Between an English Tory and a Turkish pasha one could hardly make comparisons; but there was a bond between them, for each clung, grimly or lazily, to a vanishing world. And so, while the fervent ambassador continued to talk of reform, his audience, its intuition sharpened by the approaching crisis, heard not the sense of his words but their sound: and the sound was the sound of unreformed English guns.

In this respect, the accusations against Lord Stratford were not without foundation. Everything—his personality, his innate prejudices—everything that lay in the realm of the unconscious and the uncontrollable—made him a provocative figure at such a time and in such a place. A wide knowledge of Russian maneuvers in the Near East, a distaste for Czar Nicholas (who had refused to receive him as ambassador at St. Petersburg in 1833), added some conscious bias to these unconscious promptings. Yet, oddly enough, a candid observer would have to admit that Lord Stratford did all that he could to preserve the peace; that his advice was wise and moderate; and that if the Turks had not perceived, behind his language, those anti-Russian feelings that he would have given much to conceal, some kind of a compromise might have been patched up. In fact, only one improvement can be suggested upon Lord Stratford's being at Constantinople. It might have been better if he had not been there at all.

III

When at last war came, the English people were ready for it. They had watched the maneuvers of the preceding months with an intensity all the more dangerous because it was partially blind. The Russians invaded Moldavia in July, 1853; the Turks replied with a declaration of war in October; on November 30, in circumstances of great brutality, the Russians abolished a Turkish fleet at Sinope. On December 14, Lord

87

Palmerston resigned from the Government, and a storm of unparalleled ferocity and remarkable incoherence immediately burst about the ears of all concerned. Palmerston, it is true, had resigned on a purely domestic matter; but he was a member of the war clique in the Cabinet and he was not a party man. He must have known what would be the consequences of his departure at such a time, and since these consequences meant the enhancement of his own popularity, he did not shrink from them. What did it matter if, in its rage, the public called the unhappy Aberdeen a traitor and a friend to Russia? What did it matter if, searching for loftier victims, it began to vilify Prince Albert and the Queen? Palmerston had once been dismissed from office through the machinations of those two personages; and now, when the streets of London were flooded with ill-printed broadsides, accusing the Prince of plotting with the Czar against the interests of England, he must have experienced some twinges of satisfaction. He was only human. So, alas, was the Prince. Once again, that dark melancholy, which always lay in wait for Albert, seized upon him and dragged him down. All through 1853, as the boxes piled higher and higher upon his table, he had tried to make sense of the Government's proceedings. He loved an ordered policy, but when the balance of power is at stake, English foreign policy is never ordered; and with a good but weak man like Aberdeen as Prime Minister, it was hardly surprising that, to a foreign eye, it should have lost all semblance even of control. And then, his head reeling with the effort to understand what was happening; then, when he needed all his reason and all his mental poise—there were those absurd accusations, hawked for a halfpenny under the very windows of the palace! It was too much. The English were ungrateful, they did not understand that if he remained aloof from society, or if in a somewhat unconstitutional manner he engineered the dismissal of a popular minister, he was doing it for *their* good, not for his own. And they were not only ungrateful, they were unpredictable. Two years before, a large number of the Queen's subjects had seen in her life and Albert's, as in a mirror, a resplendent reflection of their own. But let the hot breath of suspicion cloud that mirror, and what a very different image emerged from its depths—the image of a foreign prince, intriguing to destroy the country of his adoption, and about to be committed to the Tower for treason!

Palmerston returned to the Cabinet in ten days, and the storm sullenly subsided. But the return of Palmerston meant war. In March, 1854, England and France at length issued an ultimatum which the Czar declined to answer; and to the mind of the British public only one question, perhaps, remained to be solved. The war had come, and almost everyone was glad of that: but what was it all about? If the Czar seized Constantinople, he would control the two quickest routes towards the East, and then what would happen to India? The fact that the Indian export and import trades had increased by something like two hundred per cent over the last twenty years, added a certain weight to this query. But it was not the sort of query which the public, as a whole, found very comforting. Imperialism was not yet popular; and if one had to fight a war at the dictates of Leadenhall Street—well, one had to; but one might as well find other reasons for it. Other reasons, as it happened, were ready to hand. Russia was a tyranny, she had made a wanton attack upon the integrity of the Turkish Empire; and if one did not pause to inquire whether or not the Turkish Empire could possibly be said to have any integrity, all was well. The French, of course, were not the most desirable allies; they were suspect in England, and they returned the suspicion with interest; but with the destruction of the Turkish fleet at Sinope, all such thoughts were swept aside.

As a matter of fact, certain events which occurred more or less in private, and of which the public was in no position to be fully informed, gave a shadowy justification to its warlike feelings. A conference of ambassadors at Vienna; a meeting of the Czar and the Emperor of Austria at Olmütz; a modification of the Russian demands, made at the behest of Austria, and turned down by England and France—in these events, rather than in invasions by land or destructions by sea, the course of the future could be discerned. The four powers which had most consistently meddled in the Near East—England, France, Austria, Russia—were taking sides: the two liberal powers against the two absolutist powers. Austria's refusal actually to enter the war on the Russian side did not render the cleavage any less distinct, for that refusal dealt a blow at the Holy Alliance, and thus advanced the liberal cause. It might be argued, of course, that the word "liberal" hardly applied to England, and did not apply at all to France, in 1853-4; but both were susceptible to democratic influences, and in mid-nineteenth century Europe one did not expect much more than that. Thus self-interest and progress combined in their peculiar way; and behind the tactics of men there revealed itself, inscrutable and indistinct, the enormous strategy of fate.

✦

It was perhaps no more than appropriate that a conflict, whose origins and meaning were so obscure, should have been conducted in an equally baffling manner. For days, for weeks, the allied armies lingered at Varna, ripening for death in the warm, misty, sick climate of the Bulgarian coast. At length, on the 5th and 6th of September, they set sail across the Black Sea towards the fortress of Sebastopol and the mysterious peninsula of the Crimea. Nor did they travel alone: in spite of certain rather magical hopes that the sea-winds would "blow it out," the cholera—acquired at Marseilles and coddled at Varna—traveled safely across with them. Although it must have been obvious that if the lunar expanses of the Russian Empire were to be attacked at all, they would have to be attack at the naval fortress of Sebastopol; although the allied governments had given tentative orders to that effect at the end of June—the two commanders had found it immensely difficult to make up their minds. And now that the fatal step had been taken, now that the host had been landed at Eupatoria, within twenty miles of Sebastopol, they continued to display, in the most courteous manner, a perfect lack of unanimity. Their relative positions, which were calculated in any event to cause a certain amount of difficulty, were further complicated by the fact that Lord Raglan had not seen active service since the battle of Waterloo, while Marshal St. Arnaud was a dying man.

Under this direction, the campaign began. It was a campaign in which the English commander found himself, on one occasion, conducting operations in the midst of the Russian lines; in which the Russian field army, hastening out of Sebastopol, passed unnoticed across the front of the advancing allies, who had neglected to put out scouts; in which one of the most mag-

nificent and absurd of charges—led by a general who spent
every night on board his private yacht—would not have taken
place at all if an officer had pointed his finger in the right
direction. Farce and horror and courage were equally mingled
in its preliminary stages; but as the warm autumn gave way
to colder weather, horror predominated. In November, a
blizzard swept down upon the plateau where the allied armies
faced the memorable walls of Sebastopol; it swept away their
tents, it destroyed their ships and their stores on the coast below; it condemned them to a winter in the open, without those
upland supply depots which the most ordinary forethought
should have provided. When the news of its army's misery
reached England some of the blame was laid upon the gallant
and honest Lord Raglan, who at length, worn out with re-
sponsibilities and disappointments, followed St. Arnaud into
the grave. But, in truth, Lord Raglan was innocent. A victim of the out of date tradition of the English army, he had
neither the knowledge nor the staff with which to improvise
a winter campaign. And even if he had, he would most certainly have been prevented from accomplishing anything; for
those who administered the army's affairs in London presented
an extraordinary picture of well-preserved futility. What hope
was there when policies were sometimes decided by the Secretary of State for War and Colonies, sometimes by the Secretary at War? When discipline and promotions were controlled by the commander-in-chief at the Horse Guards,
equipment and armament by the Board of Ordnance, and
food and transport by the Treasury?

Since it is a British habit to be prepared after rather than before the event, some glimmers of light began, at length, to find
their way into that administrative murk; at length, too, Sebas-

topol was taken. The Russians acknowledged their defeat; the fortress and the dead (among whom were some Italian soldiers, whose blood had been spilled to further the diplomacy of Cavour) lay silent and ruined: the living departed. A blow had been struck at autocracy and legitimism. And yet, as one digs into the blood and muck of those distant records, what victor can one discover there except history, remarking, in its cynical way, the blind and intermittent progress of man? The battles that were fought in the open, were also fought in secret; the commander was on one side, the common soldier on another; the new vice of dictatorship emerged in the person of Napoleon; and in England the new imperialism struggled into light, while the old mercantilism slipped away into the past. A Treaty of Paris, the provisions of which were disregarded as soon as the opportunity arose, recorded these victories and changes; but it did not record what had really happened, for no treaty can record such things. The Crimean War, like the Crystal Palace, had a purely symbolic meaning; the long and painful birth of the nineteenth century was at last completed; and whether that process was worth one drop of innocent blood is a question to which, even today, we have not been able to find an answer.

It was only natural that the Manchester school should have opposed the war from the very beginning. Mr. John Bright was especially persistent. In Parliament and out, his voice was raised; but that amazing eloquence, in which the imagery of the Bible was blended in the most singular way with plain commercial considerations, fell upon skeptical ears. It was in vain that he summoned the Angel of Death, in vain that he invoked the Stormy Euxine. His hearers, it is true, were impressed—it would have been difficult to listen to John Bright unmoved—but, somehow or other, the impression was not a lasting one. Was it not the fact that his family business had been hurt by the war, which had raised the price of tow? Such questions were hardly fair—few men were more altruistic than Bright—but, fair or not, they fatally weakened his position. And, indeed, selfless and courageous as he was, his economic philosophy was a profoundly selfish one. An advocate of unrestricted competition, he had, as it were, taken refuge in the Crystal Palace: it was not a safe place from which to throw stones. It was all very well for him to call war a gentleman's exercise; that was no doubt the case: but did he not realize that unrestricted competition would lead in the end—precisely—to war?

Beside the bright glass hothouse of international capitalism stands the fortress of Sebastopol; and there they must stay forever, the Conservatory and the Fort, for men to ponder. They have nothing in common except the fact that one followed directly upon the other. It is their proximity that gives them their mysterious and mocking significance.

IV

If these two mighty symbols made any impression upon the Prince of Wales, it was a very slight one: the former increased his distaste for education, the latter his taste for uniforms. The Crimean War, however, did have a negative effect upon his life: it made it impossible for him to enjoy, for several years to come, the engaging hospitality of Napoleon and Eugénie.

For the war, strange to say, did not produce any cordiality

between England and France. On the contrary, a most unhappy suspicion existed upon both sides of the Channel. The
Queen and the Prince (who had now been given the title of
Prince Consort) took their six children for a surprise visit to
Cherbourg on August 19, 1857; and though everything went
off well, except for the drunken behavior of the Mayor of
Bricquebec, Albert was much disturbed by the fortifications
at Cherbourg. He examined them gravely, and wrote a serious report to the Cabinet, in which he stressed the necessity
of hastening the Portsmouth defenses. Somehow or other, Napoleon III was no longer in favor, even with Victoria. He
and Eugénie had paid a visit to Osborne earlier in the month,
and though they were as charming as usual, the Prince Consort was not deceived. He took Napoleon to task for not
bringing a Minister with him. "Où trouver l'homme?" asked
Napoleon. Albert replied solemnly that no sovereign had been
great without having great ministers. Friendships are hardly
maintained in this way.

But then who wished to be friends with Napoleon? Not
Albert, who entertained strict ideas about the behavior of
royal and would-be royal persons. Even during the war, Napoleon had been most trying: he was simply not a respectable ally. There was the time when he suddenly took it into
his head, at Mardi Gras, to visit in the most public manner
the house of Madame Le Hou, which was little better than
a brothel. And there had been that rather dreadful *fête
champêtre* at Villeneuve L'Etang, when the Emperor disappeared all evening with Madame Castiglione in the shrubbery,
and the Empress fainted with mortification, and all the gentlemen danced with their hats on. Or the time when he was
at Plombières for his kidney-trouble, the door of his carriage

jammed, and he leaped out of the window *à la Harlequin*, to the mingled delight and derision of those who were privileged to be the onlookers. Too often Napoleon was either indelicate or undignified, and the Prince Consort did not know which was the worse. Besides, his foreign policy was growing more and more sinister; it was thought that he had designs upon England; though what the designs were the Prince Consort (along with others even more qualified to state an opinion) confessed himself unable to decide. Most certainly, England would try to keep peace with France: but it was clear that Albert's family would not again visit the Emperor's dazzling and dubious court.

Chapter Three

AN EDUCATIONAL INTERLUDE

THE Prince of Wales worried his father even more than did the Emperor Napoleon. It must have been clear by now that the boy would never become a scholar, and that such gifts as he had were of a sociable description. Though he was often impatient and quick-tempered, he could be charming; but this element in his son's character failed to please the inexorable father. Albert was not charming, and he saw no reason why his son should be. And so, on the few occasions when selected boys from Eton were allowed to take tea with the heir to the throne at Windsor, and when, if left alone, Bertie might have enjoyed himself, the father was always in the room. The wretched youths trembled before that overwhelming presence, trembled even more at the ponderous teutonic jokes. The tea-parties were not a success. But except for them, and except for two walking tours in England with selected companions and one educational tour abroad, Bertie never saw a boy of his own age. On the latter occasion, one catches a glimpse of him at Metternich's castle of Johannisberg, where, the aged statesman told Guizot, he "plaisait à tout le monde," but had a very sad and embarrassed air. And well he might, for such a visit would have to be set forth with extra care in the diary—and the diary, in his father's opinion, was grow-ing more "bald, ungrammatical, and badly penned" every month.

When Bertie was nearly seventeen years old, he was given an independent establishment at White Lodge in Richmond Park, into which the outside world only penetrated in the form of eminent and elderly people, who were occasionally commanded to dinner. In addition to his two tutors, Mr. Tar-ver and Mr. Gibbs, he was now provided with three equer-ries, serving in monthly rotation. One of these gentlemen, Lord Valletort, was rumored to have some taste for music and drawing; Major Teesdale, who had won his V.C. in the Crimean War, was acquainted with French and Italian; while of Major Lindsay, who had also been decorated with the V.C., it is not known that he had any special accomplishments. Yet even if all three had been unusually gifted, and therefore equipped to train the young prince in the more pleasing ways of the world, a memorandum from the royal parents would effectually have prevented them. They were warned against lolling and lounging, slouching, dandyism, practical jokes, frivolity, pleasures which did not also instruct, etc., etc. They were told to guard against these vices, not only in the prince, but in themselves. The memorandum was hardly a tactful or a flattering document, and it served to turn White Lodge into a slightly militaristic monastery, where the living and dead languages were pursued with tedious severity, where no-body was a dandy, and nobody lolled or lounged.

When Bertie was seventeen, in November, 1858, there were festivities at Windsor; but another world, so near to Windsor and to Richmond Park, was denied him. "Bertie . . . is not to be in London during the Season," the Prince Consort wrote to his brother, "as long as he is neither fish nor flesh, as the old saying is." A memorandum was sent to the boy—"Life consists of duties" was its theme—a long, gray, pious memorandum: he read it, and burst into tears.

With the memorandum came Colonel the Hon. Robert Bruce, who was to be the prince's Governor, and who replaced Mr. Gibbs. The Prince Consort declared that the Colonel was amiable and affable, and that his expression was extremely mild; but others were not altogether of this opinion: for there was, to tell the truth, a certain dourness in Bruce's composition, while his devotion to discipline, as he himself admitted, was little short of pedantic. He was not likely to make the mistake of praising the self-willed, idle, backward and unhappy boy who had been placed in his charge: on the contrary, he disliked almost everything that Bertie said or did, and composed a number of memoranda to that effect—much to the approval of the Prince Consort, who had commanded him to be frank. The Prince of Wales had expressed a desire to enter into an active army career, but the Colonel, oddly enough, thought army life a temptation and army companions unprofitable; the royal parents agreed; and so, when they left White Lodge in February, 1859, it was to Rome that the Governor and the unwilling Bertie proceeded.

Undoubtedly there was much to be obtained, of an educational nature, from a visit to the Eternal City. On the other hand, there were some countervailing considerations. Not the least of these was the fact that Victor Emmanuel, King of Sardinia, and England's ally in the Crimean War, would sooner or later have to be encountered. A hairy man, of a virile physique, an amorous nature, and an indiscriminate affability, his visit to the English court in '56 had not been an unqualified success. His appearance was disheveled, his manners wild, and he called everyone "mon cher." The Prince of Wales had, it is true, been much taken with him, chiefly because of his boast that he could decapitate an ox with one blow of his sword; and he would doubtless have been only too pleased to avail himself of Victor Emmanuel's invitation to enter Italy by way of his capital of Turin. Victoria, however, shuddering with horror, declined.

Nor was it Victor Emmanuel's private character alone that made him unpopular with the Queen and the Prince Consort. In 1859, it was quite evident that he intended to drive the Austrians out of Lombardy and Venetia, and that he would make his attempt very soon. In this he had the support of Napoleon III, who had come to an agreement with Victor Emmanuel's Minister, Cavour, in July of the previous year. The Prince Consort was much alarmed, for, though he liked to think of himself as a liberal, he favored the Hapsburg cause; and, besides, he entertained the curious belief that the Austrian Empire could reform itself from within. No doubt Bertie would be safe enough in Rome; but even in Rome, in the early months of 1859, an air of mystery and restlessness prevailed. Pope Pius IX confided to Odo Russell that, if the King of Sardinia persisted in his inflammatory speeches, he would be obliged to "go with the faithful into the catacombs, as did the Christians of the early centuries, and there await the will of the Supreme Being." Russell hastened in great agitation to Cardinal Antonelli, the Papal Secretary of State, who was able to reassure him; it was unlikely, said the Cardinal, that events would become so grave as to drive the Holy Father underground. For it was upon Napoleon, rather than

Victor Emmanuel, that the immediate future depended; and Napoleon's relations with the French Catholics were so delicate that he would continue, at all costs, to protect the Pope.

At the Hotel D'Angleterre, meanwhile, the prince led a life not very different from that at White Lodge. Before breakfast, he learned by heart; from ten to eleven, he was closeted with his Italian master; from eleven to twelve, Mr. Tarver instructed him in the classics. Between five and six, he had his French lessons, and from seven to eight, there was private reading and music. The interval between these studies was to be occupied with sight-seeing, of an elevating and instructive nature. In this respect a number of experts had been consulted, including Mr. Ruskin, who gave it as his opinion that his Royal Highness should be taught that "one of the principal duties of Princes was to provide for the preservation of perishing frescoes and monuments." There was, to be sure, a sufficiency of these objects in Rome, many of them in a suitably perishing condition; but his Royal Highness's diary gave no indication that he had any desire to preserve them. It was in vain that Mr. Joseph Barclay Pentland took him over the Forum, the Capitol, the Coliseum, the Appian Way, St. Peter's, the Vatican; in vain that they explored the minor churches, the colleges, the museums: Colonel Bruce could only report that his young charge had given way to fits of bad temper. Even the tombs of the exiled Stuarts, even the Pope's symbolical washing of feet, made no impression upon that budding organism. Only once did the prince display any interest in what he was shown: in the studio of John Gibson, R.A., he was much struck by three portraits of a beautiful Italian woman.

There was, however, one visit from which much was ex-

pected. No other Prince of Wales had ever called upon a
pope, and on February 10, Bertie was to have that privilege:
surely his diary would rise to *that* occasion. The visit had not
been easy to arrange, though Pius IX was all courtesy and
complaisance; for in many English quarters, such an action
would only be regarded as extremely dangerous. Even Lord
John Russell shook his head; he could not forgive Pius IX
for not being a liberal, for grossly mismanaging the Papal
States, and for granting territorial titles to English catholic
bishops: but Queen Victoria had brushed these objections
aside. However, she insisted that Bruce should be present;
otherwise, she told the King of the Belgians, "they might
hereafter have pretended, God knows! what Bertie had said."
Perhaps it was just as well; for his Holiness began by touch-
ing upon the revival of Catholicism in England, and was proceeding to develop this theme when he caught sight of the
Colonel's face, from which all mildness of expression had
fled, and hastily changed the conversation. The Colonel took
his revenge by not making the usual courtesy call upon
Cardinal Antonelli; but the diary, like the interview, was
completely flat.

On the whole, the stay at Rome was a tedious and unre-
warding affair. The Colonel's reports were full of complaints.
Everything had been done that could be done; the prince
had been kept away from Roman society—but it was to no
avail. He still continued to center his thoughts upon ceremony, social standing, manners, dress. Important men had
been summoned to dinner—John Lothrop Motley, Frederick
Leighton, Lord Stratford de Redcliffe, Robert Browning. Mr.
Browning was warned in advance to "eschew compliments
and keep to Italian politics"; but it was compliments, alas, for

which the prince hankered. And it was Italian politics that drove him from Rome.

For the Emperor of Austria, having refused to take part in any congress on the Italian question which included the King of Sardinia, now declared war on that monarch. Napoleon III allied himself with Victor Emmanuel; and though his advisers had managed to restrain him from such an action in the Crimean War, Napoleon could not be prevented this time from leading his armies in person. At enormous cost he won two victories over the Austrians at Magenta and Solferino: whatever gifts he may have inherited from his uncle, military genius was not among them. He had promised his Sardinian ally that he would not turn back until Italy was free from the Alps to the Adriatic; but he soon persuaded himself that Cavour was intriguing against him; moreover, Prussia was mobilizing along the Rhine, and he himself was sick in body and spirit. And so, in July, he suddenly agreed to meet the Emperor of Austria at Villafranca, and there, on the 11th, consented to terms whereby Austria maintained her hold on Venetia, while Lombardy was added to the domains of Victor Emmanuel. The unhappy Italian king wrung his hands: he could do nothing. Pressure from England eventually gave him the duchies of Modena and Tuscany, but Venetia would have to wait for deliverance from the Hapsburg. Napoleon had betrayed the cause of Italian freedom, and though he wrested from Victor Emmanuel the province of Savoy and the territory of Nice, and thereby obtained his "natural frontier of the Alps," he had also pronounced his own doom. The Italian campaign was the watershed of his ominous career: thereafter it ran downward towards the bloody whirlpool of Sedan.

It was on April 26, at the beginning of these portentous
movements, that Colonel Bruce took his charge in haste to
Civita Vecchia, went on board H.M.S. *Scourge,* and dis-
creetly vanished from the scene.

II

The Prince Consort, though discouraged, was not deterred
by the evident failure of the Roman visit from continuing
with his scheme of education. Bertie was backward, frivolous,
vain: everybody said so; even Sir James Clark, the Prince
Consort's physician, dared to declare it openly. But Bertie
was also royal. Now royal persons are not as other men; they
may be unfitted for intellectual exercise, fond of amusement,
quite affable and perfectly commonplace—they may, in fact,
just be Bertie—but, moving as they do through a mist of
glamor, superstition, and ceremony, they have a distorted appearance in the public eye. Why not, then, distort the dis-
tortion? Why not turn Bertie into what he quite obviously
was not—a painstaking, hard-working, high-minded young
man? So the Prince Consort argued. The position which his
son would inherit, that of a constitutional monarch, did not,
surely, demand very much in the way of intellectual attain-
ments. To be assiduous in the performance of one's public
duties, to open boxes and sign papers, to obey the advice of
one's ministers—was there much more to it than that? Or
rather, would not the fact that one lived in the very midst
of the complex business of a great state eventually bring with
it experience and even, it may be, wisdom? But was that all
that there was to monarchy? The Prince Consort most de-

cidedly thought not. He was convinced that royal persons had an active, not a passive, rôle to play in world events. He himself labored night and day to inject into the Constitution an element of absolutism. He was a most energetic, a most important, even a useful personage: and the idea that he might also, perhaps, be a very dangerous one never occurred to him at all. What *did* occur to him, however, was the disturbing thought that all his fine schemes for the well-being of England and the world depended upon his eldest son. It was not for him to relax the discipline which had been imposed upon Bertie; or to admit that his son would never, never resemble himself. It might be true, but even the truth must be made to yield; if Bertie was not a paragon by nature, then a paragon he must become by application.

And so it was not into the world but into the University of Oxford that the prince was thrust. But first, since Oxford had a Long Vacation—a much *too* Long Vacation, the Prince Consort thought—Bertie was sent to Edinburgh. Here he occupied a set of bleak apartments in Holyrood Palace, where he was visited by Mr. Herbert Fisher, Dr. Leonard Schmitz, and Dr. Lyon Playfair, who strove to instill into his reluctant mind the elements of law, Greek and Latin history, and science. Invitations from surrounding noblemen were sternly refused, and the only exercise of a sociable description that the boy was permitted was to drill three times a week with the Sixteenth Hussars.

But if Edinburgh was dreary, how much drearier, when at last he reached it, was Oxford. The Prince Consort had not wished him to be a member of any one college, on the principle that he belonged to the whole University "as he will always belong to the whole Nation . . ." Dr. Liddell, the Dean of Christchurch, was obliged, however, to disagree. Oxford, he said, would insist upon his Royal Highness's attaching himself to a particular college. The Prince Consort, realizing that in the University authorities he had found a set of men as jealous of their privileges as he was of his own, beat an unwilling retreat; and the Prince of Wales was duly entered at Christchurch. But to share in its life—that was quite another thing. "The more I think of it," Albert wrote to Dean Liddell, "the more I see the difficulties of the Prince being thrown together with other young men." The only use for Oxford, he continued, "is that it is a place for *study*." This was a concept of Oxford which even Dean Liddell, it may be, found surprising; there was some notion prevalent at the time that young men went up to the University in order to learn to be gentlemen, and to fit themselves (if they had any influence) for a position in the world. A student was still just a poor man who could hope to better himself only by study. Oxford, in fact, though some reforms had been instituted, was yet to become a paradise of the middle classes. With its extraordinary class distinctions, its soft traditional airs, its odd mingling of monastic discipline and secular license, it was not at all the sort of place of which Albert could approve; and except in so far as it provided the young man with learning, he was determined that his son should avoid it altogether. Bertie, therefore, with Colonel Bruce and an equerry, went to live at Frewin Hall, a modest house in the city, whose walls effectively guarded him against the contagion of university life.

Every day some eminent hand lifted the knocker of the front door of Frewin Hall. It might be that of Sir Benjamin Brodie, the Professor of Chemistry; or of Arthur Stanley,

Professor of Ecclesiastical History; or of Friedrich Max Muller, Taylorian Professor of Modern European Languages. These gentlemen were the prince's instructors; and it would be hard to say who faced their meetings with more distaste, the pupil or the teachers. Three times a week six carefully selected companions from Christchurch gathered at Frewin Hall to listen with the prince to the words of Goldwin Smith, Regius Professor of Modern History, who strove, not always successfully, to keep his caustic tongue in check. For relaxation there were (in the words of the Prince Consort) "your convivial meetings at dinner"—where, in an atmosphere of considerable restraint, distinguished men from the university and one or two unhappy undergraduates gathered to discuss questions of a literary and academic nature. The wine flowed in driblets, and nobody was permitted to smoke.

Oxford, strange to say, in spite of the Prince Consort's hopes, failed to infuse into Bertie's character the slightest tincture of scholarship. The Professor of Chemistry, the Professor of Ecclesiastical History, the Professor of Modern European Languages, even the Regius Professor of Modern History, appeared to have uttered their wisdom into a void. The memoranda from Colonel Bruce were filled with criticisms. Perhaps it would have been better, after all, if the prince had spent his time in Edinburgh with kind Dr. Schmitz and clever Dr. Playfair; perhaps he would have been happier in the tattered but majestic shadows of Holyrood than in the more restricted gloom of Frewin Hall. But then, of course, though many experiments were tried, the experiment of making Bertie happy was not among them.

III

It was in the spring of 1860, a novel idea occurred to the Prince Consort. The Queen had promised, during the Crimean War, that the Prince of Wales should pay a visit to Canada; there had been a further invitation from President Buchanan of the United States: and Albert, putting two and two together in his own way, decided—so he told his brother—that "the Canadians wish to show the Americans how happy, free, and yet monarchical it is possible to be." He consulted Stockmar, and the baron declared that it would do Bertie a great deal of good to see Canada and America—not to mention the improvement in Anglo-American relations which was bound to result from such a condescending visit. Others were less convinced. "The tours of great personages," said Lord John Russell, "seldom have more than a transient effect; they form no real and solid relation of friendship between nations." But Lord John was careful to keep this opinion to himself.

Apart from the hopes of an improvement in Anglo-American relations, there was another political motive behind the intended visit. It was thought that the presence of a Prince of Wales in their midst might do something to quiet the Canadians who, however monarchical they might be, showed extremely few outward signs of being it.

In fact, ever since 1837 the affairs of Canada had been causing some apprehension in English circles. In that year, the provinces of Upper and Lower Canada, activated by a most inconvenient desire for self-government, burst into rebellion; and though the disturbances were easily suppressed, and though they never spread into the Maritime Provinces, it was clear that something would have to be done. Lord Durham was therefore sent out to discover a remedy. He behaved in a rather high-handed manner, and retired in some disgrace; but before he died in 1839—("Canada has been the death of him," said John Stuart Mill)—he was able to complete his famous report. This document, which conceded in principle the control of the executive by the elected body, much distressed the Whig government; but their distress was equaled, if not surpassed, by that of Durham's successor, Lord Sydenham, a candle manufacturer and a politician. Lord Sydenham found himself in the delicate position of having to put into effect some of Lord Durham's liberal suggestions, all of which he heartily disliked—so that, like Penelope, he felt obliged to undo his own work: and the dubious atmosphere which surrounded his stay in Canada continued until his death, for whether he expired from nervous exhaustion or as the result of a fall from a horse, has never been decided. He was succeeded as governor-general by the progressive Bagot, who speedily died of dropsy. Anything that Bagot may have achieved in the way of introducing responsible government was nullified by the next two governors-general, Sir Charles Metcalfe and Lord Cathcart, one of whom spent his time in fighting the reform party of Lafontaine and Baldwin, the other in suspecting the United States. At length, in 1847, there appeared upon the scene the sanguine figure of Lord Elgin. He was a son-in-law of Lord Durham, and he was determined to do justice to the principles advocated by his famous father-in-law. But alas for Lord Elgin! The repeal of the Corn Laws, the subsequent repeal of the Navigation

Acts, aroused the fury of the grain, shipping and lumber interests in Canada. There was a violent Tory reaction. Elgin
was stoned by a mob in Montreal, which also burned the
Parliament House, but he refused to answer violence with
violence; and with his liberal administration some rays of
light began to penetrate the murk of Canadian affairs. Slowly
and dimly the passage from a union to a confederation policy
took place—accompanied by religious and racial disturbances,
by demands for annexation to the United States, and by political chicaneries of a most complicated and ingenious description. It was towards the end of this process that the Prince of
Wales arrived in Canada.

Since royal tours are so contrived as to avoid unpleasant
truths, his journey was on the whole a most agreeable one.
There were, to be sure, one or two awkward moments. The
inhabitants of Lower Canada were French, not only in their
blood but in their sentiments; and the appearance of the
tricolor flying alongside the Union Jack above the Roman
Catholic Cathedral at Quebec caused a certain amount of consternation. The inhabitants of Upper Canada, on the other
hand, were aggressively Protestant. The royal steamer was
obliged to pass by Kingston, because the Orangemen of that
town attempted to greet it with some rather downright anti-
papist songs; while the mayor and corporation of Toronto,
who had substituted for his portrait a lurid transparency of
King William III crossing the Boyne, were denied invitations
to the prince's levée. On the whole, however, this part of the
tour seems to have justified Bruce's slightly acid report that
"H.R.H. acquitted himself admirably, and seems pleased with
everything, himself included." Whether it also justified Stockmar's comment that the Canadians had unquestionably derived

much benefit from the presence of the heir to the throne, must remain in doubt; for it was not until the British North America Act of 1867, which provided for the federation of Canada, that they showed any appreciable signs of being friendly toward England.

On September 20, 1860, the royal party crossed from Windsor into the United States. The Duke of Newcastle, who as Secretary of State for the Colonies had been obliged to compose the prince's Canadian speeches, breathed a sigh of relief; he was now only a sightseer, while Lord Lyons, the Minister in Washington, took charge of the tour. They moved from Detroit to Chicago, St. Louis, Cincinnati, Pittsburgh, Harrisburg, and Baltimore, arriving in Washington on October 3. The prince was now traveling as Baron Renfrew, but it was not his incognito so much as the fact that a certain Abraham Lincoln was campaigning for the presidency, that rendered the inhabitants of the Middle West somewhat less responsive to the passage of royalty than had been expected. It was true, of course, that the descendants of George III had not exactly flocked to the United States since the Revolution; in fact, the only member who had hitherto appeared there was the prince's grandfather, Edward, an insolvent martinet, who had once attended one of Mrs. Washington's receptions. But though "Baron Renfrew" stayed three days at the White House, planted a tree near the grave of George Washington, and was treated with every courtesy by President Buchanan, it was clear that the capital of the United States was too involved in the presidential campaign to bestow more than a passing attention upon him. As in Italy, so here, it was Bertie's fate to be present at the maturing of momentous events. Only in New York, which, then

as now, was a world to itself, did his presence create a satisfactory disturbance. Three hundred thousand people crowded
the streets as he drove to the Fifth Avenue Hotel; they were,
the Duke of Newcastle wrote to the Queen, "worked up
almost to madness, and yet restrained within the bounds of
the most perfect courtesy." On October 12, he attended a
ball at the Academy of Music on East 14th Street. Three
thousand had been invited, five thousand attended: "it was
not well managed," said the Duke. Mr. Edmund C. Stedman,
who recorded the occasion in verse, gave vent to some curious speculations:

> "But as ALBERT EDWARD, young and fair,
> Stood on the canopied dais-stair,
> And looked, from the circle crowding there,
> To the length and breadth of the outer scene . . .
> Perhaps he saw that we have a king,
>   The potent and silver DOLLAR,
> Able the nose of the workman to bring
> To the grindstone, and over his neck to fling
>   A heavy and feudal collar . . ."

Perhaps, but it is hardly likely. During the course of a long
and full life, such thoughts rarely troubled his Royal Highness. What he did see was that the young ladies of New York
were neither uncomely nor backward; indeed they pressed
around him in a manner which, in the Duke of Newcastle's
words, was "not in strict accordance with good breeding";
and were only deterred by the sudden collapse of the dance
floor from mobbing him altogether. The Duke may have been
disgusted; but it is not difficult to guess what must have been
the effect of such jostling beauty upon the young hermit of
White Lodge and Holyrood and Frewin Hall.

And so, at last, at Portland, Maine, on October 20, "the

Tremendous Tour" (as King Leopold called it) came to an end. Had it made any effect upon Anglo-American relations? The historian Motley contended that the prince's visit to the United States was a factor in determining England's attitude towards the Civil War. But, considering that attitude and its consequences—the *Trent* affair, the *Alabama* incident, President Grant's dreams for the annexation of Canada—Motley's remark can hardly be considered an endorsement of royal pilgrimages to the western hemisphere. In any case, it seems more likely that Lord John Russell was correct when he said that royal tours made no lasting impression; and that Lord Palmerston, in refusing to concur in any bestowal of honors upon Bruce, was acting, not as a Whig, but as a man of common sense. The Prince of Wales, in fact, passed through the United States and vanished, leaving no trace behind him except a chestnut tree planted by Washington's grave, and a persistent (and, no doubt, improbable) rumor that he had on one occasion eluded the vigilance of Bruce and Newcastle, and indulged his abounding manhood in the bagnios of New York.

IV

Madingley Hall lies four miles from the town of Cambridge. Hither, in January, 1861, Bertie repaired, to undertake a course of studies at the University. French and German ("the languages," said the Prince Consort, "in which the young man will have chiefly to correspond"), Chemistry, Law, and History were his chief studies. The dinner parties for elderly people continued; sometimes he was permitted to hunt, an exercise of which he was not particularly fond;

more often, in spite of his Governor's objections, he would visit the Amateur Dramatic Club behind the Hoop Hotel in Jesus Lane. Whatever effect the tour may have had upon the loyalty of Canada, it had put the prince himself into a rebellious frame of mind; and his father was obliged to visit Cambridge several times in order to instill into Bertie a proper respect for discipline. Ten weeks of military training at the Curragh that summer only increased this restlessness; for, as the Prince Consort very rightly remarked, the officers of the regular army were singularly uninterested in their profession, and the air of relaxation which pervaded the camp was not perhaps the best atmosphere in which to prepare for yet another winter of stern and unremitting education.

The winter, as it happened, was never completed, so far as education was concerned. To many observers, it must have been apparent for some time that the Prince Consort was not a well man. Bald, stooping, prematurely aged, he dedicated his days, with an almost maniacal intensity, to work and yet more work; and the harder he worked, the more discouraged he became. His position, it is true, was no longer a dubious one. In England and Europe alike, he was highly respected. He could no longer be dismissed as a high-minded meddler; his meticulous interference in affairs of state had given him a vast knowledge of events, if not of men; while at the same time, as a permanent and adored adviser of the Queen, he had become to all intents and purposes the King of England. And yet, in the end, it was England that defeated him. That island is an accommodating region, but it has never provided a happy home for political perfectionists. Hard as the Prince labored, high as he piled his memoranda upon the desks of ministers, he never could attune himself to the evasions, the hesitations, the perpetual compromises of English foreign policy; while the muddle of domestic affairs left him worried and miserable. He longed for order: but order could no longer be imposed upon England from above; it would have to come from below, in its own mysterious way, and at its own time. Albert had, it is true, raised the Crown to a position it had not occupied since the days of George III; but could he be sure that something, he could not say precisely what, some powerful Ministry, or sudden revulsion of public opinion, would not tear it down again? Was his dream of a reformed royalty practicable; or was it, after all, just a dream? Who could be sure of anything where England was concerned? For years he had waged an extraordinary spiritual battle with that country; he had waged it with humorless persistence and unabating courage; and now, in 1861, in the plenitude of his power, he was a prey to despondency, to strange premonitions, to sleepless nights. Such was his reward. He seemed to have lost all desire, not for work, but for life itself; and when, towards the end of the year, an inspection of some barracks in a pouring rain, followed by a hurried visit to Madingley Hall to chide his son for further infractions of discipline, brought on an attack of typhoid fever, the Prince Consort gently, even gratefully, slipped away from an ungrateful world. This shocking event, which took place on December 14, 1861, put an end to Bertie's formal education, and he left Cambridge and his books forever.

Among the disappointments which the Prince Consort had encountered in his curious pilgrimage through English history, not the least was that provided by his own son. Bertie, to be sure, was not exactly English. With his protruding eyes, his German accent, his obstinate pride of place, he was distinctly Hanoverian; but he appeared to have engrafted upon this stock some of those "idle tendencies" which, the Prince Consort declared, were typical of English youth. These idle tendencies, as it happened, were soon to blossom in an unexpectedly agreeable manner; but that was all. Albert's schemes for a new royal class had died with him. Even the education which he had imposed upon his son was speedily forgotten. Indeed, Bertie had acquired such a distaste for books that from now onwards he rarely opened one; and when he did, he was not able to concentrate upon it for more than half an hour at a time: while his handwriting—and both Albert and Stockmar had agreed that a legible handwriting was indispensable—degenerated year by year into a more and more illegible scrawl.

v

The death of the Prince Consort sent the Queen into a retirement from which she did not emerge for many years. The Victorians were apt, in the face of Death, to express themselves with a lack of restraint that they might otherwise have thought unseemly; and in this respect the Queen was even more Victorian than her subjects. Her nature was not an ambiguous one. Her grief was intense and profound, and she poured it forth to everyone—her ministers, her relatives, her children—in the most heart-rending manner. "The things of this world are of no interest to the Queen," she wrote to Earl Russell, ". . . *her* thoughts are fixed above." Such was the tenor of her correspondence; for, in the simplicity of her heart, she believed, not only in her eventual reunion with

Albert, but in his daily and hourly awareness of what was going on in the world below. "No *human power*," she therefore decided, "will make me swerve from what *he* decided or wished." The Prince Consort's decisions and wishes were to be found in the interminable memoranda that he had left behind him, and in countless other ways they had been indelibly impressed upon the mind of Victoria: the only trouble was that they were no longer in the present tense. The world must move—but would the Queen, with a ghostly adviser at her elbow who spoke only in the accents of the past, move with it? "Her determination," wrote the prescient Palmerston, "to conform to what she from time to time may persuade herself would have been at the moment the opinion of the late Prince promises no end of difficulties for those who will have to advise her."

At first, in her agony, the Queen turned towards her eldest son. There was some idle gossip in high society that she could not bear to admit him to her presence, that she treated him with contempt and hatred; but her letters indicate a contrary feeling. Indeed, she leaned upon him: yet he was a frail reed. How could he ever be made to fill, even in the most inadequate way, his father's shoes? It might have been supposed that she would now permit him some access, however slight, to the multifarious business of the state; that she would allow him to acquire some knowledge, however superficial, of the delicate relations between the Crown and its ministers: in short, that she would begin to teach him how to be a king. But no, such considerations left her cold. The Voice of Albert was particularly clear upon this subject. Had he not said many times that Bertie was undeveloped and irresponsible? Against this decision there was no appeal: and for

the rest of her long life the Queen adhered to it. Before his
death, moreover, Albert had more or less decided that Bertie
should leave Cambridge and embark upon an educational
tour in the East; it merely remained to put his wishes into
effect.

And so, the plans for an Eastern journey were set on foot.
Since the expedition was to include a camping tour through
Palestine, the Reverend Arthur Penrhyn Stanley was invited
to become a member of it. Stanley accepted, with grave misgivings—as Professor of Ecclesiastical History at Oxford he
had already had some experience of the prince. A man of rare
piety, an evangelical whose simplicity had outfaced the subtle
genius of Newman, the fierce logic of W. G. Ward, and all
the strange speculations of German theology, his mind was
most at home on those far, airy borders where the material
and the spiritual worlds meet and intermingle. He was well
acquainted with the Holy Land, and its barren spaces were
illuminated, for him, with the poignant story of eighteen
hundred years ago. Could he hope to communicate any of
this to the young prince? Well, he could try, and he *would*
try: but the attempt was not likely to be a happy one.

Stanley's letters revealed, for all the mild language in
which they were couched, an attitude towards the Prince
of Wales that was composed, in almost equal parts, of affection and distaste. The shadow under which the young man
had lived began to disperse with the Prince Consort's death;
he emerged, as it were, for the first time into the light of
day. Nor was it any longer possible to doubt that his was an
irremediably terrestrial nature. He cared nothing at all for
the things of the spirit—yet he meant well, so long as he had
his own way. And his own way, as it happened, he was now

to have. Victoria, with Albert's notes to guide her, had intended this tour to be of the usual repressive character; and General Bruce had his orders to that effect. The General did his best; but Albert's hand, stretching out from the grave to direct the little party as it moved up the Nile, was stretched in vain. Bertie was supposed to do a good deal of serious reading, and he read *East Lynne*. He was not to be encouraged to smoke, but along with the other gentlemen of the party (the disapproving Bruce excepted) he indulged in a pipe. It was he who gave orders that nobody was to shoot on Sundays—except at crocodiles, for whom there was to be no Sabbath. Even the diary, though he continued to write it, had lost its terrors—for the Prince Consort was no longer there to read and disapprove, while as for Stockmar, who had shaken his head so often over its pages, he was an old man, nodding by the fire at Coburg, wrapped in bitter dreams of the past, and dying of a broken heart.

Stanley did not entirely enjoy his passage through Egypt. It was odd but not unpleasant to preach a sermon in the great Hall of Karnak, in the shade of two gigantic pillars; or to speculate, by candlelight, in the Temple at Dendera, on the likeness between Cleopatra's sculptured face and that of the Bishop of Oxford. Yet he was glad when, on March 31, 1862, they entered Jerusalem at the head of a cavalcade of Turks, English clergy, and extraordinary Greek ecclesiastics, while groups of dusty children sang beneath the trees. The party hastened on to Bethany. "This was the one half-hour which, throughout the journey," Stanley wrote, "I had determined to have alone with the Prince." He pointed out each stage of the Triumphal Entry, and when at last, he turned around to call the attention of the rest of the party—which, with great tact, had fallen behind—"I saw, and bade the Prince look round too, the only detail which could have been worth noticing on such an occasion—a flock of white sheep and black goats feeding on the mountainside; the groundwork of the great parable, delivered also from this hillside . . ." Had he made any impression upon the polite young man by his side? "I fell to the rear, feeling that I had at least done my best." And yet—"how often I felt as if my tongue clove to the roof of my mouth!"

At the Mosque of Hebron, the shrines of Abraham, Jacob, and Joseph were opened amidst loud groans—the guardian declaring that other Christian princes would have had to pass in over his dead body—only for the heir to the Queen of England would he have done such a thing. The prince had not been unconscious of Stanley's antipathy. "High station, you see," he said reproachfully, "has, after all, some merit, some advantages." Stanley was touched; with difficulty he suppressed a smile; with difficulty, too, he suppressed a groan: of such young men are the kingdoms of this world.

But the world, and its kingdoms, were now, at last, spread at the prince's feet. The chrysalis, which Albert had contemplated with such disfavor, had burst asunder; and what emerged was a butterfly, with a remarkable facility for alighting gracefully upon such patches of sunlight as happened to present themselves. The party came home by way of Constantinople, and, although the Queen had expressed herself as being quite opposed to such manifestations, the Sultan could not be restrained from giving the prince a state breakfast. A letter exists from Sir Henry Bulwer, the British Ambassador, to Earl Russell, in which, beneath the conventional hyperbole of its language (for it was intended for the

Queen's eyes), there can be discerned a note of genuine surprise. Abdul Aziz was not the easiest man with whom to converse, especially since he knew no language but his own, and had to use an interpreter. Yet, coached in advance by Bulwer, the prince had conducted himself with extraordinary facility. "I do not think," was the Ambassador's bold conclusion, "he will study much or learn much from books, but he will attain all that is practically necessary for him to know by observation and use it with address." It was the dawn of a career; but somehow or other it is hard to believe that the Prince Consort, had he been alive, would have derived much pleasure from the Ambassador's letter.

At half past five on the afternoon of June 14, the prince came home to Windsor. Victoria noted in her Journal that he was looking "extremely well" and that he was "most affectionate." "The Prince of Wales," she wrote in a memorandum some days later, "is only anxious to do whatever his Mother and Father wish." In other words, yet another of the late Prince Consort's plans must now be put into effect: it was time for Bertie to be married.

Chapter Four

THE DYNASTIES

IN 1858, the King of the Belgians, as head of the Coburg family, had drawn up a list of seven princesses who were eligible for marriage with Bertie. Fifth upon the list was the Princess Alexandra of Denmark. Having met Alexandra at Speier and again at Heidelberg, Bertie decided that there was no need for him to bother about the other six young ladies.

Alexandra. was, indeed, a very lovely girl; she was also, though lively enough, of a gentle and modest disposition. She was born in 1844, at Copenhagen, a charming little capital, full of roses and magnolias in summer, of frost and the sound of sleigh-bells in winter. One of her earliest acquaintances was Hans Christen Andersen, who used to come to the Yellow Palace to read his fairy stories out loud. The Yellow Palace itself was anything but palatial. Alexandra's father, Prince Christian of Schleswig-Holstein-Sonderburg-Glücksburg was an impoverished cavalry officer, dependent upon the bounty of King Frederick VII and the Landgrave of Hesse. In 1852, the Treaty of London recognized him as heir to the throne of Denmark, through the claims of his wife, Louise of Hesse; but if his prospects improved, his finances did not; and it was fortunate that he had no wish to cut a dash in the world. In 1858, the childless King Frederick—whose morganatic wife looked with some natural jealousy upon the children in the Yellow Palace—bestowed the title of Royal Highness upon Alexandra and her brothers and sisters. But, Royal Highnesses notwithstanding, they were brought up in the strictest simplicity. Princess Louise taught her children the piano; Prince Christian instructed them in riding and gymnastics. Almost up to the day of her marriage, Alexandra made her own frocks. They saw very little of the world. King Frederick's court was more or less closed to them, for the king was not, on the whole, a very respectable person. A man of immense girth, and a corresponding geniality, his favorite diet was enormous quantities of pea-soup and bacon, beer and *akvavit*. He was in the habit of telling ferocious stories about the battles in which he had fought, most of which had taken place before his birth. But what else could one expect from a man whose military ardor was such that, in the war of 1848, he went about Copenhagen with his arm in a sling, though he had not himself been allowed to go near the front? He had been married twice; each marriage was dissolved; and late in life he had taken up with Louise Rasmussen, an educated and respectable seamstress, whom he raised to the nobility as the Countess Danner, and who became his morganatic wife. She was almost as large as he was; they loomed side by side in the Royal Palace; but it was not the sort of palace into which one would bring one's children. At least, that was Christian's and Louise's opinion. Alexandra's early life, therefore, was spent between the Yellow Palace, the modest summer castle among the beech groves of Bernstoff, and the yearly reunions of the enormous Hesse family at Rumpenheim.

✦

All her future relatives approved of Alexandra. And yet, such was the haste of history in the sixties, within a year of her marriage the King of the Belgians was already deploring the fact that it had taken place. This was not Alexandra's fault; but she was a Princess of Denmark; and this circumstance thrust herself and her husband into a momentous situation, which they could neither understand nor influence, and which involved on the one hand all the unimportant niceties of a family dispute, and on the other the fate of Europe.

In order to understand this, it is necessary to review some earlier events in the family life of Queen Victoria and Prince Albert.

On January 25, 1858, their eldest daughter Victoria, the Princess Royal, was married to Prince Frederick of Prussia. It was a match very close to their hearts, for the two young people were deeply in love; it was also very close to their ambitions. As reasonable human beings, the Queen and the Prince Consort would doubtless have agreed that a marriage between the daughter of one royal house and the son of another would not, in the nineteenth century, have much effect upon the course of events. But on the subject of royal marriages, the Queen and the Prince Consort were not altogether reasonable. Moreover, Prince Frederick, in the course of time, was bound to become the King of Prussia; and Albert, like other orthodox German liberals, entertained some striking views upon the future of Prussia. He believed that it was to become the corner-stone of an enlightened and constitutional Germany. Frederick's father, the Prince Regent, was, it is true, neither enlightened nor constitutional; but

Frederick himself not only possessed a sweet temper, he also showed some signs of having an open mind. If Vicky (properly advised, of course, by her father) were to play upon the first in order to enlarge the second, who could tell what might not happen?

Vicky had always been her father's favorite child. Of a quick intelligence, a ready sympathy, a romantic temperament, an impulsive and enthusiastic nature, she had taken the place in his life that might have been occupied by his son. He liked to confide in her; he felt that she understood him better than others did; and perhaps this was the case. But, as so often happens when a strong-minded father makes a particular companion of a strong-willed daughter, the result was not entirely happy. If the Princess Victoria in after life was sometimes unable to distinguish between a prejudice and an opinion, and an opinion and a truth; if she was apt to express herself with more energy than circumspection—this may have been due in part to the stimulating effect of her early relationship with Albert.

It was clear from the beginning that her position in Berlin was not to be an easy one. The court and society were prepared to dislike her; the British Minister, Lord Bloomfield, anxious to give no offense, was determined to avoid her; while a certain Otto von Bismarck, Prussian delegate to the Frankfurt Diet, summed up the general feeling in higher circles by remarking that he was against the marriage if the new Princess Frederick remained "the least bit English." Prussia was only a second-rate power; her political position in Europe had been much weakened by the events of 1848 and their consequences; and her ruling class was, therefore, unduly sensitive. If Vicky were to play any part in the enlightenment of Germany, it would be wise of her to remember a certain Latin tag about hastening slowly.

At first, to be sure, she created quite a good impression. Her gentle manner, her low voice, her old-fashioned clothes, her ruddy complexion which betrayed no trace of powder—all these were in her favor. Would she conform to the Prussian standards of womanly behavior, and retire with modest obedience into the background? Some—Field-Marshal Wrangel, for instance—were inclined to think so; but others, looking at the square jaw, the green eyes, shook their heads in doubt. And soon it appeared as if their fears were to be justified. The Princess and Prince set up their household in the Old Schloss, in a suite of ornate but gloomy rooms, which had not been inhabited for many years. Everything, the decorations, the furniture, even the humblest domestic arrangements, needed alteration; and the Princess Frederick, who had a passion for arranging things, set about this task with alacrity. And then she discovered that, even in her own house, she was not her own mistress. King Frederick William IV was sinking into imbecility; but though he was no longer considered fit to rule, his authority was still paramount in all family matters. It extended to the remotest corners, the most minute particulars; even upon the subject of the furniture of the Old Schloss he had to be consulted. Once a reactionary in politics, Frederick William now proved to be a reactionary about plumbing. The contest was prolonged and furious; and the Princess Frederick, supported only by her husband, found herself in an isolated position in the Prussian court.

Perhaps she was not very tactful. She did not disguise her aversion to the monotony, the dullness, the cumbrous and

126

over-elaborate etiquette of the court; she froze at the approach of a conservative; she began to speak of England as
"home." The suspicions of Bismarck were amply justified;
but what would he have said if he had known that one of her
weekly letters to her father contained a long memorandum
on the subject of ministerial responsibility! As it was, it soon
became apparent to her shocked relatives that the Princess
Frederick had views—the most decided views on the most
controversial topics. At this, her welcome in Potsdam, never
very substantial, was seen to be worn completely threadbare.

The birth of a son on January 27, 1859, temporarily improved matters. The birth was difficult, and in the course of
it, the child's shoulder-socket was injured and the surrounding muscles were severely bruised, so that for the rest of his
life the future Emperor William II never enjoyed the use
of his left arm. But he was a gay and vigorous baby, and
everyone was very pleased with him. The Princess could not
be sure if he resembled any member of her family; "although
now and then he reminds me of Bertie," she wrote to Queen
Victoria, "which I fear you won't like." Whatever else this
remark may have been, it was certainly not prophetic.

Two years later, the old king died, and the princess drew
one step nearer to the throne. She could never have had any
reason for loving Frederick William, but now that he was
gone, she was prepared to grieve for him. Her letter to her
mother, written on the morning of his death, was a little
masterpiece of the macabre. The sounds of the death chamber, the color and temperature of the corpse, the anxiety and
the tears, all were noted down by that avid observer; and
the avid recipient was duly grateful. The emotion behind
this missive, however, was not insincere, and the evident

sympathy of the Princess Frederick brought her closer to her
new parents-in-law. For a time it almost seemed as if har-
mony had been restored. After his coronation, the new King
William I presented the new Crown Princess with a lock of
his hair, in a charming little locket; but, alas, at the same
time he informed her that she was to be "second *Chef* of the
Second Regiment of Hussars." Vicky, who so often forgot
to think before she acted, burst into laughter, for she supposed him to be joking. A heavy frown upon the forehead
of his Majesty informed her, too late, that this was not the
case. And so the trouble spread.

The new king was sternly anti-democratic. Those features
of the Prussian constitution which filled Albert with hope
for the future of Germany were a source of grief and agitation to William. A parliament of two houses, a franchise, a
budget which had to be voted by the Lower House . . .
here, indeed, were the means of restoring the shattered liberalism of 1848! And if William had any feeling about the
shattered liberalism of 1848, it was a desire to pulverize it
completely. One consolation, indeed, he had; for the Prussian
Constitution, in spite of its liberal tendencies, failed to contain the only provision that might have made those tendencies effective. It did not demand that ministers should be
responsible to parliament. An obstinate monarch, therefore,
and a powerful minister could—and subsequently did—muzzle
the most refractory Lower House.

The Prussian liberals, of course, were anxious to tamper
with the Constitution. Nor was the king any kindlier disposed towards them when he discovered that they were beginning to gather in the Neues Palais at Potsdam, where the
new Crown Prince and Princess held their court. William I

128

had no doubt at all as to who was at the bottom of all this: it was the Crown Princess. Albert had died in November, and the long weekly letters ceased: but his death affected his heartbroken daughter precisely as it had affected her mother. Vicky was determined, more determined than ever, to put the late Prince Consort's wishes into effect; and if this led to a cleavage between her husband and her father-in-law—well, that could not be helped. The poor Crown Prince shuddered, but he obeyed her. Left alone, he might have compromised, for though he had come to wish for a liberal Prussia and an enlightened Germany, he was a dutiful son. With Vicky's relentless enthusiasm to urge him on, he forgot his scruples, and it was clear that very soon he would break with his father.

Such was the state of affairs when, in September, 1862, King William made Bismarck his Minister-President. Few people knew the nature, none guessed at the extent of Bismarck's gifts; but that gifts of a kind he had was quickly evident. He brooked no opposition, whether from parliament or press; while as for the Crown Princess, he simply disregarded her. Oh, yes, she had abilities; but she had no political experience, the "Anglo-Coburg" party that had gathered around her was weak, and if she wished to turn her husband against his father—why, that would suit Bismarck very well. On June 5, 1863, the Crown Prince proclaimed his opposition to his father's policies in the most public manner, in a speech at the Danzig Rathaus. Up to the last minute, he wavered; but the Crown Princess, as she wrote to her mother, "did *all I could*"; and it was sufficient. The speech was made, the king replied in a furious letter, and "Fritz sat up till one last night, writing the answer . . . in which Fritz says that he is almost broken hearted at causing his father so much pain, but that he could *not* retract the words spoken at Danzig. . . . He felt that under such circumstances it would be impossible for him to retain any office military or civil, and he laid both at the feet of the king." His speech, she wrote in a further letter to Queen Victoria, "was intended to convey in a clear and *unzweideutig* way . . . that he had nothing to do with the unconstitutional acts of the government." Soon afterwards, his language became even more *unzweideutig*. In an angry letter to Bismarck he expatiated upon the differences between himself and his father. "Absalom!" was Bismarck's only comment.

The Minister-President thought the Crown Prince an insignificant young man, and he had no intention of making a public martyr of him. There were other ways. None of his letters to Bismarck, for instance, was ever answered; spies surrounded him in a rather noticeable way; and when he and the Crown Princess made a tour of military inspections in Prussia and Pomerania, they were treated with studious neglect. This last method proved effective; and the pair fled to England, where they remained hidden for several weeks. The Crown Prince, it was clear, was not cut out to be the leader of the liberal party in Prussia.

II

While his eldest sister was still fighting her unequal battle with Bismarck, the Prince of Wales was married to Alexandra. She arrived in England on March 7, 1863; was met by the future bridegroom at the Bricklayers' Arms Station, and was driven through London to Paddington. The procession of six carriages was, owing to some whim of the Queen's, a very shabby affair: there were neither outriders nor trappings, there were not even rosettes. But there was nothing half-hearted about Alexandra's reception; the Londoners were delighted with the shy, slim, beautiful girl. "The Princess," said Lord Palmerston, "has made Danes of us all." The Poet Laureate echoed these sentiments in what was perhaps not one of his more felicitous poems, ending as it did with the lines:

"For Saxon or Dane or Norman we,
  Teuton or Celt, or whatever we be,
  We are all of us Danes in our welcome of thee, Alexandra!"

Years afterwards, Alexandra asked Lord Tennyson to read this poem to her. He did so; and it is much to the credit of both of them that, when he had finished, there was a silence, and then they both began to shake with helpless laughter.

The wedding took place on March 10, in St. George's Chapel at Windsor. Some people were disposed to cavil because the ceremony was taking place in Lent, but the Queen was not disturbed by such High Church notions. "In my young days," she pronounced, "there was no Lent." She herself sat in a gallery above the chancel, dressed all in black except for the blue ribbon of the Garter. Her mind inevitably went back to her own marriage with Albert, and such was the deep sadness of her expression that, as he looked at her, tears started to the eyes of Lord Palmerston. As for the wedding itself, it was "a fine thing to remember," said Mr. Disraeli, who was among the nine hundred guests, and who believed that his presence was a sign of royal favor. As a matter of fact, it was only through the persuasions of Lord

Palmerston that Victoria had consented to invite him; for in those days she still remembered her late husband's conviction that Mr. Disraeli had not "one particle of a gentleman in his composition." Another guest was little Prince William of Prussia, a restless child of four years, who was placed between his two English uncles Arthur and Leopold. Growing bored, the little boy amused himself by sinking his teeth and his nails alternately into the bare legs of his relatives, who happened to be wearing kilts; and they were only restrained by the solemnity of the occasion from uttering cries of anguish.

When it was all over, Queen Victoria drove down to Frogmore, to the Mausoleum, "and prayed by that beloved restingplace, feeling soothed and calmed." "Alix," she reflected, "is a most noble, excellent, dear creature . . . a realization of what my dear Angel so ardently wished, and I doubt not *he* sees and knows this, and that it is *one* of his rewards."

The nation agreed with the Queen. The new Princess of Wales was from the very first extraordinarily popular, and not the least of her many charms lay in the fact that she was visible. Victoria's grief, which had once aroused so much sympathy, had already begun to seem a little excessive. She proceeded, a mournful ghost and with all a ghost's regularity, from one residence to another; she was a Queen in hiding. She had hoped that her son and his wife would, to a certain extent, follow her example; would at any rate emulate the sort of life that she and Albert had led, while Albert was alive— a life, as she described it, "of right dignity without stiffness." She thought that the Prince and Princess might dine with Lord Granville, Lord Palmerston, and possibly Lord Derby;

and at Spencer House, Westminster House, and Apsley House; but "not to *all* these in the same year." Yet, somehow or other, during the season that followed their marriage, their court at Marlborough House became a center of London society, while the list of those who entertained them was an extensive one. The Prince was affable, the Princess beautiful; both were young and eager: what else could have been expected? Their life was certainly "without stiffness." But what would the Prince Consort have said if he could have seen his son and his son's guests toboganning on tea-trays down the staircase? What indeed? It was, perhaps, unfortunate that Albert's educational scheme, which had been designed among other things to remove the Hanoverian taint from Bertie's character, should have had precisely the opposite effect. Like his great-uncle George, and his more remote predecessor Frederick, the boy aspired to be fashionable; while as for reading, it has been said that all the reading he ever did was now confined to a glance at the newspapers and at the visiting-list at Marlborough House. His days were passed in an incessant round of minor functions and absolutely trivial amusements; the clouds of White Lodge and Frewin Hall and Madingley Hall were finally dispersed; and like a may-fly the Prince of Wales danced idly in the sun.

III

In November, 1863, this cheerful existence was suddenly interrupted by some momentous events from the outside world.

On the fifteenth of that month, King Frederick VII of

133

Denmark expired. He was succeeded by the Princess of Wales' father, Christian of Glücksburg, who also became (so he hoped) Duke of Schleswig-Holstein and Duke of Lauenburg. Christian was a very simple man: for the rest of his long reign his court was celebrated for its domesticity, for its practical jokes, for the milk and jellies which everyone was expected to consume before going to bed. This simplicity was handed on to his children. Alexandra, for example, positively disliked flattery; while her second brother William, who afterwards became King George I of Greece, took a peculiar delight in his old age in leading a procession of his grandchildren, on bicycles, through the ramshackle corridors of his Athenian palace. But if Christian was simple in his habits he was also, as is so often the case, extremely conservative in his politics. He disliked change; he longed for his kingdom to remain in the shape that had been imposed upon it by the treaties of 1815. But it was not to be. Whatever his faults, King Frederick had been loved, for he was a patriot. One of his legacies to the new King Christian IX was an unsigned constitution to which, two days after his accession—urged on by his Minister, Carl Christian Hall, and by the eloquent clamor of an angry crowd around his palace—Christian appended his reluctant signature. This constitution permitted Holstein to pass absolutely on every law to go into force within its own borders, but denied it any power to veto laws affecting only Denmark and Schleswig. Such a document could have but one meaning; it was the latest and most forthright of a whole series of attempts to incorporate Schleswig into the Kingdom of Denmark; and was therefore a spiritual, and possibly a literal, violation of the Treaty of London.

At the same time, at his family estate of Prinkenau is Silesia, a comparatively unknown personage called Duke Christian of Schleswig-Holstein-Sonderburg-Augustenburg formally renounced his claims to the twin duchies of Schleswig-Holstein in favor of his son, Prince Frederick. Frederick immediately set out for Gotha, where Duke Ernest of Saxe-Coburg-Gotha "recognized" him, and not Christian IX, as the rightful Duke of Schleswig-Holstein. In this way, amidst the agitations of princelings, the famous Schleswig-Holstein quarrel, which had been smoldering for many years, at last burst into flames; and from these flames there stepped, a slightly discredited phoenix, the portentous phenomenon of modern Europe.

As for the English royal family, the immediate effect of all this was to make its internal condition for a time a most uncomfortable one. But more important are the facts in the case. In them lie embedded the seeds of many of the troubles that afflict us today.

The rival claims of Christian and Frederick, though doubtless very interesting from a dynastic point of view, were not regarded as of much consequence by the great European powers. Christian's signature at the foot of the Danish constitution was, on the other hand, a matter of the first importance. For the Duchies of Schleswig-Holstein occupied a vital position on the Baltic seaboard, and for many years they had been the center of an exceedingly suggestive Danish-German conflict. Ever since the fifteenth century, the Duchies had been in personal union with the Kingdom of Denmark, whose king they called their duke but not their king; and this relationship, a curious one on any supposition, was rendered even more extraordinary by the Treaties of 1815. In 1815, the King of Denmark was confirmed in his titles of Duke of Schleswig-Holstein and Duke of Lauenburg; but this was not all. Since Holstein had once been part of the Holy Roman Empire, he was also made a member of the German Confederation as Duke of Holstein but not as Duke of Schleswig. Thus he had one foot in Germany, and a very gouty foot it was; for any attempt on the part of Denmark to draw closer to Schleswig, which was partly Danish, would cause a twinge of agony from the direction of Holstein, which was wholly German. In short, the whole monarchical structure—as rich an example of Metternichian perversity as any in Europe—was only safe so long as it remained in a state of inert absolutism; so long, that is, as it was not called in question.

In 1848, however, liberalism, magically arisen, ranged over all Europe; nor did Denmark escape. The Danes forced a liberal constitution upon the Kingdom, and were preparing to extend it to the rest of the monarchy, when the Duchies rose in revolt. This revolt, it is true, was of a most reactionary description, but it enjoyed the support of the liberal Frankfurt Parliament, which longed to bring Schleswig-Holstein within the German fold, and did not much care how this was done. It ordered a Prussian army to advance into the Duchies; there was a brief, inglorious campaign; the Prussians stumbled sullenly back into Germany; and the liberal Danes were left in control of Schleswig, while the reactionary Schleswig-Holsteiners held on to Holstein. Here as elsewhere, the curse of early nineteenth century liberalism—its tendency to degenerate into extreme nationalism—had set the Germans against the Danes, and had left nothing behind but confusion.

The treaty ending hostilities between Denmark and Prussia had provided that the King of Denmark should appeal to the German Confederation for the restoration of his authority in Holstein. In 1850, therefore, a Prussian and Austrian force marched into Holstein, in order to "hand it back" to the King of Denmark. But in 1850, alas, things were not as they had been in 1848. The reaction had set in; and Prussia and Austria made it clear that they did not intend to leave Holstein until the Danes had agreed to keep their constitution to themselves and not attempt to extend it to Schleswig. In December, 1851, the Danes assented. The monarchy, they promised, was henceforth to consist of the Kingdom of Denmark with its *rigsraad*, the two Duchies with their Estates, and the Duchy of Lauenburg with its Knights and Representatives.

It was quite clear, of course, that this agreement was at best a temporary one. The Danes still longed to incorporate Schleswig; Germany still hoped to detach the Duchies; within the monarchy itself there emerged a German and a Danish party, each bitterly opposed to the other. Such was the background to the Treaty of London of 1852, in which the six powers of France, Russia, Prussia, England, Austria and Sweden-Norway hoped to correct an almost incorrigible situation.

The Danish-German events of the past few years—the clash of passionate liberals, the intrusion of stubborn conservatives, the sudden threats to the balance of power in Europe—were such that only the most enlightened statesmanship, only the frankest and most realistic discussion, could hope to bring them to a happy conclusion. The powers were not, however, particularly enlightened, and they were certainly not disposed to be frank. Should Denmark or Germany possess Schleswig? That was the essential question; and they disregarded it entirely. They pretended that the problem was a dynastic one. Who, they asked themselves, was to succeed the childless Frederick VII? Frederick's heiress was Louise of Hesse, a member of the old royal line; and Louise had married Christian of Glücksburg. Now, while there was no difficulty at all about Christian and Louise becoming King and Queen of Denmark, there was a considerable doubt of their right to succeed to the Duchies of Schleswig-Holstein, for the Duchies clung to the salic law, which did not permit succession through the female line. It was therefore more than possible that, on the death of Frederick VII, the Duchies would pass to the next claimant, Duke Christian of Augustenburg, who would immediately bring them within the orbit of the German Confederation, leaving everything much as it had been in 1848.

In this odious dilemma, the powers were assisted by a most fortunate circumstance. Duke Christian had taken a leading part in the events of 1848; his estates had been sequestered; and he was now much in need of ready cash. For the sum of £350,000 he agreed to give up his claim to Schleswig-Holstein, to live outside Denmark, and not to interfere with the established order of succession. The powers were now free to declare that, after the death of Frederick VII, Christian of Glücksburg was to become King of Denmark, Duke of Schleswig-Holstein, and Duke of Lauenburg. Denmark, on her side, expressed herself as willing not to tamper with the structure of the monarchy.

Apart from the fact that the powers had merely recognized, not guaranteed, the integrity of Denmark, the Treaty was in many other respects a useless and dangerous piece of literature. It had restored the past: Denmark was, at least outwardly, the Denmark of the Treaties of 1815. It had taken no thought for the future: it had set up no effective machinery to prevent its provisions from being broken before the death of Frederick VII. The Duke of Augustenburg's son had not been made a party to his father's renunciation. The Estates of Schleswig and Holstein had not been consulted; nor had the German Diet, which retained federal rights in Holstein. In short, the Treaty had managed to offend the Danish liberals, the liberals of Germany, the reactionary Schleswig-Holstein party, and the German Diet; while at the same time, by maintaining the polite fiction that the whole problem was one of succession, it had not taken the only possible course—namely, to incorporate Schleswig into Denmark and Holstein into Germany. The case of Belgium in 1839 had set a precedent for this; but the powers were too divided in aims and institutions, and too busily engaged in suspecting one another, to make use of even the wisest precedent.

In the years between the signing of the Treaty and the death of Frederick, thinkers of Europe were convinced that something—they could not say precisely what, but something mysterious and alarming—would arise from the Schleswig-Holstein question to trouble mankind. The Danes, it was only natural, were doing all they could to bring Schleswig into the Kingdom before the accession of Christian of Glücksburg; and if—as their historians have subsequently admitted—they were violating the spirit of the Treaty, no disinterested mind could blame them for that. The Germans of Schleswig, on the other hand, were beginning to adopt a technique which has proved very successful in our time, but was comparatively novel then: they maintained that they were being hideously oppressed by the Danes. What would come of all this? Palmerston, in his old age, declared that only three men had understood the Schleswig-Holstein question: the Prince Consort who was dead, a German professor who had gone mad, and himself who had forgotten all about it. Whether Palmerston had ever, on this particular topic, known anything worth forgetting, admits of some doubt; but it is true that the Prince Consort had spent a great deal of time in attempting to unravel the problem.

Indeed, it was a problem very close to Albert's heart. Its remarkable complexities, its endless ramifications filled him with a peculiar delight. He took notes, he composed memoranda, he took more notes. His researches led him back to the strange events of 1721, to the Lex Regia of 1665, to the records of medieval fiefs; then, much refreshed, he plunged once more into the modern jungle of protocols and treaties, royal patents and irregular constitutions. At length he came to the conclusion that Denmark had no real claim upon the Duchies of Schleswig-Holstein. Oddly enough, this conclusion was one that he might have reached without any research at all, for it was exactly what he wished to reach, even before he began. He was now able to formulate a further proposition—namely, that the Duchies should, under Prussian guidance, become part of Germany. It had long been his conviction that a constitutional, pacific Germany would be the salvation of Europe, and that Prussia was the very instrument whereby this change could be effected. Just how Prussia was to detach the Duchies from Denmark, the Prince Consort does not seem to have decided; but he was convinced that everything could be managed in a most reasonable way, with the help of England, and without recourse to war.

Victoria had always been content to follow Albert's lead, and now that he was dead, she was unwilling to listen to any other interpretation of the Schleswig-Holstein question. She turned the pages of long, unappetizing memoranda—"his *memoranda*," as she wrote, "which are gospel now." Yes, it was all perfectly clear; one had merely to support Prussia. But even gospels have been known to mislead the faithful, and so it was in 1863. The late Prince Consort's memoranda were a monument to his industry and his powers of reasoning; but they had been written before the rise of Bismarck; and they were now of no value whatsoever.

Perhaps, if Bismarck had never lived, the Schleswig-Holstein question would eventually have been settled by giving Schleswig to Denmark and Holstein to the Augustenburgs. As early as 1857, however, in a letter to Manteuffel, Bismarck had expressed the conviction that Schleswig-Holstein should be incorporated in the Kingdom of Prussia, which would thereby acquire the enormously valuable port of Kiel. After he had become Minister-President, he repeated this conviction to King William, who thought that he was drunk. And, indeed, he was drunk; but not in the way that the simple king supposed. An extraordinary intoxication had seized upon him, so that all that was prudent and cunning in his nature, all that was arrogant and energetic too, was dedicated to the fulfillment of dreams that other men would have thought fantastic. It is easy to see Bismarck, with his huge body and high angry voice, with his fondness for large hounds and his addiction to deep potations, with his agricultural interests and his evangelical beliefs, as a calculating statesman disguised as a Junker. It is easy, too, to maintain that in many respects—in his musical tastes, for example—he was a cultured and sensitive person. Yet at the center of his being, where these characteristics might have mingled in an intelligible subtlety, there is a void, a darkness which no mind in his day ever penetrated, and no mind has penetrated since; and in which obscurely resides, if not the first, most certainly not the least of the destroyers of the liberties of Europe.

Even before the death of Frederick VII, when the new Danish Constitution was merely in its preliminary form of a royal Patent, the German Confederation had ordered an execution in Holstein, and Hanoverian and Saxon troops had marched across its border. This did not suit Bismarck at all. Trouble between Denmark and Germany, it was true, was a necessary part of his schemes; but he did not wish the German people, in so far as they were represented by the Confederation, to take the lead away from him. With the accession of Christian, and the revival of the Augustenburg claims, matters became more delicate than ever. On the one hand, Denmark had put herself nicely in the wrong; on the other hand, Frederick of Augustenburg had become, almost overnight, a hero to the liberals of Germany. There was a general demand that all the German states should recognize him; there was even talk of a united war against the Danes. It would be sad indeed, so Bismarck reflected, if everything were to end in the formation of a sovereign state of Schleswig-Holstein, which would certainly cast a vote against Prussia in the Diet. For a moment it almost seemed as if this might be the case; as if, from the crisis of 1863, there would arise the beginnings of that constitutional Germany of which the Prince Consort had dreamed.

If Bismarck were to forestall the Confederation in any move against Denmark, he would have to depend upon the friendship of Russia, the support of Austria, and a lack of co-operation between England and France. Russia was already on his side; Austria had no use for the Augustenburgs, and would not weaken her already dubious leadership of the Confederation by allowing Prussia to move alone. There remained England and France. It was almost too much to suppose that, at such a juncture, these two countries would be so obliging as to stage a falling-out. But so it was. The Government of Lord Palmerston and the English public alike entertained a deep suspicion of Napoleon III. It was not given to them to see (perhaps to nobody, not even to Bismarck, was it yet given to see) that the Emperor's hour had already struck. The Emperor himself, that puzzled enigma, still believed that he was not altogether out of touch with the Time-Spirit. The resettlement of Europe? No doubt that was impossible. The unification of Italy, the Rhenish Provinces? How remote, how inaccessible, were these objectives! Yet even now, with his sinister dictatorship disintegrating month by month, something might still be done; one might still extract from Europe, as from a rag-heap, some soiled but showy trifle. He therefore proposed a Congress which should discuss, not merely the present crisis in Denmark, but all the intricate provisions of the 1815 treaties. Lords Palmerston and Russell, however, were even more optimistic about the Emperor's future than Napoleon himself was; they, too, perceived in the European heavens Napoleon's quite invisible star. They detected in his proposed Congress a magical and destructive design; the Cabinet agreed with them; the Queen (who had reverted to the late Prince Consort's opinion that Napoleon was an immoral upstart) lent a vigorous support. Russell, employing that style of lucid asperity of which he was so unfortunately a master, turned down the proposal. All hope of Anglo-French co-operation was now at an end.

Bismarck sighed with relief. He pulled the strings in Austria as only he could. An ultimatum was sent to Denmark from both countries, demanding the immediate withdrawal of the Constitution; the Danes refused to comply; and in February, 1864, an Austro-Prussian force plunged deep into Schleswig. So far as the German liberals, the Augustenburgs, and the Confederation were concerned, they had now ceased to matter; indeed, it might almost be said that they had now ceased to exist. The resettlement of Europe was beginning, and Bismarck, not Napoleon, was its moving spirit.

We are familiar in these days with wars conducted against small peoples in order to "protect" them; but when Prussia and Austria advanced upon the Danes for the purpose of protecting them against their new Constitution, the excuse was a new one. "This horrible war," the Prince wrote to Mrs. Bruce in February, "will be a stain forever on Prussian history." From that time onwards, he was suspicious of Prussia. He had hoped that the English fleet would be sent at once to the Baltic; he apparently did not know that a similar idea had occurred to Lord Russell and that the Cabinet would have nothing to do with it. "As to Lord Russell's interminable notes," he went on to Mrs. Bruce, "nobody cares twopence for them on the Continent, and the Foreign Ministers to whom they are addressed probably light their cigars with them." Meanwhile the Danes, who had no chance at all against their adversaries, withdrew behind the Düppel lines, and demanded an armistice. The news of the fall of Düppel was read aloud by one of the Prince's equerries in the presence of the Princess, who had borne a son in January, and was still very nervous. Alexandra burst into a paroxysm of tears, the Prince berated the equerry, and altogether there was a terrible scene. A little later, the Danes gained an unexpected victory at sea; for a moment there was great rejoicing at Marlborough House; but soon afterwards it was quite apparent that further resistance would be useless. The armistice demanded in March was granted, and a conference was held in London.

Now, at this last minute, if anything were to be done to save Schleswig for Denmark, it would have to be done by the government of Lord Palmerston, and the government of Lord Palmerston was disinclined to make a move. Perhaps if Palmerston (who sympathized with Denmark) had fully understood the situation, Bismarck might even yet have suffered some astonishing political defeat. But it was too much to expect. Time, at last, had had its way with England's great Prime Minister. The statesman whose fall had once set high Vienna dancing—the latter-day Whig, whose arrogance and intuition had earned him the title of "ce terrible milord Palmerston"—the jaunty master of parliaments and princes— was now a very old man, crippled with gout, and disposed to spend rather too much of his time in writing impertinent communications to the Queen on matters of trifling importance. He was very near his death, and he longed—it was not unnatural—for things to remain stationary: the onrush of events, which had once filled him with excitement, now wearied him. "Perhaps," he said to Mr. Goschen before the opening of Parliament in February, "perhaps we may have a little law reform or bankruptcy reform; but we cannot go on legislating forever." The words were sadly filled with meaning; they indicated, not merely a Whig policy, but a state of mind. How could he realize that the Europe over which he had once wandered like a cloud, dropping unpredictable thunderbolts with extraordinary success, was now vanishing into the past? How could he hope to fathom the mind of Bismarck?

With the exception of Lord Russell, who elaborated a belligerent scheme of remarkable impracticability, there was not (in spite of contemporary hints and subsequent asseverations) a war party in the English cabinet. Palmerston, it is true, would have liked to strike a threatening attitude—it was a posture which he assumed with the ease, if not the grace, of long habit—but that would have meant acting with France; and had he not called France a runaway horse? If he could not keep her in check, would it then be wise to fight beside Napoleon against Prussia? On the whole, he thought not. Palmerston had an extreme respect for the French army; it would certainly crush the Prussians; and then Europe would be at Napoleon's mercy. These singular speculations, as it happened, were quite unnecessary: for nothing would have induced Napoleon, after the way in which his proposed congress had been treated, to enter into closer relationships with England. He was already making overtures to Prussia. And so, in June, the London conference broke up. There was much politeness, there were even, towards the end, some animated debates; and then the Danes were left to their fate.

On June 29, Alsen was captured. On August 1, in order to avoid the capture of Copenhagen, the Danes signed certain preliminary peace terms. The Duchies were made over to Austria and Prussia, who—in accordance with their treaty of January 16—accepted them as trustees for their future sovereign, whoever he might be. Bismarck had never fully exposed his hand; he had never made it clear whether or not he had gone to war to uphold the Treaty of London; so that there were many people who supposed that he would now install the Duke of Augustenburg. He was determined to keep such people in doubt for as long as possible. He needed time in which to complete his plans. To quarrel with Austria, to seize Schleswig-Holstein, to devour German principalities, to create a new Confederation under Prussian control, to overthrow France . . . such were the steps that he contemplated, and one false step would mean disaster. He must proceed, with infinite caution, along a razor's edge. He was a master of improvisation, and he would prove his mastery; he would alternate appalling truths with sweet equivocations, suddenly advance and as swiftly withdraw, flirt with his political enemies, smile at his victims; and, at last, if his nerves stood up under the strain, he would win. Did such means justify the end? How ridiculous to ask such a question! Were not the means simply the end in process of realization?

In August he discovered that his health demanded a visit to Biarritz, and there, at the Villa Eugénie, in a series of conversations, he made the first move towards ruining Napoleon. He was rather fond of the French Emperor. It was pleasant to talk with him—pleasant, too, to pierce, once again, that enigmatic surface and find the emptiness and bewilderment behind. Afterwards, he sent Napoleon a memorandum, which, since it was brutally frank, was calculated to leave the Emperor in a state of agitated suspicion. He declared that he was meditating these alternatives: either to continue with traditional Prussian policy and align Prussia, Austria, and Russia against France, or else to turn towards the free development of Prussia and North Germany. Which of the two alternatives did the Emperor prefer? He was anxious to know his Imperial Majesty's mind. But the anxiety was not very acute; for Bismarck had reached the heart of the Napoleonic mystery, he had realized the delicious truth—that the one thing that Napoleon had never known was, precisely, Napoleon's mind.

IV

The Crown Prince and Princess of Prussia, still under the cloud of King William's disapproval, were staying with Queen Victoria when Christian ascended the throne of Denmark. *Their* minds were quite made up: they supported the Augustenburgs. The Princess of Wales, on the other hand, though a sweet-natured girl, and one who did not profess to understand foreign politics, could not help repeating, her eyes bright with anger, that "the Duchies belong to Papa." The Prince vehemently agreed with her. The quarrel at length became so acute that the Queen forbade any of them to mention the words "Schleswig-Holstein" again; and in this way some kind of peace was maintained until Vicky and her husband left for Prussia in December, 1863.

Victoria's behavior as a mother and mother-in-law was considerably more discreet than her behavior as a queen. "With regard to this sad S. Holstein question," she wrote, "I can really speak with more thorough impartiality than anyone . . . my heart and my sympathies are all German." If any meaning could be extracted from this contradictory statement, it was that she had been rereading some of her husband's memoranda, and had decided, as Lord Aberdeen had once said of the Prince Consort, "to go all lengths with Prussia." The power of the Crown had considerably declined since Albert's death, but it was still far from negligible: his widow could, and did, exert a vast negative influence whenever she disagreed with the policy of her ministers. And if, as 1864 advanced, the Queen had not spent much of her time in attempting to thwart the supposed designs of Lord Palmerston and Earl Russell, it would have been a poor compliment to the memory of Albert. For Palmerston and Russell—"those two dreadful old men," Victoria called them—were certainly no friends to Prussia. She took some consolation from the knowledge that a large group within the Cabinet was determined to keep England out of war; and that one of this group was Lord Granville—"Puss" Granville—a nobleman remarkable even among courtiers for the adroitness with which he softened, or turned aside, or even stated in terms of its exact opposite, a truth which his royal mistress might find unpalatable. She had always considered him most sympathetic. This year, for example, when the reception given to Garibaldi in England had filled her with uneasiness, he had been able to assure her that, while Garibaldi was undoubtedly a hero, he was also a "goose." Upon which the Queen felt a great deal better. Now she used him as her voice in the Cabinet, and even resorted to the extremely unconstitutional procedure of sending him certain pieces of correspondence with the admonition that he was not to show them to Palmerston or Russell. Palmerston, of course, got wind of this. It did not trouble him very much, but he could not refrain from using his pen in a manner which, though distinctly Whig, was certainly not wise. "Viscount Palmerston can quite understand your Majesty's reluctance to take any active part in measures in any conflict against Germany, but he is sure your Majesty will never forget that you are sovereign of Great Britain, and that the honour of your Majesty's crown and the interests of your Majesty's dominions will always be the guide of your

Majesty's conduct. . . ." Or again. "The accompanying part of a recently set-up paper has been put into his hands. It contains much falsehood and misrepresentation and is deserving of being put into the fire. But this paper, and others which have been mentioned to Viscount Palmerston, tend to show that your Majesty has expressed personal opinions on the affairs of Denmark and Germany which have embarrassed the course of the Government. . . . Your Majesty has no doubt been duly careful as to the degree and manner in which your Majesty's opinions and views have been expressed, but it might be well that no indiscreet expression from persons about your Majesty should give any countenance to such remarks as those in this paper." The Queen replied to this dreadful language with chilling politeness, and wrote to her Belgian uncle that "Pilgerstein is gouty and extremely impertinent in his communications of various kinds to me." And she continued, whenever she could, to hamper "Pilgerstein" in his rather feeble efforts to assist the Danes.

More exasperating than the letters of Lord Palmerston, however, was the behavior of her eldest son. If only the Prince of Wales could have been more like his second brother Alfred, whose brain, the late Prince Consort had declared, was one in which "no prejudice can maintain a footing against straightforward logic." Had Bertie ever asked to read Albert's memoranda, those repositories of straightforward logic? And even if he had read them, would any prejudice thereby have been dislodged from his brain? The answers to these questions were all too obvious. Bertie was incorrigibly pro-Danish. He saw the Schleswig-Holstein question, not as an international problem, but as a family affair. It was all quite clear to him. "Fritz" Augustenburg was merely the husband of his mother's half-sister's daughter, whereas Christian was Alexandra's father. The Prince's political thinking in these days—as John Bright remarked, after an encounter at a banquet—was chiefly concerned with the acquisition of territory. The fact that Christian of Denmark was actually in danger of *losing* some territory, therefore, filled his son-in-law with deep alarm. Nor did he hesitate to express this alarm wherever he went. He poured his Danish sympathies into the ear of the French Ambassador, he declared them, in his rather loud voice, at dinner parties, he canvassed them at the club. The Queen remonstrated with him, she sent emissaries to him to beg him to desist; but even Lord Clarendon, though his reception was most courteous, and though the Prince agreed with him that caution was a necessity, seemed to have produced no effect. At last the Queen took the extreme course of keeping all foreign dispatches from her son, so that he was obliged to get his news from the daily press, just like anybody else; but since the daily press was just as pro-Danish as he, the punishment was less persuasive than it might have been.

Another source of misunderstanding between Victoria and her son lay in the fact that the Queen was so remote from her subjects. They were beginning to make unfavorable contrasts between her invisibility and her income. The excuse that she worked too hard did not move them at all—they believed that most of her working hours were spent in devising plans for the advancement of Germany. Had not Lord Ellenborough said as much in the House of Lords on May 25, when he had suggested, in a circuitous way, that she was no more English in her sympathies than the first two Georges? The Prince of Wales, it is true, was not at all well known; but he had married a charming Danish princess, and he was the father of a baby son. The danger to Victoria's position was minute, but it existed, and she was not allowed to forget it. "I cannot help saying a few words," wrote that impeccable monarch, the King of the Belgians, on June 15, 1864,

"about Bertie and Alix. You will recollect when first Albert spoke to me about Alix that he said, We take the Princess, but *not* her relations. That might have remained as he wished for years, without the death of our cousin of Denmark. That of a sudden gave us a *Danish* princess . . . Our own *dreadful* loss put Bertie and Alix *forward;* he and his wife are *constantly before the public* in EVERY IMAGINABLE SHAPE *and* CHARACTER, *and fill entirely the public mind.* . . . This state of affairs gives the young couple great influence on all classes, and is even calculated to influence the Cabinet, and to strengthen the Opposition."

The Queen, who was Albert's pupil, cared nothing for popularity; and she had long since learned that her uncle Leopold's knowledge of the English people was, to say the least, a little theoretical; but this explosive letter was not calculated to make her easy in her mind. Her affection for Alexandra was too deep to be disturbed by any such insinuations; yet could it be that Bertie, with his pro-Danish talk, was actually supplanting his mother in the public mind? The idea was an absurd one, of course; Uncle Leopold should have known better: but she waited nearly a fortnight before, in the peace of the rose-garden at Frogmore, she wrote her reply. "The third Court," she said,

"(which was quite unexpected) gave much satisfaction, but what did even more was my drive to the *station* through the *full* Park in my *open* carriage and four; it was quite *unexpected,* and, though *very painful,* pleased people more than anything; and, if occasionally done in *this* way, will I believe go *farther* to satisfy them than anything else always. I was thanked for it, and told

how kind they thought it was of *me*. . . . Everyone said that
the difference shown, when *I* appeared, and [when] Bertie and
Alix drove, was *not* to be described. Naturally for *them* no one
stops, or *runs*, as they always *did*, and do *doubly* now for *me*."

Naturally, when the inaccessible sovereign flitted for a moment before the public vision, people stopped and ran; yet
the fact that she was obliged to make this expostulation could
only mean that, in the nineteenth century, the antique jealousy
between monarch and heir was still dimly alive.

In another quarter, too, the Prince's Danish sympathies
and idle ways were received with unconcealed distaste. The
Crown Princess of Prussia was fond of her brother, but she
could not help contrasting him unfavorably with her own husband. Dear Fritz was always so busy, so useful. He had
stopped pursuing the rainbow of liberalism and was now chas-
ing the Danes, as a lieutenant-general in the Prussian army.
Before the splendor of this fact, like mists before the sun,
the obscurities of the Schleswig-Holstein question simply
rolled away. The problem, she declared in February, was "to
us Germans plain as daylight, and one for which we would
gladly bring any sacrifice." She herself, as it happened, had
been obliged to sacrifice her pride: for though, with the out-
break of the war, she had become uncompromisingly Prussian,
others were not disposed to see her in this light. German in
England, English in Germany, she had not learned—she never
did learn—how to make peace with her singular destiny. In
the very ebullience of her new patriotism there was something
—what could it be?—which reminded her relatives, more and
more, of the fact that she had come from the land of Palmerston and *The Times*. She did her best to keep the peace. She
tried not to notice the eyes which the female members of the

Prussian royal family raised to heaven whenever England was mentioned. She made no reply when the Grand Duchess of Mecklenburg-Schwerin remarked to her Aunt Charles that it was a pity that they had "an Englishwoman in the family, *et par-dessous le marché si anglaise.*" In May, life with the inhabitants of Potsdam had become so difficult that "I feel," she wrote to her mother, "as if I could smash the idiots." None the less, when the Prince and Princess of Wales saw her after the war, her colors were still flying: she was still invincibly Prussian. The meeting had not been desired on either side. The Prince and Princess had merely wished to go to Denmark, but the Queen had insisted that, for the sake of appearances, they should also go to Germany. At Cologne, there was a brief encounter with the Crown Princess and the Crown Prince of Prussia: with Vicky, who was bristling with objections to the English press and the English government; with Fritz who, more silent, displayed a new ribbon on his Prussian uniform. The Prince of Wales' knowledge of decorations was, if not a useful, already a formidable accomplishment; the ribbon spoke to him more eloquently than words. It was a reward, as he afterwards reported to Lord Spencer, for Fritz's *"deeds of valour ???* against the unhappy Danes." He eyed it with disgust.

The meeting passed off in constraint, embarrassment, and anger; and the four young people parted without regret.

V

"The Duchies belong to Papa." The ingenuous Alexandra, it was really most ironical, had after all been correct; and

Vicky and Fritz had been quite wrong. For the Prussian crown lawyers—a most respectable body of men—decided in December that Duke Frederick of Augustenburg had never possessed any legal claim to the Duchies and that Christian of Denmark had owned them all the time. From this, of course, it followed that Christian had a perfect right to hand them over to Prussia and Austria. The decision was a convenient one, but it was also, perhaps, a little confusing. Had the war been fought for the sake of the Treaty of London? Not at all; for the Treaty of London did not indicate, by so much as a syllable, that the Duchies were subsequently to be placed at the disposal of Prussia and Austria. In that case, why, exactly, had the blood of Danes and Austrians and Prussians been spilled? In what cause had the Crown Prince of Prussia won his ribbon? Could it be that Prussia, not as a state whose end was Right, but as a state whose end was Power, actually proposed to seize the Duchies for herself? To these questions, however, the crown lawyers did not provide an answer.

An answer, indeed, there was, but it lay in the mind of Bismarck, and more than a year passed before it was formulated. During 1865, with extraordinary virtuosity, the Prussian Minister-President developed his tremendous political theme; in 1866, its solution was at length made manifest. It was a task full of difficulty and danger; for there were times when even his own colleagues, even the spell-bound King, seemed about to desert him; when the Bible itself, from which his strange conscience drew refreshment, yielded no consolation; when he was a prey to moods of violent rage, to fits of nervous exhaustion, to the blackness and solitude of despair. Yet he held on his course, with courage, with exhilaration even, and with a lack of scruple so complete that before it the commonplaces of the moral judgment are best suspended.

Five stages can be discerned in Bismarck's progress through 1865 and the spring of 1866. At the end of the first, he had persuaded an infatuated Austrian diplomacy to agree to his terms at the Convention of Gastein, terms which not merely abolished the Augustenburg claims and the principle (so dear to German historians) of the indivisibility of the Duchies, but which left Holstein a useless Austrian enclave between Schleswig and Prussia. At the end of the second, he had forced the sick and disillusioned Napoleon III to agree to remain neutral in the event of a war between Prussia and Austria. At the end of the third, he had picked a quarrel with Austria over the administration of Holstein. At the end of the fourth, he had made a treaty with Italy, who agreed that if Prussia were "forced" into a war with Austria within ninety days, she would come to her aid, receiving Venetia as a compensation. At the end of the fifth, Prussia had set before the Diet a proposal for a reformed Confederation, which should exclude Austria; Austria had replied with a counter-proposal that the Diet should declare an execution upon Prussia; the Diet had most agreeably taken Austria's side by a vote of nine to six; and Prussia had thereupon declared the Confederation at an end.

During the fifth of these stages, Prussian troops advanced into Holstein; and by the middle of June, 1866, the "defensive" war against Austria and her allies was well under way, with a Prussian invasion of Hanover, Saxony, and Hesse-Cassel, whose scanty and ill-organized troops in their neat uniforms withdrew in great disorder. Italy, more punctual than particular, leaped upon Austria from the rear. As for Bismarck, he was still doubtful: the Almighty, he declared, was *sehr lauenhaft*, very capricious; and even a reading of Psalms ix, 3-5, did not entirely comfort him. For one moment, indeed, it almost seemed as if the Almighty were about to justify Bismarck's epithet; for the army of the Crown Prince was unaccountably delayed at the battle of Sadowa on July 3; and the Minister-President got ready to die in the last charge. This, however, was not necessary. The Crown Prince appeared, the Austrian flank was turned, the Austrians fled. Eight days later, when the French Ambassador, Benedetti, appeared at Bismarck's headquarters at Zwittau, the Minister-President turned upon him a face full of rage and contempt, and was barely so much as civil in his speech. For the Seven Weeks' War, which was aimed just as surely at France as at Austria, was nearly at an end.

The mortified M. Benedetti slunk away from Zwittau. Pursuing the policy of *pourboires*, he had come to demand, as a compensation for Napoleon's neutrality, the city of Mainz and the left bank of the Rhine. Bismarck replied that he would not cede one inch of German territory. If France's armies had been massed along the western frontier of Germany, it is just possible that the reply might have been different. But "je ne suis pas prêt à la guerre," Napoleon muttered to a Viennese diplomat; and it was true. The ulcer of Mexico had drained his military resources. Underestimating the ability of the Prussian General Staff, he had supposed that the war would be long and bloody; and that, when the combatants were exhausted, he would be able to offer his services as a mediator . . . for a compensation, of course. He had even taken the precaution of making agreements with both sides. Faced with a triumphant Prussia, eager for fresh conquests;

knowing that France expected him, at this last moment, to execute some master-stroke of diplomacy; sick, frightened, despairing, "the sphinx without a secret" uttered his voice. The magical syllables, so eagerly awaited, formed only the hollow word "Compensation."

As he struggled to keep his head above the waters, Napoleon III would not have been human if, like any other man in a similar situation, he had not clutched at straws. A somewhat insignificant straw, floating idly past, now caught his attention. Before the war began, the Prince of Wales, in a conversation with M. Drouyn de Lhuys, had spoken of an "entente cordiale" between England and France. The words were apt; they were reported to the Quai D'Orsay; and now Napoleon remembered them. Assuming, with the optimism of despair, that the Prince exercised more influence than was actually the case, he asked the young man to become an intermediary between himself and the new government of Lord Derby. The Prince was delighted. He did not, however, acquaint his mother with this change in his circumstances. Victoria had been obliged, it is true, to admit that Prussia was in the wrong. She had even gone further, and, seeking a husband for her daughter Helena, had chosen Prince Christian of Schleswig-Holstein, a younger brother of Duke Frederick, the ejected heir to the Duchies. The choice was largely dictated by domestic considerations; the Queen needed an unassuming, respectable son-in-law who would stay in England; and Christian, who had nice manners, a good figure, a bald head, and nothing whatever to do, seemed exactly to fit this description. None the less, the choice revealed a certain anti-Prussian bias—a fact of which Bismarck, among others, was careful to take note. Yet the Queen still believed that her eldest son was not to be trusted with confidences; and had she known of his interesting relationship with Napoleon, she would certainly have nipped it in the bud.

As it happened, the Prince, even if he had possessed any influence, would have had no chance at all of making any impression upon the government of Lord Derby. Like its Whig predecessor, it looked upon Napoleon III with suspicion and dislike. It made no effort to shore up his tottering prestige. It watched with indifference his struggle to divert the Prussian tide, brimming upon his eastern frontier. The struggle was brief and ludicrous, for after the failure of Benedetti at Zwittau, Napoleon was thrown into a frenzy of dishonest indecision. He began as a mediator: he ended as a mendicant. At last he was reduced to the extraordinary expedient of sending to Bismarck a set of terms which Bismarck had already suggested to him. When Drouyn de Lhuys heard of this pitiful maneuver, he made but one comment. "Maintenant," he said, "il ne nous reste plus qu'à pleurer."

The preliminaries of peace were signed and ratified, and Napoleon was allowed to have no hand in them. He swallowed the affront, and sent M. Benedetti to Bismarck with a demand, in writing, for the Rhenish provinces lost in 1815. Bismarck replied by revealing the substance of this demand— which was subsequently known as "la note de l'aubergiste"—to the French journal Le Siècle. And now a kind of madness descended upon the imperial diplomacy. Benedetti submitted, again in writing, the proposal for a secret convention, which should give Luxembourg to France, and provide for Prussian aid should the Emperor be obliged "to invade or conquer Belgium." This deplorable document (some of which may have originated in those conversations at the Villa Eugénie) was carefully preserved by its grateful recipient; its contents were made known to all the German states, who immediately forgot that they had ever thought of France as a protector; and it was afterwards published in the Prussian gazette on July 25, 1870.

By the end of August, 1866, Prussia had settled with Austria and her allies. After the signing of the treaty of Prague, she proceeded to annex Schleswig-Holstein, Hanover, Nassau, Hesse-Cassel, the northern part of Hesse-Darmstadt, and the free city of Frankfurt—a vast territorial accretion. She was now the head of a new North German Confederation, founded upon the debris of the old confederation of 1815; and the southern states were united to this new Bund, not only in the matter of tariffs and railroads, but through a series of secret military alliances. Like Charles V, Napoleon I, and Metternich, Bismarck was attempting to solve the Central European problem; but his solution was a new one. He proposed nothing less than that Central Europe should in future be controlled by a united nationalist Germany. That is why 1866 is an ominous date in the history of our times.

VI

"What could be more painful," the Queen wrote to her eldest son three years later, "than the position in which our family were placed during the wars with Denmark, and between Prussia and Austria?" The pain could be traced, in part, to the fact that a certain principle, much cherished by the late Prince Consort's family, had received a severe shaking in 1866. Albert had always believed that royal alliances were valuable.

Yet in 1866 it seemed as if their influence, if they could be said to possess one, was negative; that their tendency was to irritate rather than to soothe. The King of Denmark was the Prince of Wales's father-in-law, and he had lost his Duchies. The blind King of Hanover was Queen Victoria's first cousin; his kingdom had disappeared. The Grand Duke of Hesse's nephew was married to Victoria's daughter, Alice, and the Grand Duke had suffered a large curtailment in territory and revenue. The author of all this—the country which, like a broom abolishing a cobweb, had swept away this network of royal relationships—owned, as Crown Princess, Victoria's eldest daughter. No wonder the English royal family was at odds with itself; nor was its uneasiness decreased by the behavior of the Crown Princess. Vicky had not forgiven her brother. When she sent her mother some of the Crown Prince's impressions of the war (besides Sadowa, he had been present at the battles of Nachod, Skalicz, and Schweinschadel) she added: "Louise, Arthur, Major Elphinstone and Mr. Sahl and Fräulein Bauer may like to see them. I would rather Bertie did not, please . . ." Her language about the war was not calculated to give much pleasure to her English relatives. While disliking the policy of Bismarck, she tried to be a whole-hearted supporter of its results. As a feat of mental conjuring, this was more agile than admirable, but it was not achieved without anguish. Of the minor states that had supported Austria she wrote: "They might have *quite well* foreseen what danger they were running into; *they were told beforehand what they would have to expect;* they *chose* to go with Austria and they now share the sad fate that she confers on her allies." A certain shrillness in the tone of this communication suggests, to the charitable, that the Crown Princess may have been whistling in the dark.

As for the Prince of Wales, in his capacity as intermediary, he had been given a most valuable insight into the shadier recesses of Napoleon's mind. Oddly enough, this does not seem to have affected him. He continued to think of Prussia, not as a new European portent, but as the thief of his relatives' property. He continued to regard Napoleon with admiration and affection, as a monarch whose court was dazzling, and whose capital, like a siren, called more and more insistently from across the Channel.

Chapter Five

"LA GRANDE DUCHESSE," OR THE REPUBLICANS

ON APRIL 12, 1867, Offenbach's *La Grande Duchesse de Gerolstein* appeared at the *Variétés*, becoming at once the most popular entertainment in Paris. Ostensibly, it made fun of the petty vanities, the pipe-clay militarism, the loose morality of a small German state—which, in order to humor the susceptibilities of the times, had been politely banished to the eighteenth century. Everybody suspected, however, that it was aimed at the court of Napoleon III; though nobody dared to be sure. Even Napoleon, who went to see it on April 24, laughed dutifully—the guilty hero of the coup d'état, the enemy of free thought, had no defense against an opéra bouffe. The subversive opinions of *La Grande Duchesse*—if such, indeed, they were—seemed to have been distilled from the very air.

It has been claimed that Jacques Offenbach, at this stage in his career, was a revolutionary; but nothing could be further from the truth. He was simply an artist who was singularly responsive to the atmosphere of the boulevards; whose genius, like a sponge, absorbed at once the sunlight and the skepticism of the imperial capital; and whose enchant-

ing music, as indifferent to politics as a bird, prattled of the
doom of empire every evening at the *Variétés*. How could
one deal with him or with his librettists? They were the
agents of Napoleon's old ally, the Time-Spirit, which had at
length become his enemy, and which could not be censored
or suppressed. . . .

Towards the end of May, the Prince of Wales, with the
Duke and Duchess of Manchester, and the Marquis and
Marquise de Galliffet, sat in a proscenium box at the *Variétés*.
It was not the best box, for boxes were hard to come by;
and it was only through the efforts of Hortense Schneider
herself, who had bustled all morning in a frenzy from agency
to agency, that the royal party had been seated at all. At
the end of the second act, the Prince and the Duke and
the Marquis presented themselves at Hortense Schneider's
dressing room to pay their respects to the plump little Grand
Duchess; who, charming and ridiculous and surrounded by
small dogs called Puss, Vicky, Love and so forth, limited her
conversation almost entirely to a breathless reiteration of the
three words "Votre Altesse Royale." The Prince had not
met her before; but when he returned to London he carried
with him a pile of her photographs.

The visit was by no means his first of that year. The
Princess had borne her third child—a daughter, Louise—on
February 20, in the midst of an attack of rheumatic fever;
she was thereafter confined to Marlborough House for many
months; and the Prince, more idle than ever, varied the monotony of the sick-room and the dullness of his enforced
bachelor existence by taking occasional trips across the Channel. A stout young man, with thinning hair and a full beard,
he was soon a familiar figure in the gayest and most modern

of European cities. The Parisians respected his incognito; but they were far too courteous to take him for granted; there was always a gratifying whisper of "Le Prince de Galles" when he appeared at the Maison Dorée, the Café Riche, the Café Anglais, or in the more eccentric atmosphere *chez Père Lunette*, or at the baccarat tables in the Rue Royale. They noticed that, if he ate too much, he chose his meals with discrimination. They approved his taste in feminine society. They saw no harm in his rather too frequent use of *le grand Seize*—the famous private dining room in the Café Anglais—with its red and gold and crimson furnishings, and its voluptuous history. He was, they thought, most refreshingly un-English; and perhaps they were right; though, to be sure, he never went to the races on a Sunday.

His visit in May was not entirely unofficial. 1867 was the year of the International Exhibition; and he was a member of the Royal Commission for the British section. His duties were light; they involved a few balls, banquets, and receptions, at which he was able to wear his Grand Cordon of the Legion of Honor, a ribbon of which he was particularly fond. For the rest, he wished—as his Comptroller, General Knollys, wrote to the British Ambassador—"to be as unfettered as circumstances will admit of so that he can go to the Theatres."

He was not disturbed by the performance at the *Variétés*. His country was no militarist state; his mother's court was shrouded in gloom; there was nothing in *La Grande Duchesse* to remind him of home. He only wished that there were. A plump bird of passage, he fled to Paris as the swallow flies south, only more frequently; now, perched in his proscenium box, he was hardly distinguishable, physically or otherwise, from the dandies in the stalls.

Lord Clarendon, a dignified but diligent gossip, reported, after the Prince's return, that there was a story current in London to the effect that he had deserted Madame Galliffet and some other ladies whom he had invited to dinner, and had disappeared with a *demi-mondaine*. Lord Clarendon, quite correctly, believed the Prince to be incapable of such behavior; but that he had a wide acquaintance among the *demi-monde* is beyond dispute. A young man, of distinguished birth, with plenty of money, and remarkably well versed in the art of enjoying himself, could hardly have avoided it. Its leaders—Léonide Leblanc, Adèle Courtois, Anna Deslions, Guila Barucci, Silly, La Paiva, Marguerite Bellanger, Cora Pearl—flourished like fantastic plants under the kindly shadow of the Second Empire. They seemed, in their colors and their shapes, to caricature the less excessive fashions of the Empress and her ladies. But they were not merely decorative; they were also useful. They would introduce their lovers, for a commission, to the stockbrokers of Paris.

It may well have seemed to the Prince, on each occasion of his return to England, that the chance phrase "entente cordiale" had been incarnated, as it were, in the elegant French court and in its amiable underworld. How different it all was from the Lutheran solemnities of Potsdam, the suffocating crape of Windsor! And how formative! All his years of education, all the admonitions of the Prince Consort, all the vigilance of Stockmar, all the tears and the tantrums and all the punishments had come to flower—and the result was a fat, glossy, genial young man, with charming manners, no morals to speak of, and a wide knowledge of the foibles of the world. The confidences of Napoleon III in 1866 were crowned by the delights of Napoleon's capital in 1867; from them flowed the cosmopolitan tastes, the prevailing beliefs of a lifetime. The Prince's political education began on the boulevards. Forever afterwards, though he disapproved often enough of its anglophobia and its journalism, he was a lover of France.

Lord Clarendon reported to the Ambassador in Paris, Lord Cowley, a further result of these visits. "The Prince of Wales," he wrote from London, "is leading a very dissolute life here and so far from concealing it his wish seems to be to earn for himself the reputation of a roué. . . ." Lord Clarendon would probably mean rather less by the words "dissolute" and "roué" than we should today; but the Prince's taste for friends who were not exactly inhibited was already exciting comment in the press. To the vast mass of Victorian Englishmen, sunk deep in respectability or deeper in poverty, his companions would have seemed merely fabulous; at the very most—for the reading public was still small—a rumor, faint and distorted, could have reached them from his little world. But rumors are dangerous. If only a strip of water and some miles of railway separated the Prince from Paris, between him and the English public there already gaped a fissure; and the fissure showed every sign of developing into an abyss.

He was only one of many whose private lives took on an exaggerated outline against the sunset of the Second Empire. Of most of the others—the brothers Ezpaleta, the duc de Mouchy, Khalil-Bey, Prince Trubetzkoi, and so on—only the outline remains. They have become names without identities; they are like silhouettes, cut out of black paper with a pair of scissors, and so subtly different from ourselves in every detail of their clothes and manners that they are more antique than antiquity. If they move, it is not with an individual, but with an historical motion. *"Tous les étrangers vers toi s'élancent, Paris,"* sang one of the choruses in *La Vie Parisienne* (1866). It was no more than true. The dying Empire was in the grip of a complex entity called finance-capital; and the foreigners who crowded into Paris, the vanguard of a new internationalism, dimly mirrored this predicament. In search of notoriety and amusement, they expended upon the most trivial objects the money that had been gained in the shadiest of ways. The city had not lost its charm; but it had become a little feverish and more than a little theatrical. The rest of the world, less up to date but far more proper, waited with uneasy impatience for the curtain to come down. But whether it would come down on disaster or on triumph, few people as yet would have cared to predict.

II

Among the frivolous visitors to the International Exhibition, there moved some eminent figures. 1867 was an ironical year for Napoleon III. He was face to face with disaster and he—at any rate—knew it: at the same time he was enjoying, as never before, a great social success. The parvenu whom no princess would marry, the upstart whom a Czar could not bring himself to call "Mon Frère," was now host to half the crowned heads of Europe. The reception accorded them was somewhat mixed—the Austrian Emperor was greeted with cries of "Vive Garibaldi," the Czar of Russia with "Vive la Pologne." As if to give a direction to the strange excitement that possessed the capital, the royalties hurried off to enjoy the mockeries of *La Grande Duchesse*. One by one they knocked at the door of Hortense Schneider's dressing room. The Kings of Bavaria, Portugal, and Sweden, the Khedive of Egypt expressed, each in his own way, the warmest admiration for Hortense; the Czar and his son, Vladimir, almost came to blows over her. "C'est le passage des princes que la Schneider," remarked her enemy, Mlle. Silly.

Though King William of Prussia could not bring himself to visit *La Grande Duchesse*, his Minister-President was not so nice. As he sat in his box at the *Variétés*, in the heart of the Empire that he proposed to abolish. Bismarck was convulsed with laughter. "C'est tout à fait ça," he exclaimed, over and over again.

The arrival of King William, Bismarck, and Moltke cast a shadow upon that festive summer. With their drab clothes and their ramrod courtesies (though Bismarck occasionally unbent) they were altogether out of place. Their watchfulness was appalling. They studied the fortifications; they discerned in the unfinished boulevards of Baron Haussmann an admirable field for artillery fire; they gazed unmoved at the rich but inappropriate uniforms of the pick of the French army, flaunting before them at the Grand Review. "Sire," said Marshal Lebœuf, after taking Bismarck and the silent Moltke around Versailles, "I have had a terrible day with two men who hate us with a mortal hatred." Bismarck added a final touch. He called at the Quai d'Orsay, pointed out the mistakes that France had made in her diplomacy, and showed how, if she had only been more awake, she could have spoiled his game a dozen times over.

The last of the French defeats, as a matter of fact, had occurred only that May. When the Treaty of Prague dissolved the German Confederation, Luxembourg was left without legal or political status; and Napoleon III thought that he could acquire it for himself. Early in 1867, he began negotiations. The King of Holland, with whose royal house Luxembourg was personally joined, seemed willing; Bismarck was not yet prepared for a final quarrel. The ripe fruit, trembling upon its branch, was about to fall into Napoleon's hands, when he committed an absurd blunder. He insisted upon a written consent from Bismarck before entering into any agreement with the King of Holland. The news leaked out; the National Liberals of Germany shouted in wrath; and Bismarck, still engaged in framing a new constitution for his new Bund, found it politic to follow their lead. Napoleon could now obtain Luxembourg only by going to war; and Bismarck was careful to let him know how dangerous this might be by publishing the secret military conventions between the southern states and the North German Confederation. All that was needed to complete Napoleon's discomfiture was his old device of a congress; and in May, an international gathering in London duly declared that the Grand-Duchy of Luxembourg was a neutral state. Henceforth, a Franco-Prussian war was almost inevitable.

Bismarck himself, on July 1, brought to a formidable and malignant conclusion all the negotiations that had followed upon the Austro-Prussian war. On that day, the Constitution of the North German Confederation was safely promulgated. It is worth remembering that, at this period in his career, his moments of greatest triumph were always attended by the possibility of an equal disaster. The liberals and conservatives alike distrusted and even loathed him; and how to frame a Constitution that satisfied them and left him at the same time at the head of affairs, was a problem that taxed even his remarkable powers. He succeeded, however, in solving it by playing upon the weaknesses of either side. The dynasties and the particularists were made happy by the knowledge that the legislatures of the various member-states were left intact, and that their governments controlled twenty-six votes in the Federal Council (Bundesrat) while Prussia had only seventeen. The liberals were dazzled by the prospect of a Federal Reichstag, which was to be elected by universal manhood suffrage.

Universal manhood suffrage did, indeed, promise that unified Germany for which the liberals had always yearned; but the Federal Reichstag that was to be both the symbol and the agent of this unification hardly justified their optimism. There was no administration either responsible to it or representative of it; its bills could be vetoed by the Bundesrat, an appointive body, which really initiated all legislation; while the permanent Federal President—the King of Prussia—could summon or dissolve it at will. In short it was not a parliament in the English sense of the word, but a debating chamber, whose right of consenting to legislation that it had not initiated gave it the appearance, and the appearance only, of a representative assembly. The Bundesrat, of course, was by its very nature a profoundly conservative body. The President, who acted for the Confederation in all external matters and was commander-in-chief of its united forces, loomed above the whole structure like a Jove; and like a

Mercury, the Federal Chancellor descended upon it, to announce, to persuade, and to enforce.

It was in the office of Federal Chancellor that one could discern the true purpose of the North German Confederation. Appointed by the President, and not responsible either to the Bundesrat or the Reichstag, he was the only federal minister; his functions and powers were indefinite; and it was clear that if his office were held by a man of strong will, a clear purpose, and a deceitful mind—a man such as Bismarck—much could be done with it. It was necessary, of course, for the Federal Chancellor to be at the same time Minister-President of the Kingdom of Prussia; and it goes without saying that Bismarck proposed to occupy both offices.

Such, then, was the composition of the North German Confederation—President, Chancellor, Council, Parliament. It is sad to remember that such leading liberals as Bennigsen, Lasker, and Forckenbeck were ready to assist it. In exchange for the realities of representative government, they accepted the shadow of unification and universal suffrage. From then onwards German liberalism strove to express itself, more and more, in the arts and sciences: it was divorced from government. For if ever a system concealed, beneath a democratic surface, a profoundly anti-democratic bias, that system was the North German Confederation.

By a curious coincidence, July 1, the day upon which this Constitution was promulgated, was also the culminating day of Napoleon's Exhibition; when, before his royal guests, the prizes were to be awarded to deserving exhibitors. The Emperor himself was somewhat shaken. He had just received the news that one of the most vicious of his adventures had at last run its course, and that the Emperor Maximilian of Mexico had been executed at Queretaro. The news deterred the Emperor's brother, Franz Josef of Austria, from attending the prize-giving, but otherwise it proceeded as though nothing had happened at all. None the less, neither Napoleon nor the royal group was in any mood for court festivities that night. A member of their International had been done to death; and it was not just the formal period of mourning that filled them with gloom and misgiving. A cold shadow stretched out from Mexico and touched each one of them to the heart; what could happen in one place could also, eventually, happen in another. Even the Prince of Wales, who was staying at the Bristol with the Duke of Cambridge, was the victim of presentiments. "Things," he wrote to Mrs. Bruce, "don't look pleasant or quiet." But empires and hearts are resilient; and shadows pass. Once more the Cent Gardes, immense and unmoving, lined the great staircase at the Tuileries; once more, the guests drifted away to their private supper-parties in the gilt and stucco of the *Café Riche* and the *Maison Dorée;* once more the Empire turned between its habitual poles of scandal and ceremony. If one forgot the other side of the Napoleonic dispensation—the awful squalor, for instance, of the faubourgs of St. Antoine and Belleville— one might almost have been tempted to believe that it would go on turning forever. . . .

What Napoleon thought of Bismarck's new Confederation can only be guessed at; but it is fairly safe to assume that he misjudged its power. He was inclined to hope that the southern German states would have none of it, and that the Radicals of Württemberg and the Clericals of Bavaria preferred France to Prussia. It was a delusive hope. Bismarck, however, was not yet ready to engulf the south; and when Baden asked to be joined to the Confederation, he replied with dangerous humility that the Emperor Napoleon III was opposed to such a step.

III

The plans of Queen Victoria were arranged with a methodical exactitude, and she could hardly be persuaded to contemplate any change in them. Her absence in Balmoral in June, 1867, made it impossible for her to invite the Czar from Paris to Windsor; but the mere suggestion that such an invitation might have been of some small assistance to English diplomacy, filled her with uneasiness. She told the Prime Minister, Lord Derby, that invitations had never been proffered in the Prince Consort's day; that there was even less occasion for them now; and that in any case her health would not stand the strain. Lord Derby, an easy-going gentleman, of a slightly cynical turn of mind, received this communication with equanimity. The Czar had been in a hurry to go home, and no doubt he was quite contented with the Garter which had been sent to him while he was in Paris. But he was not the only visitor to the Exhibition whose susceptibilities would have to be considered. The Sultan of Turkey, Abdul Aziz, highly gratified with his flowery reception at Napoleon's court, was eager for further experiences of the same kind; and he informed the British Ambassador at Paris that he intended to visit England.

It was therefore arranged that he should see a naval review at Spithead; and the Queen observed that it would not be necessary for her to meet him until then. She was extremely reluctant to break her journey from Balmoral to Osborne. To stay at Windsor for three days in order to accord the Sultan a ten minutes' interview seemed to her an intolerable exaction; her hysteria and her self-pity were equally provoked; and she sent Dr. Jenner to Lord Derby to tell him that her nerves would not be up to it. Lord Derby was unconvinced. He persuaded Dr. Jenner to advise the Queen that her nerves would not suffer just this once; Dr. Jenner complied; and the Queen and the Sultan met on the day after his arrival.

The Prince was particularly interested in the Sultan's reception: it involved a number of ceremonies in which he himself was to play a leading part. From the moment that Abdul Aziz landed at Dover, he showered him with attentions. The Sultan, therefore, arrived at Windsor in the best of tempers; and his ten minutes with the Queen, whose manners were always perfect, quite enchanted him. He would, perhaps, have been less pleased had he known what was going on behind the scenes. The Prince was sure that nothing less than the Garter would satisfy the Sultan; the Queen and Lord Derby maintained that the Garter was a Christian Order, and that the Star of India would do just as well. The contest, as so often happened when the Queen and the Prince were on opposite sides, grew bitter; but the Prince persisted, and at last he won his case.

The investiture took place on July 17, during the naval review. The day was rough, the royal yacht pitched and tossed, and Abdul Aziz who had been "touché"—so the Khedive reported—"jusqu'aux larmes" by his reception at Dover, was now moved in a somewhat different way. He retired to his cabin, emerged just in time to receive his Garter from the Queen, and hastily went below again. Once on land, however, he appeared to be immeasurably gratified with his new Order, and the Prince, congratulating himself upon having achieved a diplomatic triumph, went off to Homburg, to recruit his energies with a course of the waters.

As for the Sultan, he returned to Constantinople, where his feelings toward England continued to be of a friendly description until the day when, nine years later, after a regime of unparalleled corruption and incompetence, he was hunted from his throne.

IV

This incident serves to emphasize one of the Prince's most characteristic preoccupations. To exchange courtesies with other royal persons, to move from court to court, to wear a variety of uniforms, to receive decorations, to endure with affability the tedium of banquets and receptions—surely, he reflected, this was a contribution towards a good understanding amongst nations. In a sense, of course, he was right; and if he over-estimated the importance of such things, his views were no different from those of a number of other idle young princes who, gazing upon the European scene from the windows of their crowded palaces, only wished that they could be of as much consequence as he.

He was even inclined to believe Mr. Disraeli when that flatterer declared, in March, 1868: "There is no doubt a great yearning in Ireland for the occasional presence and inspiration of royalty." That there was a great yearning in Ireland

176

for agrarian reform and for a dissolution of the Union with England, admitted of no doubt; but whether the Irish, as distinguished from the Anglo-Irish, entertained any notions of any sort about the presence of royalty was rather more questionable. Mr. Disraeli, however, had just become Prime Minister; and this elevation in his position had been accompanied by a similar elevation in his prose. The Queen agreed that the Prince might go to Ireland for a week; to a longer sojourn she was unalterably opposed. "Any *encouragement,*" she told Disraeli, "of his constant love of running about, and not keeping at home or near the Queen, is most *earnestly* and *seriously* to be deprecated." When she found out that a day at the Punchestown races was included in her son's program, her uneasiness became acute. "I *much regret,*" she told him on March 9, "that the occasion chosen should be the '*Races,*' as it naturally strengthens the belief, already far too prevalent, that your chief object is amusement." However, she added, she would allow him to be installed a Knight of St. Patrick; that, "and NOT the *Races*" was to be the occasion of his visit.

The week passed most agreeably. There was a state dinner, and a state ball; and the crowds at Punchestown were given an "occasion," as the Prince had already expressed it to his mother, "to display their loyalty to you and to our family, if (as is to be hoped) such a feeling exists." The display was vociferous, for the Irish are generally courteous to strangers; but of the misery of their island the Prince had no glimpse at all. It was hidden behind the waving handkerchiefs, the huzzas, the smiling faces. He returned, quite convinced that he had done something towards alleviating a situation which habitually expressed itself in Fenian outrages, riots, demonstrations, and such other ways as are at the command of a people whose standard of living has fallen well below the level of subsistence. At the Royal Academy Banquet he expatiated to Mr. John Bright upon the pleasantness of his reception in Ireland. "I told him," said Mr. Bright, "that there must be legislation as well as civilities."

Benjamin Disraeli, whose correspondence and friendship with the Queen were already verging upon the romantic, did not altogether forget that Gloriana was mortal and that she had an heir. He perceived that the Prince—"Prince Hal" as he called him in his intimate correspondence—really wished to be useful, and he tried to persuade the Queen to give her son something to do. Victoria was relentless. Disraeli, immersed in the business of keeping his government in power by stealing the thunder of his opponents, soon forgot the whole matter. The Prince plunged once more into such dissipations as the summer and his boredom suggested; once more there was comment in the press. The sentiments of the uninformed public, never very easy to gauge, may perhaps have revealed themselves in a little pamphlet entitled "A Letter from a Freemason to General H.R.H. Albert Edward, Prince of Wales," one of the curiosities of those remote days. Written by Charles Bradlaugh, an energetic republican, it is couched in terms of the most elaborate irony.

"I do not address you as Prince of Wales," wrote Mr. Bradlaugh, "for some of our Princes of Wales have been drunken, riotous spendthrifts. . . . Junius charged George, Prince of Wales, with quitting the arms of his wife for the endearments of a wanton. . . . But your pure career, your sober and virtuous life, would win plaudits even from Junius' ghost. . . .

"I do not regard your title of Duke at all in writing you. . . .

It is pleasant to think that the Duke of Cornwall and Rothesay . . . is not a runner after painted douzels, that he has not stamped cuckold on the forehead of a dozen husbands."

The pamphlet continued in this strain until the end.

On the whole, it is not surprising that it should have been thought advisable for the Prince to go abroad during the winter of 1868-9. He and the Princess, therefore, visited Copenhagen, Berlin, Vienna, Egypt, Turkey, and Greece; arrived in Paris in May, '69, to spend a week at Compiègne with Napoleon and Eugénie; and returned to an England which, everybody hoped, would have forgotten the past. This, however, was not the case.

v

At Berlin, there had been many courtesies. King William invested the Prince with the Grand Cross of the Order of the Black Eagle, while the Crown Prince and Princess, though they could hardly have been accused of cordiality, were at any rate civil. Bismarck added a sardonic touch to these proceedings, and when he was presented to the Princess before the state banquet, she noticed with disgust that he was wearing a Danish Order. He was in an excessively good humor, for he regarded with amused indulgence the frail web that the Prince was so busily spinning between one capital and another. He might have been sitting once again with Moltke at the *Variétés*, chuckling over the mummeries of *La Grande Duchesse*.

His own plans were now well advanced. Only one step was needed to complete the unification of Germany, and

that was to persuade France to declare war on Prussia. The
risks involved in such a step were, no doubt, considerable;
but he derived much comfort, not merely from the assur-
ances of the Prussian General Staff, but from the behavior
of Napoleon himself. For the French Emperor, in 1868, suddenly granted freedom of the press and freedom of assembly:
and when a dictatorship is reduced to such democratic expe-
dients, one can be fairly safe in assuming that it is growing
very weak.

Moreover, Napoleon had no allies. Russia was grateful to
Bismarck for some small favors in the matter of the suppression of Poland; Austria was helpless. Italy had begun to
realize that Napoleon wished her to remain in three parts,
each one resting upon a prickly foundation of foreign bay-
onets. England, too, was aloof. Since 1866, she had been involved in a series of internal disputes of extraordinary importance—in the metamorphosis of Whigs into Liberals—in the
passions and aridities of Reform. Without support abroad,
with disaffection at home, the Second Empire waited, like
some brilliantly dying leaf, for the storm to whirl it away.
In December, 1869, when the Emperor and Empress went
to see *Froufrou*—a play which seemed in some indefinite
and yet unmistakable fashion to mark the end of an era—the
Empress wept so uncontrollably that the rouge ran down her
face, and she dared not leave her box. Of the many intimations we have of the sense of doom that pervaded Napoleon's
court in those last years, this is the most pitiful and the most
exact.

In 1868, the abdication of the monstrous Queen Isabella
of Spain provided Bismarck with the opportunity that he
needed. He persuaded the Spanish authorities to suggest, as

candidate for the vacant throne, Prince Leopold of Hohen-zollern-Sigmaringen. Upon the qualifications of Prince Leopold for this position, history is politely silent; but one thing is certain—a German prince, connected with the Prussian royal house, was just the candidate to irritate the nerves of France beyond endurance. For more than a year the negotiations proceeded in secrecy. The prince's father, the candidate himself, the King of Prussia—all were opposed to accepting the Spanish offer. Bismarck was dauntless. At length, in June, 1870, King William consented: and then—at the last moment—it almost seemed as if Bismarck's scheme would come to nothing. For M. Benedetti hurried to Ems, where the Prussian monarch was taking the waters, and there, on July 12, persuaded him to withdraw his consent. King William confessed that he was much relieved. In spite of his subservience to Bismarck, he was at heart a Particularist—he longed for the old ways and the old days, for a Prussia that had not gobbled up other men's kingdoms and duchies, for absolutism without ambition. But the same frenzy which, in 1867, resulted in the loss of Luxembourg, once again seized upon the diplomacy of France. M. Benedetti was instructed to demand a further assurance that the candidacy of Prince Leopold would never be renewed. He accosted the Prussian king on the promenade at Ems, and William, somewhat taken aback, replied that he could make no engagements of this kind; that his government had no more interest in the matter; that, in short, he had nothing further to say. An aide-de-camp, later in the day, called upon M. Benedetti and insisted that the incident must now be considered closed. No insult of any kind had been offered to France; and the dispatch which the King sent to Bismarck made this perfectly clear.

That evening, before the dispatch was received, Bismarck, Moltke, and Roon were sitting over their wine at Berlin in an atmosphere of gloom. They could see no way of tempting the confused belligerence of France into the pit that had been dug. The dispatch arrived, and at once the light broke. Bismarck edited it in such a way that those who read it in France would be forced to believe that their ambassador had been dismissed with ignominy; and in this condition it was sent to the press. "The God of old still lives," was Moltke's comment upon this literary tour-de-force.

By July 14, Paris was shouting "à Berlin" and singing the forbidden Marseillaise; on July 15, King William ordered a general mobilization; on July 19, France declared war. So exact had been the German preparations, that Moltke found time to read French novels while the troops moved to their appointed places. Then with his sovereign he set out upon the road that led to Wörth, Spicheren, Mars-la-Tour, St. Privat, Sedan; and so to Paris and the mirrors of Versailles.

Oddly enough, most friends of Germany believed, not only that France had provoked the war, but that France would win. Queen Victoria's letters to her old friend, Queen Augusta of Prussia, were at first filled with lamentations; they were afterwards filled with surprise and delight. A similar transformation took place in the epistolary tone of her eldest daughter. Little as she cared for Bismarck, the Crown Princess could not resist the argument of a successful campaign. Her early agitations—which allowed the Prince to tell his mother that perhaps Vicky would now appreciate "what the feelings of little Denmark must have been when they heard that the armies of Prussia and Austria were against them"—soon gave way to a puritanical exultation.

The French, she declared, were frivolous, conceited, and immoral. "Where is their army," she inquired of her mother, "where are their statesmen? They despised and hated the Germans whom they considered it quite lawful to insult. How have they been punished!" Nor did she forget the family differences. "What will Bertie and Alix say," she added, rather spitefully, "to all these marvellous events?"

What the Prince said, when this letter was sent on to him, has not been recorded. He was near his mother at the time— he at Abergeldie Castle, she at Balmoral—but he was not permitted to see any of the dispatches that came pouring in to her. A few discreet excerpts from them, together with his sister's letters, comprised all the information that was allowed him. Was it true that he had given the Austrian Ambassador to understand that he wished for a speedy Prussian defeat? The Queen, at any rate, believed so. He was a violent partisan of France; and when he begged her to send him with letters to King William and the Emperor, calling for an armistice before it should be too late, she told him that, even if it were practicable, he was totally unfitted for such a task.

Nothing, of course, could have arrested the meticulous onrush of Prussia. Six weeks after the beginning of hostilities, the Emperor Napoleon III drove out of Sedan to surrender his sword to the King of Prussia. The French armies had collapsed or were collapsing; the gallantry of the troops had been equaled by the incompetence, or worse, of their commanders; and the Empire which had been founded on bloodshed and treachery was about to disappear upon the same terms. But first, before he could be admitted to the rather irritable presence of King William, Napoleon had to endure a conversation with Bismarck.

As they sat together—the tall Prussian, the small sick tyrant—they represented, in a pictorial form, the penultimate stage in the solution of a famous problem—the Question of Schleswig-Holstein. The final stage was the proclamation of a German Empire at Versailles.

VI

The fall of Napoleon III, the subsequent declaration of a French Republic, shook the English monarchy as a minor earthquake shakes a house. The floors heaved, the plaster pattered down from the ceilings, here a picture crashed to the ground, there a statue fell upon its nose; and people began to wonder whether the whole picturesque edifice would not come down in ruins.

In the first place, there were general complaints that the royal family was pro-German. On February 23, 1871, *The Pall Mall Gazette* accused the Queen and her children of a breach of neutrality through their communications to the King and the Crown Prince of Prussia. Whatever the Queen's errors may have been in this respect, the Prince was certainly guiltless. None the less, Sir Henry Hoare informed the Commons that a Captain Hozier, a Queen's messenger, "had been charged with messages to the Crown Prince of Germany from Her Majesty, the Prince of Wales, and the Duke of Cambridge, of congratulation upon the successes won by his army." Mr. Gladstone's reply was so subtle that nobody could be quite sure whether Sir Henry was correct or not.

The Prince, therefore, wrote a full explanation to Lord Granville. Captain Hozier, he said, had called upon him without notice and asked if he could be the bearer of letters to the Crown Prince or others. The Prince had written no letters, but he requested Hozier to remember him affectionately to the Crown Prince, the Duke of Saxe-Coburg-Gotha, the Landgrave of Hesse, and Prince Adolphus of Mecklenburg-Strelitz. Only the first of these personages could be said to have played an active part in the war. He had told Hozier to inform the Crown Prince that "my sympathy was great with the French," to add some conventional compliments "in a military point of view" upon the German campaigns, and to express the hope that "the bad feelings which the Germans entertained towards England would soon cease." Such communications could hardly be described as a breach of neutrality.

These accusations, however, were only the signs of a more profound discontent. All through the year 1871, republican clubs sprang into being. The Queen and her family were attacked at public meetings, in the press, and in Parliament. The attack upon the Queen, though various, was chiefly concerned with the subject of Expense. The monarchy took a great deal from the taxpayers' pockets; and what, pray, did the taxpayers receive in return? The Queen was a recluse. Half a dozen times a season, perhaps, wrapped in her repellent weeds, she nerved herself to appear in public. Her life was dedicated to the memory of a husband whom the English had never understood and whom they had almost forgotten; her long hours of work were absorbed in advancing the cause of Germany; she spent nothing on ceremony; she was damaging the millinery trade. Such were the arguments of the republicans; and to these there was added yet another. She was a very wealthy woman—her savings from the Civil List, it was believed, must amount to a considerable sum every year—yet she did not scruple to ask Parliament to grant a dowry to a daughter and living expenses to a son. Why should Princess Louise receive £30,000 and £6,000 a year; what had Prince Arthur done to deserve an annual allowance of £15,000?

The public resentment at length came to a head on July 28, 1871, when a great mass meeting submerged the fountains and the lions in Trafalgar Square and flowed from the steps of St. Martin's Church to the entrance of the Barracks. Here Charles Bradlaugh—it was just a week after the Queen had asked Parliament for some provision for her son Arthur—protested against "any more grants to princely paupers," and shouted that the House of Brunswick should take warning, for the patience of the English public was almost exhausted. Mr. George Odger, who followed, struck a similar chord. It might have been possible—though it would certainly have been unwise—to dismiss Mr. Bradlaugh and Mr. Odger as demagogues; there were others who could not be so lightly treated. When Sir Charles Dilke attacked the "miserable political and moral tone" set by court sinecures; when he inveighed against the prejudices of the Duke of Cambridge and the promotions of the Duke of Edinburgh; when he maintained (wrongly as it happened) that the Queen paid no income tax; when he declared of the republic that "I say for my part—and I believe that the middle classes in general will say—'let it come'"—the friends of Victoria were seriously alarmed. As for Mr. Joseph Chamberlain, the radical mayor of Birmingham, he went even further: "the republic," he asserted, "must come." No doubt Mr. Chamberlain's political views—his desire, for instance, to obtain decent housing for the poor of Birmingham—were sadly warped. But his monocle, his impeccable frock-coat, the orchid in his buttonhole! In those days, when a somewhat exaggerated value was set upon appearances, there was something portentous about democracy in fine linen.

Much as Victoria contributed towards the rise of republicanism in England in those two years, the Prince contributed a great deal more. The Queen's errors—her thrift and her grief—were, in a sense, errors of virtue: the same accusation could not be leveled against her eldest son. The Prince's income was around £100,000 a year; and while it required a pamphlet called *What Does She Do With It?* to suggest the nature of the Queen's expenditures, no such research was necessary in the Prince's case. The court gazette and the comic papers, an accidental but effervescent alliance, combined to give the public a rough idea of where his money went. His progress through the year was almost astronomical. Ringed about by dubious satellites he moved, with a planetary obedience, from London towards Goodwood, from Goodwood to Cowes, from Cowes to Abergeldie, from Abergeldie to Homburg, from Homburg to Sandringham, from Sandringham to the Riviera, from the Riviera to London. The orbit might differ from year to year; but it represented, to that shocked and inquisitive Victorian public, the same round of racing-debts, gambling debts, purely social pleasures, and—and worse.

On February 16, 1870, Sir Charles Mordaunt, of Walton Hall in Warwickshire, applied for a dissolution of his marriage with Harriet Sarah, Lady Mordaunt, on the grounds

187

N

of her adultery with Viscount Cole, Sir Frederick Johnstone, and "some person." The two co-respondents were friends of the Prince, and the "some person" was himself. He was haled into the witness box, and though the evidence against him consisted of a few absolutely innocuous letters, his appearance in such a trial created the most unfortunate impression. It gave, as it were, a body to the airy rumors upon which the public had hitherto been fed; and his appearances that summer were sometimes greeted with hisses. Then, on August 10, the editor of the *Sheffield Daily Telegraph* was accused of libeling Lord and Lady Sefton and the Prince of Wales; his paper had stated in April that the Earl was divorcing the Countess and that the Prince was to be co-respondent. The case was tried at the Leeds Summer Assizes; the statement was proved to be untrue; but once again the Prince's reputation suffered a miserable eclipse. By the autumn of 1871 it can only be said to have existed in a negative way; and when Charles Bradlaugh publicly announced in October that he "trusted that [the Prince of Wales] may never sit on the throne or lounge under its shadow," any number of Mr. Bradlaugh's fellow-countrymen would have been inclined to agree.

Royalty in those days was strangely insulated against the shocks of public opinion. The Queen made no attempt to appear more frequently; or the Prince to disappear. Together they descended, by very different routes, to the same level in the public affections; and, since the turn of the century, perhaps only George IV had reached a lower one.

Towards the end of November, at Sandringham, the Prince fell ill of typhoid fever. By December 11, he was raving with delirium, and it was universally believed that there was no chance of his recovery. The Queen watched by his bedside, and sometimes he stopped shouting and singing and appeared to recognize her: ten years before, she had been at Windsor and the Prince Consort had been dying of the same illness. On December 14, however, the anniversary of Albert's death, the Prince began to mend: it was said that he asked for a glass of beer, drank it, and sank into a refreshing sleep. The story may have been apocryphal, but it was related with gusto and affection in the public-houses. Indeed, all over the country there was a sudden change of feeling, and expressions of loyalty poured in from every side. When the Queen, summoning up her courage, drove to St. Paul's in February, 1872, to render public thanks with her son for his recovery, she was given a deafening welcome by vast and enthusiastic crowds. From then onwards, the tide of republicanism steadily ebbed away.

VII

It is true that nothing is more calculated to restore royal popularity than a prolonged illness or an attempted assassination. Yet the Prince's restoration to favor—which, in any case, did not last very long—was only an effect of the decay of republicanism: it was, at most, a rather obvious symptom of a quite obscure condition. The English republicans attacked the monarchy on the grounds that it was too expensive. Now expense—even expense combined with idleness and immorality—was hardly a strong enough reason to compel the overthrow of a constitutional monarchy: it was a

189

reason that appealed to a class of tax-paying persons whose revolutionary appetites had been satisfied, nearly thirty years before, by the Repeal of the Corn Laws. Nor was the French Republic, which gave the English republicans their momentum, an inspiring affair. It had stepped into power over the wreckage of the Commune: and England, in 1871, would have needed the spirit of the Commune, not the spirit of the Republic, to bring about any change in her institutions.

It would be an exaggeration to suggest that the Commune of Paris enjoyed a wide support at this moment among the English lower classes; or that its fall occasioned them any excessive grief. It had received a remarkably bad press. Its divided counsels, its jealousies, the destruction of property, the murder of a prelate—these had been stressed. About its heroisms and aspirations little had been said. Yet a movement so dynamic and so prophetic could not fail to have its effect; and its immediate effect upon England was to reduce by degrees the enthusiasm of the working classes for the republican movement. An instinct, an intuition, informed them that they would gain little by the substitution of, shall we say, Mr. Joseph Chamberlain for Queen Victoria; that conditions would probably remain pretty much as before, only with a group of rather less picturesque people at the head of affairs; that, in short, one can get rid of one's monarchs, and still retain one's masters. As the English working class, in 1871, had become the only revolutionary class, there was not much more to be said.

The voice of the people, rising spontaneously, is one of the voices of history. As the crowds cheered Queen Victoria, driving to St. Paul's, they were expressing a decent

English sympathy for a mother who had almost lost a son; but they were also giving vent to a profound, unconscious distaste for middle-class republicanism. There was, no doubt, a great deal of good sense in the arguments of Mr. Joseph Chamberlain and Sir Charles Dilke and Professor Fawcett and Mr. Taylor. But the people had the last word.

Chapter Six

A VOYAGE THROUGH THE CANAL

ON FEBRUARY 20, 1874, in his seventieth year, Benjamin Disraeli became Prime Minister for the second time. The ruling passions of his life, he admitted, were "Power and the Affections"; and he was now able to satisfy the first in the distribution of patronage, and the second in a rococo communion with the Queen. Yet how often he told his friends that his honors had come too late! What were power or fame or fortune or the affections, without the gifts of youth and health? Nothing but dross and tinsel. He was a lonely widower; there was no one now to inspire his imagination or to supervise his diet; nor was there anywhere in the world a single person who, "were I to die tomorrow, would give up even a dinner party." Such were his reflections when, tortured by gout or exhausted by asthma, he lay for days at a time in his bedroom at No. 2, Whitehall Gardens.

They were not his only reflections, however; nor, perhaps, did they convey his inmost feelings. The letters which he wrote from his confinement seemed often to reiterate, in their playfulness and their malice, the vivid impulse of his youth; his taste for worldly success had grown less keen, but it was also less agonizing; and nothing—not even pain, not even unhappiness—could dull the edge of his delight in himself. Lying back on the pillows, with the blinds drawn, in silence and in darkness, he would review over and over again the vanished episodes of his extraordinary career. It was his favorite romance, and he was his favorite hero. Were there not still some sunset pages left to him, through which he could see himself moving, impassive and melancholy—a hero to the end?

And then once more—a thin, strange, bent old man, with a yellow face and lizard eyes—he would emerge into the world: to preside with shrewdness and tact over a Cabinet, to dominate a debate—to drive from dinner party to dinner party, from country house to country house—to laugh with the Duchess of Edinburgh, to flatter the Queen. His lot, he told Lady Chesterfield, was "a terrible [one], almost intolerable"; he was "wearied to extinction and profoundly unhappy." Lady Chesterfield was duly sympathetic, but not unduly so. She was quite devoted to him, and she knew—none better—that he savored his despair with all the relish of an incurable romantic.

Those who like to speculate upon history's habit of suiting the man to the times, may derive some interest from this second administration of Benjamin Disraeli. The country had grown tired of the incessant legislation of Mr. Gladstone, a middle-clash divinity, all wrath and flame, who hurled reforms like thunderbolts. If his successor had any domestic blessings to provide, it would clearly be advisable for him to drop them like manna; this procedure as it happened was the one which Mr. Disraeli found most agreeable; and it was discovered, by the middle of 1875, that he had quietly effected a considerable improvement in the relations between worker and employer and in the laws that dealt with public health. Yet it was not upon measures such as these—much as they appealed to his vestigial radicalism—that Mr. Disraeli wished the country to dwell. His oriental imagination began to dally with high visions of imperial splendor: and it was with these that he hoped—and for a time managed—to bedazzle the public.

The fabric of these visions, whatever else it may have been, was certainly not baseless. It was nimbly woven out of vulgar necessity—out of the need for raw materials and markets and opportunities for investment. Because he transformed these gross realities into agreeable romances—romances, moreover, which he himself believed—Mr. Disraeli became, during the seventies at any rate, a man of the hour. He did not initiate an imperial policy: the movement of the times did that—a movement too complex and too compelling for either Liberals or Conservatives to resist. He simply made, with all the histrionics at his command, a choice of gestures. Should one go through the motions of swimming against the tide? Or should one glide conspicuously along with it? Mr. Disraeli chose to glide: so conspicuously, indeed, that in the end it brought about his downfall.

II

When the Prince of Wales revived his long-cherished desire to make a tour of India, he found, therefore, a ready supporter in the new Prime Minister; and if ever he needed support, it was for just such a project as this. Disraeli, of course, as Prime Minister, was the official confidant of the Royal

Family; but he was not the man to leave things on an official basis. His romantic friendship with the Queen is a familiar story; it admitted him to an intercourse which no other Prime Minister since Melbourne had ever enjoyed; and even for Melbourne the etiquette was not relaxed as it was for Disraeli. In the bosom of the Family, the strange old sorcerer would persuade the Princess Beatrice to show her wit, or open a confidential conversation with the Princess of Wales by praising the shape of her slipper. With such an advocate at headquarters, the Indian tour had at least a chance of becoming a reality.

With the Prince himself, Disraeli was less at ease; "male society," he said, "is not much to my taste." As a connoisseur of the world, however, he found "Prince Hal" not unworthy of attention. High birth and amiable manners were no bar to Mr. Disraeli's interest; and if their owner happened also to be "a spoilt child" who "can't bear being bored," that simply made the spectacle more piquant. He was, he told his friends, always glad to meet the heir to the throne in society: he rarely bestowed a higher compliment than that.

As for the visit to India it could not do any harm, in Mr. Disraeli's opinion, and it might easily do some good. He was engaged in reversing Mr. Gladstone's rather tepid policy in Afghanistan; and if any good feeling could be promoted on the Indian side of the Khyber Pass, so much the better. For the truth was that India in the 1870's was sadly disaffected. The government of that country, since the suppression of the Mutiny, was the most businesslike that it had ever known; but this state of affairs, strange to say, did not satisfy the Indians. So long as the East India Company had been in nominal control of their lives, they had accepted the presence of the English with resignation. The Company was the successor of Akbar and Aurungzib; it was an occupying power; and though it was curiously addicted to prayer-meetings and other forms of missionary endeavor, there hung about it a faint but unmistakable air of the desperado and the freebooter. As such it was, if not a pleasant, at least an intelligible phenomenon. But the new Government of India was quite another thing. It was not even its own master; there were times when it was obliged to accept the criticisms and bow to the commands of a Secretary of State in London; the Secretary of State was himself, to a certain extent, the servant of Parliament; and in this way the voice of democracy began to make itself heard in India. At such a time, it was at best a faint and freakish voice; but it was audible. Here and there, among the teeming peoples of the sub-continent, little groups began to talk and learn about self-government; slowly the Indian mind awoke. One of the consequences of nineteenth century imperialism was that, the more firm and efficient it became, the more it seemed—not of its own volition, but by its very nature—to instruct its subject peoples in the art of doing without it.

Whether Mr. Disraeli ascribed these or other or any reasons to the unrest in India—or whether he left such speculations to the Secretary of State, Lord Salisbury—is not known. It was perhaps enough for him that the unrest existed, not merely among the peoples but among the princes, whom he considered of far more consequence; and that an ingenious attempt on the part of the Gaekwar of Baroda to poison the English resident, Sir Robert Phayre, had recently emphasized it in the most agitating manner. He thought that a royal visit, with all its accompaniments of gifts and civilities, would soothe the princes; Lord Salisbury agreed with him; and on March 17, 1875, the Viceroy added his formidable endorsement.

The tour, however, was by no means a certainty. The Queen's peculiar jealousies were aroused, and she bristled with objections. On May 19, Disraeli wrote to Lady Bradford that he had "received a most extraordinary letter from the Faery today. . . . She dies hard, and will prevent the Indian visit, if possible, yet." As the summer wore on, caught between the objections of the Queen and the complaints of the Prince, he had a very hard time of it. On one occasion, he felt obliged to absent himself from a dinner party at Stafford House for fear of what the Prince, who was also to be present, might say to him. In August, he penned a humble expostulation. "I regret," he wrote, "that relations between your Royal Highness and Her Majesty's Government with respect to your Royal Highness's Indian tour have been unfortunate. I will not stop to speculate on the cause. There have been many cross-purposes."

This was no exaggeration. The cross-purposes, which perhaps deserved a harsher name, might be grouped as follows.

(1) The Queen's interference in every detail of the program. It is probable that, if Mr. Disraeli had not been there to influence her, the program would never have survived her attentions. As it was, the Prince was not consulted at any point. This was one of the chief sources of his complaints.

(2) The Viceroy's insistence (in which he was backed by the Queen) that he should take precedence of the Prince. The Prince and his friends—or "the Marlborough House banditti"

as Disraeli preferred to call them—maintained that he could travel only as the Sovereign's representative, and must therefore take precedence of the Viceroy. This dispute was further embittered by the intervention of Lord Salisbury, who had some scores to pay off with the Viceroy (a Gladstonian appointee), and who ranged himself on the side of the banditti. By the end of June, the whole project seemed doomed to split upon the remarkable rock of who was to take the *pas* of whom. Eventually a compromise was reached. The proposed Durbar was to take the form of a Special Chapter of the Star of India; and the Viceroy, as Grand Master, was to read a special commission from the Queen deputing the Prince to preside on so exceptional an occasion. The Queen found this compromise most distasteful, and it took all Mr. Disraeli's cajoleries to persuade her to agree to it.

(3) The Prince declared that he ought to choose his own suite. Lord Salisbury demurred to this. The Cabinet, he said, had decided to treat all arrangements as official questions. After endless disagreements, and in ways too circuitous for investigation, a large staff was selected; it turned out to be composed, for the most part, of congenial persons; and the Prince further consoled himself by having his personal jester, Lord Charles Beresford, appointed an aide-de-camp.

(4) The Government thought that £60,000 ought to be enough to cover the Prince's expenses, since he was not to be traveling as a formal representative of the Sovereign; and Parliament accordingly voted that sum. The Marlborough House banditti were filled with wrath. "What a shabby concern this vote is!" exclaimed the Duke of Sutherland. "If I were you, Sir, I would not take it. I would borrow the money of some friends at five per cent." "Well, will you lend it

me?" was the reply—"which," Disraeli reported to Lady Bradford, "shut him up. If H.R.H.," he added wryly, "knew that I had so successfully proved that he was a wit, he would pardon me." The Prince, however, continued to remark that £60,000 was an insufficient sum.

Such, in brief, were the difficulties which had to be met before anything could be done about soothing the princes of India.

As for Mr. Disraeli—without whom the tour could hardly have escaped the clutches of Victoria—he was at length forgiven. He spent a week-end at Sandringham; and on October 19, on the eve of the Prince's departure, he received a communication from that repentant personage, declaring: "I know that you will always be a friend to me." Disraeli thought it "a very touching letter." And in this way the controversy ended.

Soon afterwards, H.M.S. *Serapis*, bound for India with the royal party on board, entered the Suez Canal. "It is an everlasting pity," wrote the Prince to Lord Granville, "that it [the Suez Canal] was not made by an English company and kept in our hands, because, as it is the highway to India, we should (*sic*) be obliged to take it—and by force of arms if necessary." The words were, no doubt, prompted by those simple, acquisitive instincts which, years before, had so shocked Mr. John Bright; but they were just as suited to the spirit of the times as were the visions of Mr. Disraeli. They echoed, in a somewhat ruthless manner, the sentiments of any number of well-informed people; they were filled with dire presentiments; and they evoked, above all, a very curious past. Why was the Suez Canal "not made by an English company"? As the *Serapis* moves on through that unique water-way towards a reconstructed India, it might not be without interest to pause and inquire.

III

In the year 1855, Ferdinand de Lesseps paid a visit to London. It was in June, the height of the season; everybody was in town; and M. de Lesseps, whose manners were delightful, and who was distantly related to the Empress Eugénie, enjoyed a great social success. It was not for this, however, that he had come to the English capital. He had with him the plans for an extraordinary project—nothing less than the piercing of the Isthmus of Suez—and he was in search of English backing. He was fresh from a visit to Constantinople where, he admitted, he had not been very successful. But he had the support of the Viceroy of Egypt, Mohammed Said, and he was sure that if he could persuade the British Government to agree with him, he would have no further difficulty with the Sublime Porte.

In his youth, M. de Lesseps had been influenced by the doctrines of Saint-Simon, whose program for universal peace included the construction of a canal at Suez. In 1846, a company was actually incorporated for that purpose; but its directors quarreled among themselves; and its plans came to nothing. De Lesseps, fired by the ideals of Saint-Simon and the efforts of the company, and armed with a survey completed when Bonaparte was First Consul, was determined to dig a canal by the most direct route. In spite of some diplomatic experience, he was in many respects a very innocent man. He was neither an engineer nor a financier, nor did he wish to make any money for himself out of the canal. His project was a legacy from the noble liberalism of the early nineteenth century. Did it not require a great deal in the way of imagination and not much in the way of machinery? Did it not hope to promote the brotherhood of man by bringing the East many weeks nearer to the West? High idealisms and strange romanticisms were mingled in it; it was the child of impractical economics and poetical yearnings; but it was itself practicable. And that is why, when de Lesseps inherited it, he found himself plunged into all the difficulties that obstinacy could summon or intrigue invent for him.

In the winter of 1854, when Mohammed Said, before the assembled consuls-general at Cairo, announced his intention of granting a concession to de Lesseps, that gentleman noticed that only one member of the gathering seemed uneasy. It was Mr. Bruce, the British representative. De Lesseps knew that England had never been "canaliste," but he was quite convinced that the merchants and the bankers and the politicians of England had but to see his maps and his graphs to change their minds. His reception in London in '55 and '56 seemed at first to justify this prediction. The merchants and the bankers immediately grasped the salient points in his argument; the Queen, the Prince Consort, Mr. Gladstone, Mr. Cobden were all condescension and enthusiasm. But suddenly de Lesseps' happiness was checked in the most startling fashion and from a pre-eminently powerful quarter. Lord Palmerston had come into the picture.

The violence of Lord Palmerston's language with respect to the canal has caused almost as much astonishment to posterity as it did to M. de Lesseps. He referred to it as "one of the many bubble schemes that from time to time have been palmed upon gullible capitalists." He was convinced, he said, that it was outside the realm of practical engineering. Were not the Mediterranean and the Red Seas upon exactly the same level; and did it not follow that any canal between them must inevitably became a foul and stagnant ditch? "There are three authorities," he wrote in the margin of a dispatch from Paris, "adverse to the execution of this scheme. The English Government, the Turkish Government, and Nature. The two first are not likely to change their views, the third is inflexible." At the same time, he offered de Lesseps his support, if de Lesseps in turn would give the English Government full control of his project. De Lesseps, strange to say, did not accede to this mocking proposal; but then he was not expected to. He made one more attempt, in 1857, upon the common-sense of Lord Palmerston; Lord Palmerston retorted in a speech which had—said the *Daily News*—only the merit of frankness; and de Lesseps realized that all his hopes of obtaining English capital or English support had now vanished forever.

We have every reason to suppose that it was not because he doubted the practicability of the canal, but because he believed in it, that Lord Palmerston opposed M. de Lesseps. He was convinced that Egypt, a weak and corrupt state, would fall prey to some great power if such an international highway were to pass along her borders; that both the integrity of the Ottoman Empire (so essential, he believed, to the peace of Europe) and England's communications with the East would thereby be endangered; and that in any case the railway then in process of construction would prove a sufficient link between the two seas. Such were Lord Palmerston's convictions; and yet it was not from his convictions, but from his intuitions, that the violence of his opposition proceeded. His imagination was appalled by the immense upheaval in world geography which such a canal would effect. He was full of contradictions. It was one thing to support the liberals of Italy, and to entertain Kossuth; it was quite another to be cordial with Mr. Cobden, or to acknowledge the existence of Mr. Bright. And would not men like Cobden and Bright—men with ungentlemanly notions and tasteless energies and unpredictable appetites—be the very ones to gain the most from de Lesseps' scheme? To the end of his life, Lord Palmerston was a Whig, guarding the portals of a Whig-conceived world. When he opposed the canal, it was just as if he were protecting Rosings Park against a threatened expropriation by some assorted characters out of Charles Dickens.

De Lesseps, undismayed, went back to Constantinople in 1858. Lord Stratford de Redcliffe, to whom any innovation was anathema, was no longer Ambassador; he had been succeeded by Sir Henry Bulwer; and de Lesseps thought that British influence at the Sublime Porte would now be weakened—at any rate, so far as his canal was concerned. In this, however, he was mistaken. Sir Henry put forth all his energies, and the Sublime Porte declined to ratify Mohammed Said's concession. There was only one thing to do, and de Lesseps did it. He proceeded with the incorporation of the *Compagnie Universelle du Canal Maritime de Suez;* the 400,000 shares were taken up, partly by small French investors, partly by Mohammed Said; and with 200,000,000 francs as his working capital, he prepared to start operations.

And then, in April, 1859, the Sultan—as suzerain of Egypt—commanded his Viceroy, Mohammed Said, not to permit any work to be done.

It seemed as though Lord Palmerston had triumphed after all.

If relations between Egypt and the Ottoman Empire had not been, to say the least, imprecise, the world would have had to wait many years before it obtained a Suez Canal. On April 25, however, the work began. It began in a fashion that would scarcely have pleased Saint-Simon; for there was another side to the innocence of M. de Lesseps; and it was through the *corvée*—the hideous system of forced labor—that his prophetic trench was being dug. In the intensity of his enthusiasm he disregarded this unhappy circumstance. It was enough for him that Mohammed Said was on his side; that Mohammed Said had blandly informed the Porte that the work was nothing more than a preliminary exploration; and that his canal, with its flogged and sweating slaves, was advancing further and further into the desert. Indeed, the "preliminary exploration" was so active that, on November 18, 1862, at Ismailyia, M. de Lesseps was able to declare: "In the name of His Highness, the Viceroy, and by the Grace of God, I command the waters of the Mediterranean to flow into Lake Timsah." The canal was in its forty-seventh mile.

Yet it was not in the desert that the issues were to be decided. A diplomatic conflict of remarkable virulence was being waged at Constantinople and Cairo and London and Paris. Sir Henry Bulwer and M. de Moustier whispered contradictory admonitions into the ears of the Turkish pashas; Mr. Colquhoun and M. Tastu were engaged in a similar task at Cairo; M. Drouyn de Lhuys was much agitated; Lord Russell girded himself for battle. The existence of the canal, it seemed, was now mingled with the political independence of Egypt, and England and France were drifting once again into an historical opposition.

Towards the end of 1862, Bulwer paid a visit to Egypt, in the course of which he delivered himself of some remarkable observations. He did not consider the canal, he said, of any importance either strategically or commercially; but he was convinced that it ought to be opposed upon humanitarian grounds. Twenty-thousand *fellahin* labored upon it in monthly shifts; which meant that—if one assumed that twenty-thousand were proceeding from their homes towards the canal and that another twenty-thousand were returning from it— as many as sixty-thousand human beings were being taken away from the pursuit of agriculture. Since the pay of a forced laborer was one franc a day, while that of an agricultural laborer was between twice and three times as much; and since the war in America had given an added importance to the cultivation of Egyptian cotton—it was obvious that, whether one considered the question in the light of ethics or of economics, a great injustice was being done. These were the opinions of Sir Henry Bulwer, and he let it be known that the conscience of the Sublime Porte, generally a dormant organ, was as much exercised as was his own. Lord Palmerston, in short, was still full of fight.

At this critical moment, Mohammed Said died and was succeeded by the Viceroy Ismail, a potentate whose two statesmanlike qualities appear to have been an odd personal fascination and a well-developed capacity for intrigue. He was supposed to be "canaliste" in his easy-going way; but nobody could be certain. The French reassured themselves with the knowledge that his favorite resort was the card-tables of Biarritz; the English took comfort in the reflection that his Minister for Foreign Affairs, Nubar Pasha, was distinctly anglophile. Ismail was not in a very easy position; and it is hardly surprising that he should have attempted to play off England against France, in the hopes that something —he could not say precisely what—would come of it. And so, while he first delighted the French by offering an unqualified support to the Company, he then veered towards the English and the Porte by professing a stern opposition to the *corvée*, and declaring that he was most uneasy about the amount of land granted by his predecessor to de Lesseps. In 1864, as if to emphasize both his own importance and the equivocal nature of his sentiments, he sent Nubar Pasha, who was no "canaliste," to converse with M. Drouyn de Lhuys, who was. The conversations were proceeding in the utmost obscurity, when everything was suddenly complicated by the intervention of the Duc de Morny, Napoleon III's half-brother, and the most influential man in France. Morny, it was rumored, was anxious to liquidate the present Company, and form another one, composed of large bankers and himself. He therefore opposed the *corvée*. The London press thereupon burgeoned with articles about the evils of forced labor; all work on the canal was abruptly suspended; and it appeared as if the hopes of de Lesseps were at last to be extinguished. For it was generally believed that, without forced labor, he could not expect to continue.

De Lesseps, however, was not an easy man to suppress. He hastened to Paris, and made his way to the Tuileries, to the apartments of the Empress herself. The result of his activities was swift and it was unexpected. Brushing aside the claims of England and the Porte, Napoleon III agreed to arbitrate the matter, as though it were nothing more than a quarrel between the Viceroy and de Lesseps. By this ingenious device, the tables were suddenly turned upon London and Constantinople; and Napoleon's verdict completed their discomfiture. He pronounced the *corvée* to be illegal, and declared at the same time that the Company must be paid an indemnity of 84,000,000 francs. He granted Ismail's claim to lands, to the extent of 150,000 acres; but ruled that the sweet-water canal, though Egyptian property, could be used by the Company. Above all, gently usurping the functions of the Sultan, he declared Mohammed Said's original concession to be valid.

It was a triumph for de Lesseps, since the indemnity would enable him to hire free labor. It was, so far as England was concerned, the end of all hopes of preventing the canal from coming into existence; and though Bulwer described the verdict as "subtle and unjust," he did not see any way of getting it reversed.

In a sense, that verdict was a watershed in English imperial diplomacy. The Palmerstonian theories ran backwards from there until they disappeared into the distant eighteenth century sea of mercantilism; and forwards from that point ran the beliefs that England would have to exert herself, not to abolish the canal, but to prevent it from falling under French control, or any control but her own.

Sir Henry Bulwer paid another visit to the Isthmus in 1864, and when he returned to Constantinople, reported to the Grand Vizier that Bedouins, those notorious haters of the Turks, were established on all that remained of the Company's lands. His object, of course, was to hamper de Lesseps as much as possible; but the Grand Vizier, though a timorous man, declined to take alarm. The French star was in the ascendant. Further hints from Bulwer that de Lesseps was trying to colonize the canal probably did prevent such a plan from being attempted; but when a French-Turkish-Egyptian Commission was appointed to examine into the whole question of the Company's lands, no British member was admitted to its consultations. Bulwer was thereupon replaced by Lord Lyons; but the delaying tactics of the new Ambassador proved to be no more successful than those of the old; and on March 19—after so many years of hesitation—the Porte at length granted its firman to the Company.

Meanwhile, Ismail had grown tired of sulking, and had decided to become friendly with de Lesseps. As a result, one hundred thousand wretches, always without pay and often without implements, labored upon the sweet-water canal. This oblique defiance, both of Napoleon's verdict and of the English Government, proved that de Lesseps need fear no more interference; and, although the English Admiralty rather ostentatiously increased the harbor at Malta, his peace of mind was never seriously disturbed after 1866. Nor were his remarkable energies at all impaired by his labors: for in 1869, a few days after the official opening of the canal, at the age of sixty-four, he married a young lady of twenty-one. She subsequently bore him six sons and six daughters.

As for Ismail, his dearest ambitions were realized. In 1867, he received the title of Khedive, and during the Paris Exhibition of that year he was treated in a most royal manner. In 1869, on November 17, the Canal was officially opened amidst scenes of extraordinary splendor, and the Khedive—who had expended £20,000 in order to ensure a favorable press in Europe—received his royal guests as their equal. On the day before, there had been religious ceremonies of a most elaborate nature. Three pavilions were set up outside Port Said. In the one on the left, the Mohammedan hierarchy offered up prayers; a group of Christian ecclesiastics were similarly occupied in the one on the right; while in the central pavilion the Khedive sat enthroned between the Empress Eugénie and the Emperor of Austria, listening with royal attention to a mellifluous discourse from Monsignor Bauer, the Empress's Jewish almoner. The English, it was noticed, were represented only by Mr. Henry Elliott and several warships.

The Prince of Wales, during his long absence from England in 1868 and 1869, paid a visit to the Khedive at Cairo, and was afterwards privileged to open a lock on the canal, thereby admitting the waters of the Mediterranean into the Bitter Lakes—the ancient Gulf of Hieropolis. He was deeply impressed, and would often allude thereafter to the extraordinary mistake that England had made in not associating herself with the canal from the beginning. He probably did not know that this mistake had originated in the odd notions of Lord Palmerston. But Lord Palmerston had vanished, and his high Whig prejudices had vanished with him. Lord Granville himself—who had been a member of Palmerston's Government—no doubt agreed with his august correspondent that it was "an everlasting pity that the canal was not made by an English company." The times were moving fast; and, as he passed towards his momentous destination, the Prince was moving with them.

IV

The motion of the times, none the less, brought him to rest at last upon a quite fantastic shore. His concept of India, and of his mission to India, might appear to us today to be just a little far-fetched. Even so, it was substantially in agreement with that of Mr. Disraeli. For Mr. Disraeli, in spite of his political wisdom and his wide information, was temperamentally unable to think of India otherwise than as a land of ivory and apes and peacocks. The Prince, more earthbound, believed himself to be going to a country full of big game and suspicious but hospitable potentates. There was nothing, really, to disabuse him of these ideas. The crowds that lined his route, when he drove through Bombay on November 9, were most self-effacing. As Lord Northbrook, the Viceroy, put it in a letter to the Queen:

"The anxiety of the people to see his Royal Highness was very marked. Lord Northbrook could observe them pointing him out one to the other. This somewhat interfered," he went on, "with the cheers and clapping of hands."

Lord Northbrook, even though he was a Gladstonian appointee, need not have been so very tactful; for the truth was that the Prince had not come for their sake. Nor did they take a very large place in the imagination of those who were governing them. They were as yet an administrative rather than a political problem; their discontents, though noticeable, did not become coherent until the first Indian Congress of 1885. The Prince, who invariably did his best when confronted by any large concourse of human beings, never failed to acknowledge their presence with repeated military salutes; but they were rarely more to him than an anonymous huddle of onlookers, a Face without features, an innumerable emanation from the bazaars and the plains. Sometimes, but only sometimes, they would assume an individual form; becoming, for example, a group of ragged pensioners at Lucknow, or a choir of children, seated upon the grass at Bombay, and shrilling this singular refrain:

"What can we render but our loyal love
And hope that all thy life may noble prove?"

His real business, of course, was with quite another set of persons. A committee of them waited upon him on the day of his arrival. They were dressed in every variety of oriental magnificence—in yellow hats and pink turbans, in white silks and violet velvets, in ropes of pearls and panoplies of diamonds. These were the princes. They were not a representative assembly; that would have been impossible; for there were over seven hundred native states, covering rather more than two-fifths of the peninsula, and varying in size from Hyderabad, which was larger than Great Britain, to the few hundred ragged acres of some small Orissan state. But though the princes and chieftains differed one from the other in almost every respect—in title and rank, in wealth and customs and religion—in one respect, at any rate, they were quite alike. They were all dedicated to the past.

Here and there some original ruler might interest himself in education or in health, might evolve a Constitution or publish a Budget; but these were mere illusions, the creations of fancy, behind which he ruled with the moodiness and absolutism of nature herself. His subjects held him in much the same regard as, in England, is accorded to the weather; they were grateful for sunshine, but quite resigned to rain. A British Resident, it is true, maintained a certain check upon the caprices of the more important rulers; excesses of cruelty and extravagance were mildly discouraged and it was because he had shown an inconvenient curiosity about the less pleasing habits of that prince, that Sir Robert Phayre had been nearly poisoned by the irritated Gaekwar of Baroda. The Gaekwar was deposed, for his had been a somewhat obvious misdemeanor, and so the authority of the Resident was upheld. But the Residents, however influential some of them might be, could not effect any essential changes in the character of the native states. Though something might be done to improve the worst of them, their peculiar feudalism remained unimpaired.

This feudalism, in so far as it expressed itself in a respect for the Crown, had been somewhat shaken by the Gaekwar's fate. Many of the rulers thought deposition too heavy a punishment for so small an offense as an unsuccessful poisoning. Since the Mutiny, only one other prince—the Nawab of Tonk—had been similarly treated: and *he* had staged a successful massacre. Others even went so far as to confess themselves unable to believe in the Gaekwar's guilt. Under these circumstances, all the Government of India could do was to press on with its policy of leaving the princes alone as much as possible, and of binding them—with gifts, with decorations, with the arithmetical discharge of ceremonial cannon—closer and closer to the Crown. It was the object of the Prince's tour to further this policy.

For such a task he was especially fitted. There is no doubt at all that he could exert, towards those whom he wished to please, a great—indeed an historical—charm of manner. In private life, he was often short-tempered, impatient, self-indulgent; in his public capacity, he was all courtesy and long-suffering. Popular enthusiasm, it is true, seemed to be in inverse ratio to the amount of distance covered; if there was little of it in Bombay, there was less in Colombo, and even less in Madras; the inhabitants of Lucknow were sullen, the inhabitants of Indore put up their shutters and closed their jalousies; and so it went. But though the living embodiment of the Raj meant very little to the peoples of India, to the princes he was a most gratifying apparition. They came to him with profuse compliments and incomprehensible complaints; he listened with the utmost good humor; and in this way the wrongs of the Gaekwar were quite forgotten. He found himself at times in rather odd and even delicate situations. At Baroda, he was driven under a triumphal arch adorned with living angels—ten shivering youths, their bare brown bodies covered with some white substance, their backs decorated with gauze wings, and their heads with auburn wigs and gilded coronets. He was just about to laugh when he caught the eye of Sir Madahva Rao, the new Gaekwar's able Prime Minister, and the designer of this preposterous conceit. At Madras, he sat with the Maharajah of Travancore, the Rajah of Arcot, and the Prince of Cochin, who listened with approval while an old gentleman in a green gown and a purple turban led a curious Hindu sextet—violin, pipe, tom-tom, and three conches—in a sixty-minute rendering of "Bonny Dundee." At Calcutta, there was an embarrassing encounter with the Maharajah of Patiala, who was covered all over with the recently acquired jewels of the Empress Eugénie. Princely India, in short, was in its usual condition —half jumble, half dream; where the chief ornament of some great palace could be a marble pedestal, carved with all the elaborations of Eastern fantasy, and supporting a toy tin donkey that wagged its head; where lovely white fountains exuded, when pressed to do so, about a cupful of dirty water; and where unimaginable treasures were guarded by ragged sentries, armed with old flint fowling pieces. Many of the denizens of this extraordinary world—rulers and chieftains whose families, sometimes, had never met before except upon the field of battle—gathered at the great Calcutta Durbar on New Year's Day. The Viceroy ceased to be Viceroy on this momentous occasion; the Prince took his place; and two maharajahs were invested with the Grand Cross of the Star of India, while seven chiefs were turned into Knights Commander of that Order.

On the whole, it was agreed, the visit had been a most beneficial one—at least as regards its effect upon the imagination of the princes. "A sentiment in their feudalism," wrote Sir Henry Daly, the Agent in Central India, "has been touched"; nor was Sir Henry exaggerating. When, on March 13, H.M.S. *Scorpion* left Bombay with the Prince and his suite, it was loaded with their gifts—daggers, tea services, swords, shields, lances, shawls, carpets, jeweled cups, a small fleet cheetah, a gray Arab horse, five tigers, seven leopards, four elephants, three ostriches, and a Himalayan bear.

V

While the Prince was passing through India, a vagrant symbol, Mr. Disraeli had emphasized, in an even more symbolic way, yet another aspect of his Eastern policy. . . .

At the roots of modern Egypt, the historian cannot fail to find, if he cares to dig, the debts of the Khedive Ismail. Ismail was much addicted to French mistresses and to public works, but his affections in either case were transitory, and vast sums of money—wrung from his unhappy subjects in the most expensive and agonizing ways—simply disappeared. As his European creditors swiftly increased, and the productive capacity of the Egyptians no less swiftly diminished, the infatuated Ismail began to divest himself of any property that could be turned into cash. At last, in 1875, he was reduced to the desperate expedient of offering to mortgage his 177,000 shares in the Suez Canal; and a French syndicate was preparing to close with him on ruinous terms. The rumor of these transactions appears to have reached Mr. Disraeli on Sunday, November 14, at a dinner party at Baron Lionel de Rothschild's. On Tuesday, General Stanton called upon Nubar Pasha in Cairo to ask if this story were true, and to insist that Her Majesty's Government could not view such a sale without extreme uneasiness. On Wednesday, Mr. Disraeli talked his Cabinet into agreeing to purchase the shares, without consulting Parliament; the price was to be £4,000,000 with interest of 5%, and Rothschilds were to find the money at a commission of 2½%. On the 24th, the Egyptian Government agreed to this arrangement; the French Government, who were much indebted to England for support against Bismarck after the Franco-Prussian War, did not feel strong enough to resist; and two days later the shares were deposited at the British Consulate-General in Cairo.

Disraeli was highly elated; for this was just such a coup as his soul most hankered after. Here was no laborious piece of diplomacy, no lengthy and delicate negotiation, but a conjuring-trick, performed single-handed, under the brightest lights, and with himself at the center of the stage. And, like a conjuring trick, it was quite insubstantial. The control of the Suez Canal had never been in the hands of the shareholders —it was a question of naval supremacy and of influence at Cairo. Nor were the shares themselves exactly remunerative, since the Khedive, in some previous entanglement, had already pledged the coupons for twenty-five years in advance. But these considerations did not perturb Mr. Disraeli; and though Mr. Gladstone thundered against the purchase in Parliament, and Sir Stafford Northcote grumbled that it wasn't quite the thing, it was very generally applauded. In its swiftness and its daring, in its disregard for democratic punctilios, it appealed to that new mood which Disraeli had helped to foster. Since it gave notice, in the most dramatic fashion, of England's interest in Egypt, it might be called nothing more than a political gesture. But it had its economic significance as well. The hour of the bond-holder and the Dual Control was at hand; not long afterwards, strict inquiries were being made into the baffling jungle of the Khedive's accounts; and that unhappy spendthrift was soon exercising his powers of fascination, and exercising them in vain, upon the chilly presences of M. de Blignières and Mr. Rivers Wilson.

The Prince was delighted when the news of the purchase

reached him in India. "In the eyes of the whole world," he wrote to Disraeli, "it is a step which has met with the highest approval and one which must bring the highest credit and honour upon the First Minister of the Crown (if you will allow me to say so). I only hope," he went on, "that the day is not far distant when *all* the shares will be in our hands."

It was just as well that cordial feelings had been promoted in this way; for very soon afterwards, relations between the Prince and the Prime Minister became somewhat strained. On February 8, 1876, the Queen opened Parliament in person, a rare gesture with her, and one which generally intimated that Her Majesty had something up her sleeve. In this instance, it was an announcement in the Speech from the Throne to the effect that a Royal Titles Bill would shortly be laid before the Lords and Commons, conferring upon Her Majesty the style of Empress of India. In the streams of messages which she had discharged at her son as he traveled through India, and which were generally of a somewhat scolding nature, she had not mentioned this impending change; nor had the Prime Minister thought fit to give him an inkling of it. As a result, he heard about it only when it appeared in the newspapers, and since it affected him somewhat intimately, he was justified in feeling put out. The Queen had most certainly been unkind, and the Prime Minister impolite; but the Prince's wrath, which in any case did not burst upon him until several weeks later, was among the least of Disraeli's difficulties. He had also neglected to inform the Opposition of his intentions—a course which, in a matter affecting the dignity of the Crown, was more or less obligatory —and it was clear that the Bill would have a stormy passage through Parliament. This complication was tiresome enough, but what rendered it even less endurable was the fact that Disraeli himself did not care very much for the Royal Titles Bill. He had thrown out the suggestion rather carelessly in 1874; it had been little more than one of the blossoms that he loved to scatter; and he had not expected Victoria to pick it up. But Victoria was fascinated. The high notions of royalty which her new Prime Minister, in his letters and his audiences, perpetually impressed upon her—notions so agreeably spiced with a romantic adoration—were having their effect. The Queen saw nothing but what was appropriate in the title of Empress. Day in, day out she urged Disraeli to fulfill his promise; and at last, with a sigh, he yielded. The public, as well as the Opposition, was far from pleased. Disraeli's opening speech, with its constant reiterations of the word "imperial," somehow conveyed the idea that the Queen was to be styled Empress of Great Britain—and to the Victorian mind "Emperor" suggested either the coarseness of Prussia or the debauchery of Napoleon. As for the Commons, their behavior during the second reading of the Bill—which, to be sure, they had no intention of rejecting—was most unseemly. Disraeli pointed out that, according to Gibbon, mankind was never so happy as under the Antonines, who were emperors; but this argument, oddly enough, failed to quiet the Opposition; and the trouble spread to the Lords, where the Earl of Shaftesbury was extremely caustic, and the Duke of Somerset insinuated that the Queen desired her new style because her children would get a higher position at the German courts. Worse still, from Disraeli's point of view, which was that of an assiduous diner-out, the best London society was altogether down on the Bill.

It was while he was in the midst of these distresses, that he received a letter from the Prince, complaining most bitterly of the treatment that he had received. Disraeli did his best to turn away this wrath by saying that his Royal Highness could soon call himself Imperial Highness; the Prince retorted that nothing would induce him to adopt such a title; and it took all the flatteries of the Minister to bring about a reconciliation. At last, on January 1, 1877, Disraeli (now Earl of Beaconsfield) gave a rather noisy banquet; the Prince and Princess attended; and the quarrel was made up.

Once the Prince's vanity had been salved, there was certainly nothing to quarrel about. The Royal Titles Bill, the Prince's tour, the purchase of the Suez Canal shares . . . they were all fragments of the same unfinished, imperial mosaic. So, too, in its unromantic way, was Lord Salisbury's famous quarrel with Lord Northbrook over the Indian import duty on Manchester cotton piece-goods. The mosaic had, no doubt, a more brilliant appearance in the seventies than it has to-day; but even today it is still unfinished; and nobody can tell what the design will be in the end.

Chapter Seven

THE ABSENTEE

FROM 1877 until his death in 1881, Lord Beaconsfield was on very cordial terms with the Prince. We know from the old statesman's correspondence with Lady Bradford and Lady Chesterfield that he grew more and more particular about the characters who should be permitted to play a part in his life, now winding into its last chapter. The Prince was now among these characters. He was, to be sure, only a very minor one; his appearances were infrequent; but Beaconsfield savored them with the relish of an artist. Like some novelists, and all gifted letter-writers, he was inclined to create people rather than to report them. The Prince was too masculine and too robust for Beaconsfield to turn him into one of those gracefully eccentric figures with which he liked best to people his world; there was something of the Falstaff about Prince Hal. As such, however, he was a source of affectionate amusement. His genial energies seemed to enchant that infinitely weary spectator. Beaconsfield related with glee to Lady Bradford how his secretary, Montagu Corry, was commanded to dine with the Prince and Princess Louise and some rather quiet people; how they went on to see "Diplomacy"; how the Prince and Corry slipped away to a supper party, the chief ornament of which was Mrs. Langtry ("the Jersey beauty whose name begins with an L"); how this continued until almost dawn; how Corry, exhausted by conversation and champagne, began to nod on a sofa; and how the Prince then announced that he was going to the Turf to play some whist. Yet reality did not always obey the waving of Lord Beaconsfield's wand. His days were a series of transitions, of imperceptible adjustments, between the world as it was and the world as he would have it be. His life was not invariably a romance, all roses and thunderclouds. People often stepped out of the rôle that he had assigned to them; often he stepped out of his own. Thus, in the course of everyday affairs, he would forget that the Prince was supposed to be an amusing character; and, especially after the Indian tour, there were encounters of a more serious kind. The chain of events which, with an ominous rattle, like an iron adder, uncurled itself from the Balkan revolts against the oppression of Turkey seemed, at one time, about to lead to war between England and Russia. The Cabinet was divided. Lord Beaconsfield believed in supporting the Turks; Lord Salisbury and Lord Derby were inclined to favor Russia. Meanwhile Mr. Gladstone had quite emerged from the retirement into which his defeat of 1874 had consigned him, and was raging against Turkey in a manner which, said the Queen, "can't be constitutional." In short, Lord Beaconsfield's days were full of perplexity, and he would turn to the Prince for occasional comfort and advice. When at last the issues were left to the Congress of Berlin, the Queen—who had been breathing fire and slaughter, and threatening abdication, and vowing that her sex alone prevented her from giving "those Russians such a beating"— ceased to be Bellona, and became, once more, the Faery. She

declared that she could not spare Lord Beaconsfield, that he
was ill, that she dared not take the risk of letting him go to
Berlin. Everybody knew that it was the Prince who persuaded her to change her mind. And so the Prime Minister
went off—to be tortured by the gout—to be disgusted with
Bismarck's tobacco and his rabelaisian talk—to ruin his diges-
tion at banquets—and to come home in triumph. There are
people who say that it would have been better if he had
taken that special train which, in a moment of exasperation,
he ordered to be in readiness to carry him back to Calais. But
the threat was enough; the train waited for another week;
and the Congress proceeded to lay some part of the foundations of the war of 1914-1918.

The nature and extent of the Prince's influence in these
years have never been determined. His incessant encounters
with eminent personages, at home and abroad, spatter the records like spray, and dissolve, and leave no images behind.
Only at long intervals, and for brief moments, can we catch
a steady glimpse of his activities. In March, 1878, for example, a curious scene was acted in Berlin. After the wedding of
Prince Charlotte of Prussia with Prince Bernhard of Saxe-
Meiningen, the Prince had an interview with Bismarck. The
Imperial Chancellor, with his ogrish frankness, suggested that
England might profitably occupy Egypt, and that Germany
would support her against France if she did so. He then extracted from the Prince an admission that England would
come to Germany's aid, if Germany were compelled to move
against Russia. But why did Bismarck trouble to bandy provinces and alliances in this extraordinary way? Was it because
he respected the Prince's ideas? Or was it because he had

found an extra-diplomatic channel—august and gossipy—through which his own ideas could be spread over England?

And then, after the Congress had ended, it was revealed that one of the by-products of the "Peace with Honor" was a quiet understanding between England and Turkey, whereby England was to receive the island of Cyprus. The French Chamber shouted with wrath, and one of the chief objects of its execration was the Prince himself. He had been to and fro all summer—1878 was an Exhibition year—making the friendliest speeches, and all the time his country's Government was plotting against France in the eastern Mediterranean! He responded to these attacks in a manner which was afterwards to become famous. He invited M. Gambetta, the most influential member of the Chamber, to luncheon at a quiet restaurant, talked with him all afternoon over brandy and cigars, and convinced him that an English occupation of Cyprus could not do any harm. The influence of good brandy may be detected in this success; but it was a success on any terms, and a grateful letter from Lord Salisbury was the result.

Such incidents, however, could only provide the Prince with a temporary consolation. He was still denied any access to the secret business of the State. He still knew less than did the secretaries of Ministers about the contents of those boxes that were piled upon his mother's desk. There was the tree of knowledge, there the fountain of wisdom; they were just out of his reach; and occasional confidences made his predicament all the more tantalizing. His, indeed, was a galling position. Surrounded on every side by all the outward signs of consideration and respect, sent out from time to time upon missions of apparent importance, he never knew with any certainty what was toward. His rank and his interests made him—as was only to be expected—a storehouse of unwinnowed information: but that was all.

A more systematic, a less self-indulgent man might perhaps, by sheer persistence, have broken down the Queen's opposition. But the Prince was fond of his pleasures, he was not dissatisfied with his royal progresses, nor with his personal successes. It pleased him to be agreeable to the radical Mr. Chamberlain. He formed a lasting friendship with "Citizen" Dilke. In 1882, there were several meetings at Sandringham; and, in a vague atmosphere of conspiracy, Sir Charles Dilke was smuggled into Mr. Gladstone's Cabinet. If he had not been instinctively conservative—and if it had not been too much trouble—the Prince might have become a Radical figurehead; there were plenty of precedents for such a move. But domestic politics held only an intermittent interest for him; and even that was generally of a very personal kind. Lord Beaconsfield once said that whenever he had a place or a living of any importance in his gift, the Prince never failed to ask it for one of his friends—"and always the least qualified candidate." As for domestic engagements, their frightful debris mounted higher every year—the trowels in the morocco cases, the golden keys, the illuminated addresses. He longed for something more—to be really useful, to be really important; but he did not quite know how.

II

It was not that there did not exist, in the ordinary way, any number of claims upon his time. Committees, commissions, boards of trustees—these, quite apart from the Drawing Rooms, and the Levees, and the ceremonial openings and unveilings, lay in wait for him in his spare hours. Sometimes he attended them, always punctual, always courteous, but never very attentive. They were unimportant; at any rate, they were dull, which amounted to the same thing. Yet here and there, in that desert of tedium, there appeared an oasis— a patch of harsh shade in which he might have lingered, a bitter well from which he might have drunk.

In 1884, for example, he was a member of a Royal Commission. It was, in some respects, the most important Commission of the decade. It examined certain ruins, and exposed certain horrors, for the first time in official history. It was called the Royal Commission for Inquiring into the Housing of the Working Classes. Now to the mind of the '80's there was something just a little offensive in such a subject: for this was an era of solid wealth and substantial comfort; and if people lived in filth and disease was it not, in some obscure but awful way, a judgment upon them? Could one be sure that the inquiry—quite apart from the fact that it showed an alarming tendency to encroach upon private enterprise—was just an inquiry into housing conditions? Might it not almost be called an examination into the workings of Providence itself? A Royal Commission, of course, was a comfortable entity; it pursued its researches in private, and published its findings in a thick book which nobody bothered to read. And a Royal Commission with a Prince of Wales upon it, even a somewhat profligate Prince of Wales, was not merely comfortable, it was consoling. It seemed to elevate the whole subject. If the public had learned that the Prince was seldom present after the first five sittings, and that some of his fellow

Commissioners were not much more assiduous, it would not have been surprised or critical. For Royal Commissions, it was believed, not always incorrectly, were intended to bury probblems, not to raise them.

To us, as we look back, it does not appear unseemly in a future sovereign—at whatever inconvenience to himself—to learn about the miseries into which thousands upon thousands of his fellow-countrymen were plunged. But the '80's did not see things in that light. Nor did the Prince. He had a remarkable memory for faces, but almost none for facts; and the facts which were laid before the Commission were so numerous and so repulsive that they would have wearied even a trained mind. If we read the *Report* in which the evidence is printed, we can almost re-live the experience of those who listened to it. Our interest, at first so intense, is blunted and dulled by that cold weight of human misery; and it is only with an effort that we can plunge on into what is, after all, little more than a morass. The *Report* is, nevertheless, a remarkable document. Through the efforts of the more persistent commissioners, a gray light leaks into the darkness; and figures, unrelieved by fancy or imagination, begin to stir, and to speak to us with the authentic voice of half a century ago.

The evidence dealt with certain country districts, with Edinburgh and parts of Scotland, and with Dublin and Waterford; but the largest part of it was devoted to London. There are many aspects of London. There is the London whose lovely buildings and curious ceremonies attest the quiet continuity of English history. There is the London which, at this moment of writing, is an heroic and immortal city. And there was the London as it revealed itself to the Commission

—a city which, *inter opes inops,* contained the greatest and
the worst of nineteenth century slums.

Vast areas of sordid brick were delivered over to pecu-
lation and to anarchy; disease and famine grew fat in an
atmosphere of medieval ingenuity and licensed *laisser-faire.*
Occasionally, in the earlier part of the century, some bold
hand, armed with a little legislative broom, had stretched
itself out towards those Augean slums. A Common Lodging
Houses Act, a Laboring Classes Lodging Houses Act, a
Laboring Classes Dwelling Houses Act, a Nuisances Re-
moval Act approached and were defeated by the fearful
wilderness. In 1868 and 1879 the two Torrens Acts made an
effort to deal with the demolition of single houses; but they
were administered very largely by the vestries and local
boards, whose members' chief concern was to see that nothing
was done. The Cross Act, even after its amendment in 1879,
never got very far with its ambition to demolish and recon-
struct whole areas of insanitary hovels. When we consider its
machinery, this is not surprising. A Medical Officer of Health,
or two Justices of the Peace, or twelve London ratepayers
had first to make a representation to the Metropolitan Board
of Works (or, in certain cases, the City Commissioner of
Sewers). The Board (or the Commissioner) considered the
matter, and passed a resolution that the area was unhealthy,
and that an improvement scheme ought to be made. After a
suitable interval, the Board then drew up a scheme, the scheme
was submitted to the Secretary of State, the Secretary of State
issued a provisional order, and the provisional order was confirmed by Act of Parliament. It was somewhat unusual, therefore, for anything to happen at all.

In 1882, the Artisans' Dwellings Act, Part I, consolidated

and amended the two Torrens Acts; while Part II consolidated
and amended the two Cross Acts. But Part I and Part II still
overlapped, and where they did not overlap they were consistently hindered by the vestries, the local boards, and the
Metropolitan Board of Works. Sir Richard Cross and Mr.
W. T. M. Torrens were both members of the Royal Commission, and both were prepared to defend their Acts with
their dying breath.

III

The Commission met first on March 11, 1884, at No. 8,
Richmond Terrace, Whitehall. The Chairman was Sir Charles
Dilke, who, it appears, had made some preliminary investigations into certain slum areas. The Prince, following Sir
Charles' example, had also made two or three visits. The
other members of the Commission had not put themselves to
this trouble. It was clear from the beginning that the Commission was divided into two schools of thought: one, headed
by the Marquess of Salisbury, holding that the poor were attached to their slums; the other, headed by the Chairman,
maintaining that the poor were attached to their slums only
because they were given no chance to be attached to anything
else. Midway between this conflict of Heredity and Environ-
ment stood Cardinal Manning, who was interested in the moral
aspects of the evidence, Sir Richard Cross and Mr. Torrens,
who were preoccupied with the defense of their Acts, and
the Prince of Wales, who did not express an opinion. After
five sessions, the Prince disappeared. He re-emerged in Paris,
staying *incognito* at the Bristol; and then went on to Wiesbaden where, however, the weather was very bad.

Although it would be impossible to condense into anything like a short *précis* the mass of evidence which was laid before the Commission, one might perhaps, hovering here and there above its grim prolixities, present a few glimpses of that London upon which the Prince so quickly turned his back.

The very first witness was the Earl of Shaftesbury. A radical Tory, a social Hegelian who believed in changing society without changing society, Lord Shaftesbury had spent much of his life in a state of uneasiness, bordering upon bewilderment. He was, however, a most upright man; he was also a very active one. He had explored the jungles of London when they were still as unknown as Dark Africa; he had pushed his way into lanes so narrow that one could touch the houses on each side with extended arms; lanes so noisome, so "tremendously terrible," that one could not struggle to that further end where the "single accommodation" squatted and discharged its poison up and down; lanes whose inhabitants lived in such unimaginable squalor that one could only speak to them through the windows. These, he thought, had disappeared; there was no longer a Frying-pan Alley to horrify the occasional fanatic, or fatten the intrepid rent-collector. Overcrowding, on the other hand, had increased; plumbing was not much improved. More and more people thronged the slums, not because (this in answer to a question from Lord Salisbury) they were "enamoured of their filth," but because a man had to find a house near his work. And if the house was filthy, what other consequences could one expect but sickness, drink, and despair? As for the migratory classes, "I have never been able," he confessed with horror, "to see any mode, except by complete alteration of the state of society,

229

in which we could benefit them." A railway company, or even the Torrens Act, sometimes demolished an insalubrious area; but few buildings, except public houses, arose to take its place; and the people most in need of relief simply migrated to some adjacent rookery, where the landlords were not over-nice and the authorities had not seen fit to act.

In spite of the brief and almost hopeless picture which he had executed in his evidence, Lord Shaftesbury confessed that he would not be willing for the Government to interpose with state money. He believed that if "people will be content with four or four and a half per cent," decent dwellings could be built by private enterprise; and that "local authorities may safely be charged"—perhaps by raising money upon the security of the rates—"with doing that which private enterprise cannot reach."

When the Commission proceeded to inquire into the nature of the local authorities, it began to seem as if Lord Shaftesbury had been, perhaps, just a little optimistic. There was something about the vestries (a vestry was the parliament for a large parish) and the local, or district, boards (a local board was the parliament for a collection of small parishes) which made one wonder if the destinies of the poor were in quite the best hands. On the Clerkenwell Vestry, for example, the fourteen most active members were all interested in bad or doubtful property. Ten of these house farmers were members of the important Works Committee, seven of the equally important Assessment and Appeals Committee. Ten more members of the vestry (otherwise an inactive body) were publicans who, for reasons of their own, did not frown upon bad housing. From other parts of London came complaints that vestries and local boards were controlled by traders in unsanitary property. In short, those whose duty it was to see that a better state of things existed appeared to be the very people most interested in keeping things as they were.

It was true that when the local authorities defaulted, the Metropolitan Board of Works was empowered to act for them. The Metropolitan Board of Works, however, was composed of two representatives from each of the vestries and local boards—a circumstance which did not make for excessive activity. Owing to the rather curious way in which it disposed of valuable frontages, it was also known as the Board of Perks.

Should the local boards, the vestries, and the Board of Works refuse or neglect to act, a memorial from complaining householders could be sent to the Local Government Board, which otherwise—at least in the metropolis—had no powers save those of suggestion and protest. No complaining householder, strange to say, had yet sent in a memorial to the Local Government Board.

Another figure, almost as high-minded but not so experienced as Lord Shaftesbury, soon wandered into the evidence . . . Lord William Compton, a younger son of the Marquess of Northampton. Lord William was in a great state of distress. His father was the ground landlord of a large area of Clerkenwell, and the son had just discovered what this meant. He had, in fact, been making investigations. There were six hundred tenements on the Northampton property; some were leased by the house farmer directly from the estate, in the case of others a complicated system of sub-leases separated the landlord from the house-farmer. All the tenements that Lord William visited were filthy; but the worst were those built around 1830 in the courtyards of houses built at an earlier date. He recited cases of families of seven, eight, and nine all living in one room; of six families living in six rooms with one W.C. between them; of a family of nine adults living in two rooms, one of which had neither windows nor ventilation. It did not appear that any repairs had been done in these warrens for many years; not, at least, until the horrified and despairing visitations of Lord William had been reported to the house-farmers, who thereupon slapped a great deal of paint and whitewash over the worst abscesses. Their sanitary endeavors, however, did not go further than that.

From his son's evidence it would seem as if Lord Northampton rather prided himself upon owning, in Mr. Decimus Alfred Ball, one of the most respectable tenants that a landlord could hope for. Mr. Ball was Vice-Chairman of the Assessments and Appeals Committee, he was very well spoken of in the neighborhood (that is, among his fellow-vestrymen), and it was not until Lord William had examined some of the houses of which Mr. Ball was the lessee, that the family complacency became a trifle disturbed. For if other house-farmers were niggardly with their repairs, Mr. Ball was a miser with his. His tenements were rotten through and through; and "I do not pretend to say," Lord William confessed, "that we are not disappointed in Mr. Ball." This estimable gentleman, whose yearly profits were enormous, was generally admitted to run the affairs of the Clerkenwell Vestry. His second in command was a Mr. Ross, another house-farmer, and Chairman of the Works Committee.

The inhabitants of the tenements were hard-working, said Lord William, if the ones whom he had encountered could be taken as representative of the rest. Most of them were literate. All were "very much of the class for whom anybody would be very anxious to legislate." It was upon his family's poisoned acres that they lived; but somehow or other Mr. Ball, and the vestry, and leases, and sub-leases, made them very inaccessible. "In fact," asked Sir Charles Dilke, "there are no relations between the people and the large land-owner?" Lord William sadly admitted that this was the case.

The goodness of Lord Shaftesbury and the unhappiness of Lord William Compton were soon balanced, though not out-faced, by the appearance of Mr. H. T. Boodle, Lord North-ampton's solicitor. Royal Commissions have no *dramatis personae;* all witnesses receive the same, or nearly the same, treatment; and one can only guess, from a slight, an almost imperceptible, austerity in the tone of the questions, that this Commission as a whole did not approve of Mr. Boodle. Out of his answers, given nearly sixty years ago, there still arises a spiritual dustiness, which settles again upon the reader's mind in an even gray pall. He admitted that the effect of the middleman upon poor property was to divide houses, once inhabited by single families, into tenements—single-room tenements which paid more profit all around. But then the leasing powers of Lord Northampton, as tenant for life of the family property in Clerkenwell, demanded that "he should get the best or most improved rent that can reasonably be obtained for the same." The Commission squeezed from the witness the information that, by executing a deed of appointment, Lord Northampton could become absolute owner of the property at any time; but the law did not oblige him to do this, and Mr. Boodle was not the man to steer his client towards dangerous philanthropies. Mr. Boodle, indeed, was exceedingly cautious—even to the point of prevarication. He said at first that the ground landlord could effect no improvements until the leases expired; he then admitted that a clause did exist in all the leases whereby the landlord could insist if he pleased (but only if he pleased) upon repairs and sanitary improvements. But, alas, the sanitary rules of the metropolis were very complicated; they were almost as difficult to understand as the Church Building Acts, and those, said Mr. Boodle in a legal ecstasy, nobody had been able to understand at all. As a result, Lord Northampton never insisted upon repairs or improvements, and the middlemen made profits amounting to as much as 150% a year. As for overcrowding, there was nothing in the leases which empowered the ground landlord to do anything about *that*.

There were model buildings, called the Compton Buildings, upon Lord Northampton's Clerkenwell property; but since their lowest rent was 6/6 a week, they were beyond the means of the very poor; while the moderately impoverished persons who did inhabit them were banished if they got one week behind in the rent. Why was this? Because the Buildings had to pay 5% to the shareholders of Sir Sidney Waterlow's company, which built them. The directors of Sir Sidney's company did not take any fees, and Lord Northampton charged only 2.01 pence per foot as ground rent instead of threepence or fourpence a foot: to this extent, the Compton Buildings might be called a charitable enterprise. But Mr. Boodle thought that kindness and business ought not to be mixed together; and when he was asked why Lord Northampton did not erect model buildings himself, at a modest profit, he replied that a tenant for life could not be expected to spend many thousands of his income for the benefit of the settled estate, and that even such a gesture as lowering the ground rent for charitable purposes was a questionable transaction in law. He then retired.

Thus it appeared that, so far as Lord Northampton and his man of business were concerned, the poor of Clerkenwell were caught in some unhappy limbo between the tenant for life and the settled estate; where they could rot forever, so long as the rents improved. And rot they did; for when Mrs. Sarah Bates, a London School Board visitor, called the attention of the sanitary authorities to the conditions in Northampton Street, where families of nine lived in two exiguous and pestilent rooms, the reply was "Oh, throw a little water down." The property in question was leased by a Mr. Hill, a vestryman. In Wynyatt Cottages, the court was entered by an archway, through which one descended some fifteen steps from the street level, and so reached a number of dark and damp cellars, almost every one of them inhabited by a family. Such a place should be condemned, said Mrs. Bates, for it was beyond redemption; but it was leased from the Northampton Estate by Mr. Decimus Alfred Ball; and where Mr. Ball was the lessee, property was almost never condemned.

The visits of Sir Charles Dilke had, however, stirred some of the middlemen into action in Clerkenwell and Holborn; but no amount of hasty work could conceal the fact that two W.C.'s were insufficient for the eight houses of Three-King Court; or that it was perhaps not the most sanitary arrangement to keep the water supply directly over the closet which served, in solitary squalor, *all* the six houses of Cherry Tree Square. Mr. Henry Windebank, another London School Board visitor, who gave evidence about these two places, remarked with a gentle irony that he did not believe that the sanitary inspector had ever bothered very much about them.

But then the sanitary inspectors of Clerkenwell were not men whose experience or loyalty would incline them towards a very rigid interpretation of their duties. One had been an assistant schoolmaster, another was an assistant clerk in the Vestry office, a third had descended from the jewelry trade to the combined position of sexton of the church, coroner's officer, and messenger to the Vestry. Not one had the slightest knowledge of the principles of building; all were dependent upon the Vestry. The Commission discovered that only one sanitary inspector had been discharged by the Vestry of Clerkenwell in twenty-eight years; the nature of his crime had been "neglect"; but whether the neglect was too much activity or too little, the Commission could not discover.

The Vestry of St. Pancras, according to its medical officer, Mr. Shirley Forster Murphy, was resolutely determined not to adopt those tenement provisions which permitted visiting at night—and visiting at night was the only way of discovering how serious overcrowding actually was. This tenderness for the liberty of the individual did the Vestry of St. Pancras much credit; but the fact remained that, somehow or other, overcrowding did not meet with the disapproval of the most active vestrymen. Theirs was an amorphous body, constantly changing; the majority of the one hundred and thirty members was not in the least aware of conditions in the underworlds of St. Pancras; and when the visits of Sir Charles Dilke stirred Mr. Charles Robinson, head of the Sanitary Committee, into doing some inspection on his own, he was ready to declare that the slum district of his parish was "an infamous filthy colony." But it was not with Mr. Charles Robinson, or with the inactive majority, that the fate of the St. Pancras poor resided. The house-jobbers controlled the most important committees; and overcrowding was very much to their taste. For instance, if a man who rented two rooms got behind with his rent, he could be persuaded, in return for a remission of his debt, to give up one of his rooms to another family; and thus the two rooms could be made to produce twice the rent. The result, said Mr. Murphy, was an encouragement of typhus and consumption; and a typical overcrowded house could be compared, in his opinion, only to the Black Hole of Calcutta.

The rapid increase in population, the decrease in the number of houses, had raised rents as high as fifty per cent over the last ten years; the middlemen did no repairs of any kind—or did no repairs without raising the rent; the tenants were afraid to complain, for if they complained they were generally turned out. Excuses that the raising of the rates was responsible for the raising of the rents—and the middlemen, when cornered, often took refuge behind such defenses—could not be entertained, for the latter rose above the former in a fantastic disproportion.

It was the aim of the middleman to abolish, wherever he could, the occupancy of houses by one family. Not that such occupancy was unprofitable. In Smith's Place, Pentonville, for example, on the estate of Captain Penton, there were ten quite typical houses. Each contained two rooms, ten feet by seven; there were no back windows and therefore no back ventilation; there was no wash-house; and one cistern, in the center of the court, from which the water could be fetched in tubs, served all ten houses. The ten families who lived in this horrible rookery were further accommodated with two W.C.'s, approached by one door; but the water had not run for many years and they were used as receptacles for rubbish. For each of these houses—houses without water or plumbing, houses where not even the most superficial repairs were ever done—the middlemen charged five shillings and sixpence a week; and one of them had written, in an indignant letter to the Sanitary Committee of Clerkenwell, that, "I do not think more healthy and comfortable dwellings for the poor than these can be found in the parish of Clerkenwell."

The less corrupted vestrymen, members of such comparatively helpless entities as the Sanitary Committee, seemed actually to welcome the intervention of a Royal Commission; and it was one of these, Mr. Samuel Brighty, who revealed the unhappy process by which the middleman came into his own. Mr. Brighty said that when leases fell in on the Northampton Estate, the tenants who, owing to their circumstances, had managed to avoid the middleman, were now requested by Lord Northampton to pay £40 instead of £35 a year for a seven years' lease, to bear the cost of repairs themselves, and to pay an additional £5 for the cost of the lease. The tenants—small jewelers, policemen, postmen, and so forth—were unable to meet this additional expense; and, though some of them were tenants of twenty and thirty years' standing, they were obliged to move away. If they were obdurate, Lord Northampton took the violent course of leasing the house over their heads to a middleman, who thereupon raised the rent as much as £19 a year, as in the case of Mr. Willkins of 8 Goswell Terrace; while raises of £12 and £14 a year were quite the usual thing. In short (said Mr. Brighty) the Marquis and Mr. Boodle, in their unseemly haste to let to middlemen, "deal exceedingly hard with respectable people." The result of all this was the triumph of Mr. Decimus Alfred Ball and his tribe.

Mr. Boodle returned; but his attempt to rebut the evidence of Mr. Brighty was not very successful. He maintained that he would not let to occupiers only when such occupiers were not substantial people—that is, when they could not be relied upon to execute the necessary repairs. Why, then, he was asked, did he let so eagerly to Mr. Ball, a gentleman who, though very substantial, never executed any repairs unless driven to do so by rumors of a Royal Commission, by the visits of Sir Charles Dilke, and the anxiety of Lord William Compton? Having no reply to this, Mr. Boodle—like the squid, who emits an inky fluid when attacked—contented himself with a few general remarks about the filthy habits of the poor; after which, he troubled the Commission no more.

The problem of overcrowding was, of course far beyond the power of the landlord to alter or the middleman to intensify to any very great extent. Its roots lay deep beneath years of official neglect and administrative corruption; it had been fed by astonishing inefficiencies, by gross habits and outworn prejudices; it had grown fat upon the increase in population and the extension of enterprise. Here and there some enlightened official might, through an unusual exercise of his antiquated powers, halt the rot in some isolated alley; but, expunged from one spot, it appeared, doubly virulent, in another. The Royal Commissioners, whose labors were to be crowned by an Act of Parliament, might well have wondered whether such an outcome would prove sufficient; might well have asked themselves whether an earthquake, an inundation, an Act of God might not be the only practicable solution of the problem which they were investigating. And yet, to expose the stained sources of such incomes as Lord Northampton's, and the predatory nature of such lives as Mr. Ball's; to search for palliatives, to propose reforms—was it not by these means, in the nineteenth century, that the work of the world got done? They were not the best means, to be sure; they were full of hesitations and timidities: but they were better than none at all.

As the Commission delved on into the fungoid housing of Clerkenwell, the evidence became more and more appalling. The Rev. M. Dawes, Vicar of St. Mary Charterhouse, complained that the medical officer of health had declared that no area existed in the parish in respect of which any official representation was called for under Mr. Torrens' Act. And yet, in Playhouse Yard, the children all had "the blight"— or ophthalmia; and the smell arising from the closets in the cellars poisoned every house, so that "in some cases, until you had been in the room a little while, you could hardly bear yourself, the stench was so bad." At No. 4 Red Lion Market, in Lion Row, in Norman Cottages, the same state of affairs existed as Mr. Dawes could testify from personal experience; and as for the children, "they go to school in a half-starved condition, and having slept in this foul air, I do not think they are in a condition to use their brains." Oddly enough, however, Mr. Dawes confessed to the belief that much of this was due to the extravagant sums of money spent in the public-houses; that it was drink which drove people deeper into misery, not misery which drove them deeper into drink. This ingenuous point of view was amplified by another clergyman, the Rev. A. T. Fryer, who, after expressing his indignation at the ghastly overcrowding in the neighborhood of his church of St. Philip's, remarked, none the less, that "it is of greater consequence that people should have the moral principle than increased accommodation."

The official definition of overcrowding was not always an exacting one. Inspector John Bates, T Division, Metropolitan Police, inspecting under the Common Lodging Houses Act, gave an account of the Italian Colony in Holborn, in the course of which he stated that nineteen persons, eight adults and eleven children, slept in three rooms in Half Moon Court. He was asked if he would not characterize this as overcrowding, and replied: "I think not. They were small children. Under the Lodging Houses Act, we require 300 cubic feet for every adult male lodger, and two children under ten count as one person." Inspector Bates's ideas of justice, however, were not limited entirely to considerations of cubic feet, for in the course of his evidence he succeeded, with an unconscious artistry, in creating an enduring vignette of the habits of London house-farmers in the 1880's. A great deal of property around Gray's Inn Road was owned by a Mrs. Flight. At one of these houses—No. 10, Prospect Terrace, Gray's Inn Road:

"I spoke" (said the Inspector) "to a woman who was living in the parlor on the left-hand side. She looked very ill. She and her husband and four children were occupying this room. One little boy was lying on the floor, and the woman told me that they had not seen meat since Christmas time (this would be about three weeks ago), and her husband was breaking stones in the stone yard; but on that day he was not able to get work, being very poorly; and I could not see a particle of food in the house. She told me that the landlord refused to take her money because she was a halfpenny short in the rent. She had 4/5½ wherewith to pay 4/6, and the landlord, or rather his agent, positively refused to take the money, and told her she had better put it in a flower pot until it grew; and she sold her bedstead to raise the money for the rent."

The most dismal element in the lives of the Flights, or of Mr. Decimus Alfred Ball, or of Mr. Ross, or of any of the house-farmers who figure in this *Report*, was the fact that their whole economy depended upon wringing the last halfpenny from destitute and diseased people. They never indulged in spectacular operations; they dealt in the sordid, and the colorless, and the infinitesimal. One feels that if Mrs. Flight's agent had remitted that one halfpenny, the whole house-farming system (so far as single-room occupancy went) would have been dealt a severe blow; that the reverberations would have shaken the sanitary inspectors and the medical officers of health and the Vestries and even the Board of Works; and that some faint tremor might even have been felt in the mansions of Lord Northampton and Captain Penton and all the other owners of that unfruited earth.

The Rev. Robert Claudius Billings, B.A., Rector of Christchurch, Spitalfields, was a vigorous and determined opponent of overcrowding. Unlike Mr. Dawes, he believed that poverty led to drink, and that if you banished the former, the latter would disappear with it. It was true that some categories of human being were more inclined to take refuge in drink than others. The Jews, for example, who were constrained to take in the victims of persecution abroad, "arriving by waggon loads from the docks every night," only overcrowded; they rarely took to drink, and there was little disease among them. None the less, said Mr. Billings, if you encountered intemperance, immorality, and incest; if you found men living upon the prostitution of their wives and their daughters; what else could you expect when two families lived in one room, without the means of moving elsewhere? A laborer's wages on the docks or about Spitalfields Market averaged eighteen shillings a week; he simply could not afford to rent decent rooms. He was obliged to huddle his family into quarters so rotten with filth that all the scrubbing in the world would have made no difference. Sometimes, too, families not only lived and slept in one room, but worked there as well. This was true of the fur cleaners and sack-makers; and of the match-box makers, in whose work "the little children are employed"—and who were obliged to provide their own paste and to keep it warm, so that the smell was very bad. "There are two classes of the very poor in our neighborhood," said Mr. Billings. "I would guarantee that a certain number of them would break the windows and pull down the doors, for I have had experience of them myself, having made some little adventures in my own humble way. But there are a class distinct from these, a very large class, the majority of the people, who would be only too glad to get into rooms [i.e. model dwellings], and who would be proud to keep them in order and clean."

The worst house in his parish, he thought, was 35 Hanbury Street. It was a nine-room house, with one family to a room, and an average of seven persons to a family. Since there was never more than one bedstead to a room, adult sons and daughters slept together on the floor. There was one W.C. for the whole house, and that was on the ground floor. He could also tell of innumerable cases of people sleeping on staircases—" 'appy dossers," they were called—but he never thought it of any use to inform the police, for such people had nowhere else to go. If they were young people, he would, when he discovered them on his weekly visits, "take them"; otherwise, if the police discovered them and turned them out, such boys and girls without shelter "must go under a railway arch, or into a water-closet, or into a dust bin, or under waggons and carts." He believed, he said, that there was only one remedy for this state of affairs: the whole local government of a metropolis should be thrown upon some Government Office.

This touched Mr. McCollough Torrens upon a very sensitive nerve; his own Bill was being called in question; and he felt obliged to expostulate. "I understood you to say," he remarked, "or rather, I hope I misunderstood you to say, that you thought the remedy for that state of things lay in more central authority and power." In the subsequent argument, Mr. Billings—no dialectician—seemed about to yield; but he recovered his ground at the end. He was a man of conviction, a very good man, one of an increasing number of London clergy who believed that the basis of religion was goodwill. As for the poor, whom he served to the best of his ability, and whom he admired, he did not believe—he repeated—that they were at all resigned.

"They are not content as they are?" asked the Bishop of Bedford, one of the Commissioners.

"Not at all."

"You consider that this is a happy thing?"

"Yes," said Mr. Billings.

Another witness was the Rev. A. Mearns, author of "The Bitter Cry of Outcast London," a pamphlet which dealt with St. George the Martyr, Southwark, a parish lying on the boundary between the St. Saviour's District Board and the St. Mary, Newington, Vestry; and enjoying the maladministration of both these authorities. Queen Victoria herself had read "The Bitter Cry"; and it was because she had been moved by its simple arguments that she had permitted the Prince to become a member of the Royal Commission. He does not appear himself to have perused "The Bitter Cry," nor was he present to hear Mr. Mearns' evidence. It was dreadful evidence. Mr. Mearns spoke of places like Falstaff Yard, Tabard Street, Unicorn Street, Bull's Court, where the furniture was nothing but a heap of rags; where the closets were choked up and running down the staircases; and where dead bodies lay for as long as nine days or more, before they were moved. He spoke of lodging houses which let furnished apartments to men whose furniture had been seized to pay the rent; and said that the furniture in these apartments— they fetched from four shillings to six and sixpence a week— was too awful to deserve the name. He spoke of the Mint—the worst district in London, where thieves and prostitutes and liberated convicts lived side by side with the working people—and said that the houses here were all decaying, with great holes in the walls and roofs. There was a Mint Committee, especially concerned with this district, but its leading members were vestrymen of St. George the Martyr and St. Mary Newington; and since these vestrymen were all interested in bad property, no Mint house had ever been demolished under Mr. Torrens' Act. A gentleman with the not inappropriate name of Mr. Roach collected the rents throughout the Mint.

Mr. Mearns had once, in the course of his investigations, encountered the owner of some of the worst houses in Falstaff Yard. This was a Mr. Henry Levy, a member of the Vestry of St. George the Martyr. Mr. Levy had threatened to pitch him out of one of the courts in Falstaff Yard, because he had been obliged to expend £50 on account of what he called Mr. Mearns's "whims."

Mr. Mearns agreed with Mr. Billings that the inhabitants of these pigsties were far from accepting them as part of the natural order of things. In answer to a question from Cardinal Manning—were they not "very susceptible on the subject of rich and poor, and so on"?—he replied that this was undoubtedly the case, and that such susceptibility took a political form among the more educated. "Did you find," asked Mr. Samuel Morley, another Commissioner, "any of that sort of discontent which would show itself in the event of political disturbances?" "I have had men say to me that the thing could not last long—that they were strong enough if they could unite to alter the whole state of things." The Commission did not press Mr. Mearns for any further developments of this theme.

Oddly enough, in spite of the evidence, Mr. Samuel Morley still seemed to believe that drunkenness was largely to blame for all this. He said as much to Mr. G. R. Sims, author of a series of letters to the *Daily News* called "Horrible London." Mr. Sims replied that sweated labor, high rents, and rapacity might also have something to do with it. He pointed out that it was not uncommon for rents to be raised three-pence a week for "repairs" and that the repairs might be nothing more than the lid from a box of Cleaver's Soap tacked over a hole in the wall. He said that rents were in any case altogether too high; and that people who earned twelve to fifteen shillings a week should not be expected to pay more than one shilling and sixpence a week. This excited the animosity of the Hon. Lyulph Stanley, Lord Stanley of Alderley's son, another member of the Commission. Mr. Stanley maintained that rents could not be managed that way at a profit, and that a rent of one shilling and sixpence a week was nothing more than a subsidy of sixpence a week, an idea which struck him as totally repulsive. Lord Salisbury added that if rents were to fall, wages would fall also, a theory which Mr. Sims did not bother to attack. He simply pointed out that wages were disproportionate to rent; and that if wages fell, thereby preventing people from going further afield in search of accommodation, rents immediately rose; and that "the poorer the district, the higher the rent."

Obviously, those who made from twelve to fifteen shillings a week as sweated laborers, or those whose casual work on the docks or the markets might bring in eighteen or twenty shillings a week, could not hope to escape from their ver-minous and insanitary surroundings. But those who were better off, who belonged more to the artisan class, might if they were fortunate move into the model lodging houses which were sometimes to be found in London. These build-ings did not cope with the problem of housing, since they turned away the very poor, while at the same time, for fear of overcrowding, they denied accommodation to large families. But they attempted, none the less, to bring some order into the surrounding chaos, and the men who promoted them were actuated by the best intentions. The trouble was that the Peabody Buildings paid 5% to its shareholders, so did the Improved Industrial Dwellings Company; so that, in a more elevated way, they behaved like Mr. Ball, Mr. Ross, Mr. Levy and Mrs. Flight. They never. allowed a tenant to get more than a week behind with his rent. The South London Dwellings Company, on the other hand, which paid only 4%, allowed a two weeks' arrears of rent; though with tenants employed in seasonal trades this was hardly a generous arrangement. In another respect, too, the model lodging houses were not exactly ideal institutions. Their erection had been entrusted to builders who were self-made men, men without much education; and in consequence they were more like barracks than blocks of apartments. There was no trace of beauty in them, not a curve or a line that could possibly soothe the eye or the spirit. Solid and dismal, harshly regulated, with precipitous staircases of slippery stone and iron, they repelled that enthusiasm that a man has a right to feel for his home. And they were not always well guarded: in the Peabody Buildings of Clerkenwell, a little town of three thousand inhabitants, there was only one watchman; and when the gaslights were turned out at eleven o'clock, unfortunates crept in from the outside and slept all over the staircases. All that one could say for these model lodgings was that they were sanitary, and that one could keep one's apartment clean. Since they had very few sets of four rooms, very few families with many children ever found a haven in them; and such families with children as there were, were generally assigned rooms on the lower floors. Here another unhappy circumstance arose. The buildings were too high. It was upon this point that a brief but terrible piece of dialogue occurred between the Rev. J. W. Horsley and the Marquess of Salisbury:

THE REV. J. W. HORSLEY: "Those who live in the lowest rooms are found to suffer in health, especially the children."
LORD SALISBURY: "From the shadow?"

As a matter of fact, it was not from the shadow that these children became pale and listless so much as from an absence of air. It was generally remarked at the schools, said Mr. Horsley, that one "could tell the difference between the children who lived at the bottom, and those who did not live at the bottom of the model dwellings."

If the shareholders had been satisfied with 2½%, would the buildings have been less high? Perhaps. But it would have taken an even more profound change in social thinking for the buildings to have become kindlier and more beautiful.

Upon only one occasion did the Commission question someone who represented the house-farmers. This was Mr. Robert Paget, who, for twenty-eight years, had been Vestry Clerk of Clerkenwell. He was asked if he did not think that to have men upon the Vestry who were interested in doubtful housing might produce bad results. Mr. Paget most decidedly thought not. "Those who hold property, and have something at stake in the Parish are the most suitable men to be elected to administer its local affairs . . . I am inclined to think," he added later, "that men of property are the most suitable. I do not care what that property is, whether house property or property in the funds, or any other property, but give me men who have something at stake in the Parish." Sir Charles Dilke went on to say that he could not resist the conclusion that the central parts of London, including part of St. Luke's, nearly the whole of Clerkenwell, the southern part of St. Pancras, and the eastern part of Holborn were by far the worst parts of London, both structurally and as regarded overcrowding. The witness had an answer for this.

"I believe I may say that our vestry is generally of the opinion that Clerkenwell is not so bad as it is represented or made out to be, and especially if the death rate is to be taken as any criterion, and most people hold that to be at least some criterion. . . . Our intraparochial death rate, within the parish, is 16.9; and making allowances for everything else our doctor says that he cannot bring it to above 21 at the very outside, and he says that is too high."

"You are not prepared to deny, are you," Sir Charles asked, "that there is an immense amount of overcrowding in Clerkenwell?" "Query what is overcrowding," was Mr. Paget's rather cryptic reply. "I suppose you would call eight people in a room, the size of the rooms in these houses, over-crowding?" "I daresay I should. It depends upon the size of the rooms. Query are the people members of one family or of different families. Then again, query, does not the over-crowding take place even without the owner of the property becoming aware of it." This argument—that overcrowding took place without the knowledge of the owners or of the vestry—was soon disposed of by Sir Charles. The witness was also obliged to agree that Messrs. Ross, Osborne, Thaine, Henry Hill, Sans, Abrahams, Hasleham, Coker, Gibson (the agent for the Penton estate) and Javens—all members of the vestry—were interested in house property. But he could not be made to agree that it was bad or doubtful property. "It is a question then," he argued, "of what is bad or doubtful property. Some people may think a very good class of house a bad and doubtful piece of property; others may have a very different opinion. The question is what class of property are the poor expected to be able to obtain and to live in? Naturally the smaller, poorer and inferior class of property, I take it."

Such was the mind of the local governments of London in the '80's.

IV

The Royal Commission labored on until the end of August, 1884; adjourned until November 21; and adjourned again until February 20, 1885. In April of that year, it was in Edinburgh, and in May it was in Dublin. Even from the few glimpses of the evidence that have been given in these pages, one can see that such evidence was both undramatic and terrifying. That was as it should have been; and even though the Commission was unduly tactful—it examined the Prince's model estate of Sandringham, but not the Duchy of Cornwall's holdings in South London—much was done. Or rather, much *occurred*; for it was in the minds of the Commissioners, rather than in the results of the Commission, that something like a minor miracle can be seen to have taken place.

They had spent much of their time in exploring the evils of London. They had discovered that all existing legislation was suffused and sodden with the fogs of *laisser-faire*. It suggested and pleaded, but it never enforced. Any man, with a little ingenuity, could circumvent the Dwellings Acts in the

R

'80's. They had discovered, too, as a necessary consequence of this, that it was easier to demolish a tolerable house than an intolerable one; for if a house was rotten, if no repairs had been done upon it, the middleman was making such profits out of his lease that he demanded an impossible compensation; and so a kind of Gresham's Law ruled the slums, and the bad houses drove out the good. Moreover, the ground landlord, that distinguished parasite, was not willing to sell or lease his ground for less than the highest price that could be obtained.

In their interim and final reports, therefore, they recommended that legislation should be more coercive; that compensation should never amount to more, and might often be less, than the market value of a house; and that ground for housing purposes should be leased on a Fair Rent principle, not at the best price but at the most reasonable price. The last two suggestions were embodied in a Bill, and presented to Parliament during the Salisbury Administration of 1885-6. The House of Lords, a predominantly Tory gathering, shuddered with horror to hear Lord Salisbury advocating such measures; were they not the first step towards state socialism? Lord Salisbury, himself, perhaps, was more than a little astonished by the words that were coming out of his mouth. But the words were spoken.

Indeed, it was astonishing that the Commission, by no means a radical body, should have made, as it did, a whole series of mildly radical recommendations. It is true that when a Housing of the Working Classes Act at length, in 1890, found its way into the statute book, it brushed aside most of these recommendations, and hedged the rest about with too much caution and too many qualifications. It was not until the 1930's that any real progress, so far as London was concerned, began to be made in slum-clearance; and it is only today, in the hour of her greatest ordeal, that we feel in London a determination never to let the slums come back.

Yet the fact remains that the Royal Commission was inspired to make demands which the complacency of the times could not accept; and which the Commissioners themselves, it may be, soon forgot. To judge them by their results, these demands were futile. Yet must we always judge historical facts by their results? Must we assume that these interim and final reports, put out by a group of men against the instincts and interests of the majority of that group, were simply a kind of *ignis fatuus*, dancing over the morass? Or could it be that here one of those little fires was lit which seems to prove, before the darkness quenches it, that man has actually a feeling of goodwill towards man?

After attending the first four sessions, the Prince was rarely present. Between March 25 and August 8, he was only once in his seat at No. 8 Richmond Terrace; and between March 25 and August 8 some of the most effective evidence was given. This evidence, it is true, was never very easy to follow; the method of question and answer led it up many blind alleys and along many a fruitless road; yet merely to have subjected himself to it would have been a valuable education for a man who hoped one day to ascend the English throne.

Was it not to equip his son for just such experiences as this that the Prince Consort had drawn up his formidable scheme of education? Albert himself, no doubt, would have plunged with alacrity into such a subject as the Housing of

253

the Working Classes; but of the strange fires that burned behind his frosty exterior not one particle was inherited by his son. The Prince's reaction to the little evidence that he bothered to hear was of a less vigorous description. In a vague but kindly way, he had been touched; and when, in 1891, another Royal Commission was gazetted for the purpose of inquiring into Labor Problems, he asked to be allowed to sit upon that, too. This was not thought politically advisable, but when a Royal Commission for the Aged Poor sat in 1893, he became a member of it, and his attendance was much more assiduous. He was present at all but three sessions; asked several pointed and sensible questions; and occupied his spare time—as a fellow-commissioner, Mr. James Stuart, informs us—by filling the paper before him with Union Jacks drawn in red and blue pencil. The Aged Poor Commission was not exactly a success; its recommendations were inconclusive, and it fell into discredit: but that was hardly the Prince's fault.

As for the Royal Commission of 1884-5, it was his first engagement in an important domestic inquiry; for previous efforts of this nature had been limited to two House of Lords Committees—one on Cattle Plague, the other on the Scarcity of Horses. . . . And yet, during the spring and summer of 1884, when the Royal Commission was wrestling with the dismal problems of London, we find him in Paris, in La Bourbole, in Baden, at Koenigstein; or attending the races at Newmarket ("which calls," said *The Times*, "for very slight comment") and at Goodwood; or sailing his yacht at Cowes. Perhaps this should not cause us any surprise. During his Indian tour, in the hinterland of empire, had he ever bothered to inspect the hovels of the Black Town at Madras? And was the Black Town at Madras so very different from Falstaff Yard, and Wynyatt Cottages, and Three King Court? Besides, people in the '80's did not really wish their royalty to be too inquisitive about the lower levels of society; there was no outside force strong enough to mend the deficiencies in the Prince's own temperament. In short, it would be idle to criticize him for not doing what few people, least of all himself, expected him to do. One has merely to report, as an interesting and even an illuminating circumstance, that there was a Royal Commission on Housing in the years 1884 and 1885; and that the Prince was, on the whole, an absentee. . . .

Chapter Eight

THE SIGNIFICANCE OF A TIFF

ON JUNE 21, 1887, Queen Victoria celebrated her Golden Jubilee. It was not merely a ceremony, but an awakening. After so many years of misunderstanding, indifference, and dislike, the Queen, emerging at last from her rusty solitude, discovered her people; the people discovered their queen. Victoria was accustomed to applause whenever she appeared, but she was not accustomed to enthusiasm; and as she drove through the extraordinary clamor of the streets on her way to Westminster Abbey, the resentments of the past years finally melted away. The people, on their side, had not known what to expect; but what they found, in the tiny old bowing figure, was not so much a woman or a queen as a Myth. It was a very ancient, a prepotent myth—it had attached itself in the past to a number of personages, some human and some legendary; it was the myth of the Universal Mother. There was, in fact, something timeless and beautiful about the prosaic Victoria in that brief moment of English history. Nor was she ever again to be criticized or disliked by the English people.

Yet the Universal Mother who drove through London on June 21, 1887, was at the same time an entirely English phenomenon; indeed, she was a creation of the 1880's. Squired by a glittering assembly of sons and sons-in-law and grandsons, she was preceded by a concourse of kings and heirs-apparent; by a group of Indian princes, like jeweled and painted idols; and by a small flock of drab colonial dignitaries. Such a procession seemed to express the essential ambiguity of England in the waning years of the nineteenth century. Solid and industrious, and clothed in the plain textures of everyday life, England none the less stretched out her hand into the marble palaces of India; she ruled among the Pyramids; her voice was heard in the islands of the Pacific; and she sent her armies plunging into the Afghan mountains and the gloomy forests of the Gold Coast. The romance of Empire was still a vague concept, only partly exploited—its actors had not yet emerged from the pages of those little gray books, called the Railway Library, with which Mr. Rudyard Kipling was soon to enchant a susceptible public; but the Golden Jubilee did much to give it a shape. As the procession moved towards the Abbey, a consoling light fell and grew upon the gray lives of those who watched. They felt themselves to be the heirs of Africa and the Orient; and all the kings of Europe had come to do them honor.

At the head of the procession of princes rode the Prince of Wales and the Crown Prince Frederick of Prussia and Germany. The two afforded a contrast upon which Mr. W. T. Stead, in his rather scurrilous way, was quick to seize. He remarked upon the difference between the "fat little man in red" and "his splendid brother-in-law." And, indeed, the Crown Prince Frederick, in the white uniform and gilded helmet of the Pomeranian Cuirassiers, was a most rewarding sight. The spectators, looking at that bearded, benevolent and handsome face, were filled with pleasure. It was a noble face—and yet—and yet—was it a very forceful one? The old Emperor could not live much longer; an astute observer might well have asked himself whether the Crown Prince, when he came into his own, would prove quite strong enough to fulfill his ambitions; would ever be able to oust Bismarck; would ever lead Germany into the paths of representative government.

An answer, as it happened, was not to be provided. During the previous winter, the Crown Prince had developed a persistent soreness of the throat; a stay at Ems, in April, 1887, did not effect a cure; and when he returned to Berlin, his medical advisers began to fear that something very serious was the matter with him. It was decided to call in the English throat specialist, Dr. Morell Mackenzie; Dr. Mackenzie detached two small fragments from the throat and sent them to the eminent pathologist, Dr. Virchow; Dr. Virchow reported that he could discover nothing malignant in them; and Dr. Mackenzie thereupon gave it as his opinion that no operation was necessary, and that a few weeks in England under his care would restore the Crown Prince to complete health.

Acting upon this advice, therefore, Frederick came to England a week before the Jubilee, prepared for a longer stay: but, as if he had been granted some premonition of disaster, he brought with him three boxes full of his private papers, in order to deposit them for safe-keeping in Buckingham Palace. The premonition, if such it was, was correct; and Dr. Mackenzie was in error; for when the Crown Prince—a figure of radiant vitality beside his rather obese brother-in-law—rode through the streets of London on Jubilee Day, he was already a doomed man.

His voice reduced to a whisper, he lingered for two months in England under Dr. Mackenzie's care; then, searching vainly for health, he and the Crown Princess moved to the Tyrol, to Venice, to Baveno. November found him in a villa at San Remo, whither Mackenzie was summoned; and Mackenzie saw at once that his patient's condition had undergone an appalling change since the last examination. The Crown Prince was suffering from an incurable cancer.

A group of German doctors, sent down by the Emperor, confirmed the fatal opinion of Mackenzie; Frederick heard them out with composure and thanked them with courtesy; then, at last, he began to despair. He gave way to terrible fits of depression, and his wife, ceaselessly on guard, tried to interpose herself between him and the world . . . the visitors, and the officials, and, above all, their eldest son William, who had hastened to San Remo, in order to carry back a report to his grandfather.

The sudden change in his fortunes had completely gone to Prince William's head. A pupil of Bismarck, a favorite of the old Emperor, he had been estranged from his parents for some time; he had nothing but pity and contempt for his stricken father; and now, while the Crown Prince, a whispering ghost, shrank away from his son in cold dislike, there were scenes of furious recrimination between William and his mother. At length a reconciliation of a sort was patched up, and Prince William returned to Berlin, where he occupied himself in military pursuits. Meanwhile, outside the Villa Zirio, reporters lurked day and night; for the Crown

Prince's tragic predicament had stirred the German press into a virulent attack upon the Crown Princess. It was being said that she had connived with Dr. Mackenzie not to permit an operation earlier in the year.

All through the winter, the attack persisted; and when the Emperor William died in March, 1888, and the new Emperor Frederick dragged himself from the sunlight to the cheerless plains of Berlin, it greeted the Empress Frederick there, too. An English wife, an English doctor, a burning ambition not to let anything, such as an operation which might prove fatal, interfere with her husband's accession to the throne—these were its ingredients. Its origins and motives were, however, less fantastic. The former lay buried in the jealousies and intrigues of the Prussian Court, where the new Empress, who was neither very tactful nor very reticent, had made herself remarkably unpopular; the latter could be traced to the official home of the Imperial Chancellor. Prince Bismarck could have silenced the press, if he had wished to do so; he had small respect for its liberties: but since the Empress Frederick was a Liberal and an Englishwoman, he found it politically convenient to let the slanders go on. And so it was in an atmosphere of malignant gossip that the Emperor Frederick spent his last days on earth. Just before the end, he summoned Bismarck to his presence. He could not speak; but he took his wife's hand and laid it in the hand of his old enemy; as if to beg that formidable and treacherous personage to protect her against her own eldest son.

On the night of June 14, 1888, the lamp of German constitutional government began to flicker out in the New Palace at Potsdam. Early on the morning of the 15th, the Emperor

Frederick died; and immediately all the whispers and the stealthy movements, which had filled the palace in the night watches, organized themselves and announced the new reign in their own fashion. Soldiers surrounded the building, soldiers hunted through its mournful interior, and the new Emperor William, dressed in the red uniform of his hussars, and with a saber in his hand, himself investigated his mother's room. He and his search parties were looking for his father's papers (another consignment of which had been smuggled out of the palace the day before, and was already on its way to England); and particularly for the War Diary of 1870-1, with its revelations of imperial policy. But they do not seem to have found it, though it stayed in Germany.

The Empress Frederick would have been the first to admit that in the depths of her grief there lurked a grim and bitter disappointment. To have waited so long, to have come so far, and to be cheated at the end! Never would she help to reform the broken ranks of the National Liberals, never would she see the realization of "beloved Papa's" dream of a parliamentary Germany! There was nothing left to her but the empty title of Empress. She could precede a few more people through a few more doors; she would be called "Majesty" by courtiers whose formality scarcely concealed their dislike and contempt; and when she and her mother met in public, they would greet each other with a mutual instead of a unilateral curtsey. Such were the rewards for more than thirty years of confused but unremitting struggle. With her sad heart and her unsatiated ambition, with her barren honors, she prepared to leave the arena to the volatile William, who would lead the Germans—where?

✦

When the Prince of Wales received the news of his brother-in-law's death, he was on the racecourse at Ascot. He hurried back to London, and reached Berlin on the eve of Frederick's funeral. He was genuinely grieved. The old quarrel about Schleswig-Holstein and the Danish war had long since evaporated; and he felt, as he wrote to his mother from Berlin, that he had parted "from the noblest and best man I had ever known, except my ever to be lamented father." As for his nephew Willy, his feelings towards that young man were somewhat less clear. Willy's behavior during the past months had been most disconcerting, to say the least, but on the day of the funeral he showed himself, the Prince reported, "quiet and reasonable and only anxious to do what is right." This was more than could be said for Prince Bismarck, with whom the Prince had an interview, and who gave vent to a number of offensive remarks about the dead Emperor.

The Prince reported all this to his mother over the tea-table at Frogmore on June 26; and the Queen hastened to tell Lord Salisbury—as her Journal puts it—about "Prince Bismarck's violent language, when talking to Bertie, which showed how untrue and heartless he is, after . . . poor Fritz had placed Vicky's hand in his, as if to recommend her to him!" She was deeply perturbed, and took no pains to conceal her agitation; so that when General Winterfeldt came to announce her grandson's accession, she received him very coldly indeed. Then, in her best grand-maternal style, she composed a letter to the new Emperor. She was much concerned, she said, about the problem of his mother's future home: "Uncle Bertie told me that you had mentioned the Villa Liegnitz, but that is far too small."

"Mama," she went on, "does *not* know that I am writing to you on this subject, nor has she ever mentioned it to me, but after talking it over with Uncle Bertie he advised me to write direct to you. Let me also ask you to bear with poor Mama if she is sometimes irritated and excited. She does not mean it so; think what months of agony and suspense and watching and broken and sleepless nights she has gone through, and *don't mind it.* . . .

"There are many rumours of your going and paying visits to Sovereigns. I hope that at least you will let some months pass before anything of this kind takes place, as it is not three weeks since dear beloved Papa was taken and we are all in such deep mourning for him . . . GRANDMAMA V.R.I."

It is not difficult to imagine what effect such a missive would have upon a young man whose head had been turned by his sudden elevation to an imperial throne. The liberal sprinklings of "Uncle Berties" and "Mamas" and "Papas," the bland intermingling of the grandmother and the queen, the gentle advice on family matters leading almost imperceptibly into advice upon affairs of state—would not all this remind the new Emperor that, whatever he might be in Berlin, at Windsor and Sandringham he was just a junior member of a very large family? This was not quite what the Queen intended; but then she did not know that her matriarchal propensities had long been the subject of some of Bismarck's heaviest witticisms. William, who was still his Chancellor's protégé, was determined to teach his grandmother a lesson. He therefore replied that at the end of the month (July), he proposed to inspect his fleet and sail on into the Baltic:

"where I hope to meet the Emperor of Russia, which will be of good effect for the peace of Europe . . . as I deem it necessary that monarchs should meet often and confer together to look out for dangers which threaten the monarchical principle from democratic and republican parties in all parts of the world. It is far better that we Emperors keep firm together with Italy, than that two of them should go pitching into one another without any earthly reason except for a few miserable villages more or less! Which would only be arranging and preparing the way for anarchists at home and abroad."

But the Queen was not a very amenable pupil. Her reaction to this letter was one of shocked amazement. "Trust we shall be *very cool*," she telegraphed to Lord Salisbury, "though civil, in our communications with my grandson and Prince Bismarck, who are bent on returning to the oldest forms of government." To her son she was more explicit. "How sickening it is," she wrote on July 24, "to see Willy not two months after his beloved and noble father's death going to banquets and reviews! It is very indecent and very unfeeling."

But worse was to follow.

The Prince had been invited to stay with the Emperor of Austria in September; and he wrote to his nephew, who was to be in Vienna at the same time, to say that he looked forward to this meeting. William did not reply. The Prince departed from England in the best of humors. Though his appearance in uniform was such as to justify the criticisms of Mr. Stead, he was none the less very fond of this portion of his wardrobe; and he looked forward to greeting William in the disguise of a Blücher (5th Pomeranian) Hussar, of which regiment he was Colonel-in-Chief. Great was his surprise, therefore, and even greater his mortification, to learn upon arrival at Vienna that the Emperor William II had expressed a desire not to meet him. When Sir A. Paget, the

British Ambassador, told him of this, he could hardly believe his ears. He hastened to Crown Prince Rudolph, who confirmed the news. Since William was a reigning sovereign as well as a nephew, there was nothing for the Prince to do but to pack up his uniforms and depart, in high dudgeon, in the direction of Rumania.

The reasons for this imperial snub had already been reported by Count Hatzfeldt to Lord Salisbury; and, on the day after the Prince's retreat from Vienna, Lord Salisbury sent them to the Queen. Neither the Prime Minister nor Count Hatzfeldt had, of course, expected William to behave in such a drastic fashion; though the reasons for his displeasure were, if true, far from inconsiderable. The Prince of Wales, according to William II, did not behave at all well at the funeral of the Emperor Frederick. In the first place, he told a Russian Grand Duke (who hastened to the new ruler with the story) that if Frederick had lived he would have restored part of Alsace to France, part of Schleswig to Denmark, and part of Hanover to the Duke of Cumberland. He and the Princess of Wales had then pressed the Cumberland claims upon Prince Bismarck.

If the Kaiser's complaint had been limited to these two particulars, it might have extracted a soft answer from Victoria, who never needed to be convinced that her eldest son was indiscreet. But William, whose attitude towards public affairs was nothing if not personal, pressed a further charge. The Prince, he said, treated him like a nephew and not like an Emperor. At this, the Queen's wrath knew no bounds. She perceived that William's attack was aimed, not merely at his Uncle Bertie, but also, obliquely, at herself; that she, with all her private claims upon him, was being put in her place. "This is really too *vulgar*," she burst out to Lord Salisbury on October 5, "and too absurd, as well as untrue, almost *to be believed*. We have always been very intimate with our grandson and nephew, and to pretend that he is to be treated *in private* as well as in public as 'his Imperial Majesty' is *perfect madness* . . . If he has *such notions*, he had better *never* come *here*. The Queen will not swallow this affront."

Lord Salisbury replied with a telling comparison between the behavior of the young Emperor and that of the German imperialists in Zanzibar; but he soon began to fear that this family quarrel would encroach upon his own preserves. The Queen was determined to invite the Empress Frederick over to England. Lord Salisbury protested that this would have an adverse effect upon Anglo-German relations, and that the Prince of Wales agreed with him. The situation was clear to all three of them:—the nervous exasperation of the Empress, the unfilial animosities of her son, and behind it all—directing this psychological conflict for his own purposes—the remorseless figure of Prince Bismarck. But the Queen was in no mood to abandon her daughter; and she realized—as Lord Salisbury and the Prince of Wales did not—that Bismarck had never really understood the limitations of the English monarchy; that he was always inclined to confuse the Queen's private actions with her public and official ones. It was a confusion very much to Victoria's taste, and she held on her course. She telegraphed to Lord Salisbury that to postpone the Empress Frederick's visit "would be of no use and only encourage the Emperor and the Bismarcks still more against us. You all seem frightened of them, which is not the way to make them better. Tell the Prince of Wales this, and that his persecuted and calumniated sister has been for months looking forward to this time of quietness. Please let no one mention this again." When the Queen spoke in this manner, it was generally best to comply with her wishes. Lord Salisbury, therefore, reluctantly withdrew his objections, and the visit took place. The Prince of Wales fetched his sister from Flushing, and Victoria (who had hitherto never stirred beyond her own door even to meet the greatest sovereigns) herself went down to Port Victoria to meet her daughter. On her birthday, the Empress received Count Hatzfeldt, the German Ambassador, and all his staff; and when at last she left England, it was with a Sovereign's Escort that she was ushered out of London.

This family solidarity was re-affirmed a few months later in a manner which, though less spectacular, was equally striking. In April, 1889, the Queen paid a visit to Sandringham—the first since the days when she had watched the Prince through his typhoid, so many years ago. Knowing her passion for the theatricals, he had his ballroom turned into a theater; and on the evening of the 26th she saw "The Bells" with Henry Irving, and the Trial Scene from "The Merchant of Venice" with Mr. Irving as Shylock and Miss Ellen Terry as Portia. It was a most successful visit. Moreover, her anger with her grandson had blinded her to the fact that the Prince himself had not come any too well out of the Vienna incident. He totally denied that he had ever said a word to a Russian Grand Duke, or that he and the Princess had pressed the Cumberland claims upon Prince Bismarck; but he did admit that, in a conversation with Count Herbert Bismarck, he had inquired whether the late Emperor Frederick had not thought of restoring part of Alsace to France and of Schleswig to Denmark. Though the

Kaiser's revenge at Vienna was characteristically juvenile, there is no doubt at all that the Prince had been exceedingly tactless in Berlin; that Count Herbert, Prince Bismarck, and William II did quite right to be angry; and that, if William's arrogance had not provoked her, the Queen would have visited one of her severest scoldings upon her son. As it was, after the Prince had journeyed to Balmoral to make his explanations in person, she merely noted in her Journal that it was "very dear and kind of him to come."

This stiffening of the ranks in the English Royal Family did not fail to have its effect upon William II. His was a nature that oscillated between pride and panic; and when he realized that his grandmother, of whom he was genuinely fond, had turned against him, he hastened to bring about a reconciliation. He was, he said, most anxious to visit the Queen during the summer of 1889; and Count Hatzfeldt was instructed to convey this information to Lord Salisbury. Lord Salisbury, who had been extremely uneasy throughout this period of family tension, and who questioned the propriety of allowing the disputes of relatives to interfere with international politics, rubbed his hands and hurried off to the Queen: but Victoria was adamant. "William must *not* come *this* year," she wrote to the Prince on February 7. "*You* could not meet him and I could not, after all he has said and done."

Lord Salisbury, however, was persistent; and Lord Salisbury was Prime Minister. Three weeks later the Queen agreed that William might pay her a visit if—and only if—he made some sort of apology to the Prince of Wales. The Prince was ready to be forgiving upon these terms—"the close relationship between him and me," he said, "would render an estrangement between us a matter of serious importance": and as his brother-in-law, Prince Christian of Schleswig-Holstein, was about to journey to Berlin, he asked him to "sound out" the Emperor. The unfortunate Prince Christian, whose business in life it was to make himself agreeable to everyone, accepted this mission most reluctantly. It was true that the Prince required no more from his imperial nephew than "a few lines to express his regret"; but even this was more than Prince Christian felt himself able to accomplish. Nor was he unduly pessimistic; for the Kaiser, on being sounded out by his embarrassed relative, blandly denied that there had ever been a Vienna incident. How then, he asked Prince Christian, could he apologize to Uncle Bertie for something that had not occurred? Prince Christian wrote to his brother-in-law, suggesting that this explanation might take the place of an apology. The Prince replied that he must either have an apology or else refuse to meet his nephew in England.

As late as May 12, the Queen's secretary was still telling Prince Christian that Her Majesty had been "extremely dissatisfied throughout" by the Emperor's treatment of his uncle. On May 25, however, she had decided that the squabble must cease; and that the Kaiser's explanation—foolish and insincere as, no doubt, it was—must be accepted. Pressure was therefore put upon the Prince; and, though he complained that he was being sacrificed to political expediency, he agreed to pretend that nothing had happened at Vienna, and prepared to meet his nephew with as good a grace as he could muster.

The Queen always kept a soft spot in her heart for her

grandson. In spite of his behavior to his mother and uncle, she now forgave him completely. She accepted from his hands the Honorary Colonelcy of the First Regiment of Dragoon Guards, and made him in turn an Admiral in her Navy. When the Kaiser heard of his new rank from Sir Edward Malet, the British Ambassador in Berlin, he was quite overwhelmed. "Fancy," he wrote to Sir Edward, "wearing the same uniform as St. Vincent and Nelson; it is enough to make me quite giddy. I feel something like Macbeth must have felt when he was suddenly received by the witches with the cry of 'All hail, who art Thane of Glamis and of Cawdor too.'"

"I beg to be allowed to remark," he assured Sir Edward in a postscript that already seemed to betray a trace of vertigo, "that I do not look upon you as a witch, but more as a good fairy."

It was in an expansive mood, therefore, that William II arrived at Osborne on August 2, dressed in the uniform of St. Vincent and Nelson, and bringing with him an escort of twelve warships. Since the Queen rarely saw him except at night, he spent his days with his uncle, whom he submerged beneath a flood of nautical information. The two men did their best. The Prince made the Kaiser a member of the Royal Yacht Squadron; the Kaiser bestowed a Black Eagle upon the Prince's younger son. But the Vienna incident still hovered between them, like a dissatisfied spirit. It had revealed an essential antipathy; and no amount of determined geniality on the uncle's part, or determined condescension on the nephew's, would ever conjure it away.

II

Whether men shape events, or whether events shape men, is a question which might be debated forever. If as the years went on the nephew had grown fonder of the uncle or the uncle had been less irritated by the nephew—or if either or both had been more clairvoyant—they might have done something to postpone the war which broke out in 1914. Yet it is hardly probable—it is, indeed, most unlikely—that, even if they had been miraculously endowed with wisdom and statesmanship, they could have done more than that. Their significance lies elsewhere: in the way in which their personal quarrel seemed to attend upon the maturing of a dreadful conflict; in contrasts of character, and divergences of circumstance.

At the time of the Vienna incident, the Prince had come to represent not a few of the social changes which resulted from the shift of power from Land to Capital. One has only to repeat that the Repeal of the Corn Laws was no more than a legislative framework around an immense and, at the time of the Repeal, quite unfinished picture. The framework fell away and was forgotten—the agonies of Peel, the virulence of Disraeli vanished into the past; the picture, endowed with its own mysterious life, continued to grow. The poverty which Peel had hoped to dispel became less abysmal and more widely diffused; the monopolies which he had attacked assumed a different form and fell into more dangerous hands. Elsewhere, in the upper regions of politics, the picture produced the later Gladstone, whose timidities and passions were those of the middle class; in the upper regions of society, it brought forth the Prince.

Between 1846 and 1890, polite Society managed not to reflect the profound changes in the world beneath and around it. On the whole, it retained its aristocratic character of the days before Repeal. It was still an oligarchy, unresponsive to the claims of wealth or wit. And yet, now and again, it was shaken; the mirror, with its rather pompous reflection of the past, trembled on the wall. Nor would it have required a very accurate seismograph to detect the centers of these disturbances: they were, all too often, at Marlborough House and at Sandringham.

As early as 1873, good Bishop Magee of Peterborough noted with surprise the composition of a house-party at Sandringham. "I find the company," he wrote, "pleasant and civil, but we are a curious mixture. Two Jews, Sir Anthony de Rothschild and his daughter; an ex-Jew, Disraeli; a Roman Catholic, Colonel Higgins; an Italian duchess who is an Englishwoman, and her daughter, brought up a Roman Catholic and now turning Protestant; a set of young lords, and a bishop." The mixture grew more experimental with time. Years later, Czar Nicholas II found that his stay at Sandringham coincided with the auction of some of the Prince's horses; and the Autocrat of All the Russias, that nerveless but implacable tyrant, fled, in gentle disgust, like a horrified cloud, before the horsy guests who were assembled under his uncle's roof. The Prince became more and more addicted to the company of people who amused him—brilliant Jews, vivid Americans—people whom Society still regarded with a certain uneasiness. There were guests at Marlborough House during the season whom one would never have found in the houses of those almost legendary "tall duchesses" of the late Victorian era; at Constance, Duchess of Westminster's, or at the Duchess of Sutherland's, or Lady Suffield's.

It would, of course, be an exaggeration to pretend that the Prince allowed his somewhat cosmopolitan tastes to get out of control, or that he did not maintain his place at the head of Society. Marlborough House remained at the very apex of that structure; and it was the aim of every ambitious mother to have her daughter appear there, when the great striped tent was spread away from the ballroom, and young people sat upon the staircase under the commemorative frescoes of the Duchess Sarah.

Indeed, the Prince and Princess of Wales, in that close world, where there was as yet no restaurant life, and where people dined and danced only in their own houses, quite dominated the scene. Important ladies might protest against the "fastness" of the Marlborough House set and the questionable antecedents of some of its members; but they did not venture to ostracize that brilliant little court. The Princess had not a little to do with this. The Prince's infidelities, which had caused such a scandal during the republican agitations of the '70's, increased rather than diminished as the years went on; but he was, in his own way, a courteous and affectionate husband. The Princess, who never dreamed of making a public issue of her wrongs, and who remained until the end a devoted wife, was a recognized beauty. She was somewhat lame, the result of an earlier illness; and while some ladies imitated her dresses and her coiffure, others, in the intensity of their devotion, cultivated an "Alexandra limp." But the Princess was possessed of something more than beauty: she had an instinctive kindness and an almost child-like zest for life which were quite irresistible. Those who found their way into her private apartments could testify to this. Her rooms were littered with pictures, miniatures, photographs, books, bibelots; her very dressing table over-flowed with scent bottles, flagons, gold pencils, more photo-graphs, more *souvenirs*. She had a personal feeling for every-thing that came her way; she seemed to make no distinction between a precious trinket, the gift of some Indian magnate, and a trout-fly presented to her in an expansive moment by an affectionate Scots gillie. Her passion for keeping things, once they had drifted into her possession, was quite as strong as that of Queen Victoria; but whereas the Queen had all her possessions catalogued and numbered, as though they were, by their very fixity, a bulwark against time and change and even Death itself, the Princess kept hers in an indiscrimi-nate confusion, out of sheer affection for life. Charming, gay, simple, with her courage and her kind heart, often unhappy, always sympathetic, Alexandra was a successful mediator be-tween the vagaries of her husband and the virtuous disap-proval of his times.

The Prince, too, was a mediator, a link between the rigidi-ties of the old Society and the laxity of the new Wealth. His friendship with a Baron Hirsch or a Thomas Lipton—("He is boating with his grocer," said the Kaiser once, when he heard that his uncle was on Sir Thomas' yacht)—caused more surprise in foreign than in English circles. England is never averse to compromise or to idiosyncrasy; and if the Prince tried to make the best of two worlds, most people agreed, with a shrug or a smile, that it was the best of them that he made. In purely English circles, moreover, he was a great deal more at home than any of his male predecessors had been—with the intermittent exception of the Regent. In the charm of his conversations and the informality of his after-dinner speeches, in his ability to mingle the easy-going with the conventional, in his love of horse-racing and his distaste for intellectual pursuits, in a thousand and one less obvious ways, he might almost have sprung from some polite English family. Almost, but not quite. Oddly enough, he was also slightly foreign: foreign in his passion for uniforms, foreign in his almost fanatical preoccupation with the details of ceremonial dress, foreign in his accent, foreign in his too abrupt transitions from the good-humored *viveur* to the freezing heir to the throne. Above all, he was foreign in his love of what the Queen called "running about"—in his fondness for Europe, and the ease with which he insinuated himself into the European scene. It was this faculty for being at once an Englishman and a European that filled the Kaiser with envy. Very soon, the envy turned into suspicion. There were moods in which the young monarch seemed to see, in his mind's eye, only his uncle: his uncle chatting agreeably on the lawn at Cowes, or dining the Jockey Club on Derby Day; or shooting with Baron Hirsch among the ostentations of St. Johann; or infusing a little warmth into the numbed solemnities of the Austrian court; or hobnobbing with politicians in German watering places and Parisian *cafés*. Small wonder that William mistook these cosmopolitan tastes for something more; and that, when at last he came to believe in the "encirclement" of Germany, he perceived in his mobile relative the agent of this policy.

The Prince, of course, wanted to be useful to his country.

The form that this usefulness was to take was constellated in his actions as a Royal Commissioner in 1884. He was touched, but not deeply, by the immeasurable woe of the slums: and he turned from that spectacle, with all its possibilities of social service, to the more exciting *milieu* of a German watering-place. He came to put more and more reliance upon Wiesbaden and Homburg as resorts where one could pick up a great deal of interesting information. The same purpose can be discerned in his September and October pilgrimages, when, after enduring a fortnight of purely domestic amusements in the unaffected court of the King of Denmark, he would leave his wife in the bosom of her family, and wander at large in Europe. In Dröttingholm and Sinaia and Athens, or wherever his engagements happened to lead him, there was always something to be learned. It was the education of a hedonist who was also an extrovert: but that it was an education of a kind can hardly be doubted.

As a hedonist, the Prince could not realize that his private life might become embarrassingly public: even though in 1871 and again in 1891 this fact was brought home to him in the most unpleasant manner. He once wrote in a confession book: "I am happiest when . . . I can, like plain Mr. Jones, go to a race meeting without it being chronicled in the papers next day that His Royal Highness the Prince of Wales has taken to gambling very seriously and yesterday lost more money than even he can afford to pay." This rather naive confession, with its faint touches of bravado, shows him in his least agreeable light. On the other hand, in his official appearances, he tried hard to please, and almost invariably succeeded. In another respect, more expressive of an attitude to life, he appears to advantage: in his behavior towards eminent men—even if he thought them dull or disagreeable or politically dangerous—he was always deferent. Living almost entirely in an unreal atmosphere, in which tradition, protocole, and snobbery were subtly intermingled, he accepted compliments and flatteries as a matter of course: but one compliment, the greatest of them all, he never seems to have swallowed. The words "By the Grace of God" were a convenient formula in proclamations and looked well, in Latin, on coins: and though the Queen, with her simple piety and her profound self-confidence, may sometimes have believed that they expressed the truth, the Prince was obliged to admit that his titles and his income were in the gift of a less exalted authority. His family was royal, in every way that mattered, only by Act of Parliament; and what Parliament had bestowed, Parliament could take away.

III

William II, on the other hand, lived upon intimate terms with the Almighty. He could see a providential design in the history of his family since the days when it had cooled its southern blood in the damp airs and dismal politics of the March of Brandenburg. There was no doubt about it— a Hohenzollern ruled by Divine Right. Nor had his education failed to drive the lesson home by pointing out, in the devious triumphs of Bismarck, further evidence of God's special care for the ruling house of Prussia. Yet, close as William felt himself to be to the ruler of the Universe, the relationship was an uncertain one. Sometimes he saw himself as a protegé, sometimes as a victim. From a sovereign who is temperamentally insecure, and who believes in the Divine Right of Kings, such uncertainties are to be expected; but they do not make him easy to live with.

It is in his insecurity that the key to William II's peculiarities can be discovered. Perhaps the circumstances of his childhood had something to do with this. From the quiet mausoleum at Frogmore, where the Prince Consort lay buried, there radiated a strange influence: the educational notions of the Crown Princess were, like her political beliefs, distinctly Albertine. The Crown Prince submitted to his wife; and so the little Prince William was brought up in a strict and disparaging fashion, as though nothing but discipline and more discipline could cure the defects in his character. They were the defects of a clever and sensitive child, whose sensitivity was rendered all the more acute by the fact that he had a withered arm. Yet the Crown Princess could not altogether conceal the genuine warmth of her nature; she would often show an involuntary tenderness, a deep but galling pity; and sometimes, in the intensity of her emotions, she would smother her son with caresses. The Crown Prince, at heart the gentlest of men, occasionally unbent. It was, to say the least, a confusing childhood.

At a very early age, Prince William was committed to the care of a tutor called Hinzpeter, a gentleman who proceeded to crush his charge into the iron apparatus of German education. If Hinzpeter had ever shown signs of relenting, the royal parents would certainly have admonished him: but then Herr Hinzpeter was not by inclination a relenting teacher. The boy's days—from six or seven in the morning until bedtime—were spent in a round of grinding mental tasks and appalling physical exercises. He was then sent to the Grammar School at Cassel, where—though his rank forbade him from entering fully into the intimacies of the place—he was obliged, as he wrote years later in his Memoirs, "to learn with strange boys in a public school, to compete with them, and—to come out lower in the list!" In these shocked phrases are revealed the fundamental tendencies of a lifetime. However deeply he may have suffered from the bewildering behavior of his parents and the negative vigilance of Hinzpeter, the boy was convinced that Life owed him deference. It was a conviction that increased with the years.

When he was eighteen William left the Grammar School and went to the University of Bonn for a few terms. After that, there was an end of study. He joined his regiment. Here, in the very heart of Prussian military life; here, where one either did not relax at all or relaxed too much; where there was no moderation; where, at every turn, one saw oneself reflected and glorified in the faces of one's companions— William learned what it was to be a Hohenzollern. At the same time, he began to receive the attentions of the old Emperor and of Bismarck. The young man could easily be weaned from the progressive ideas of his father; all that was needed was a little flattery; and he was therefore entrusted with work which should rightly have been given to the Crown Prince. But long before he was sent upon those inflating missions to St. Petersburg and Brest-Litvosk, the estrangement between himself and his parents had taken place. The Crown Princess, who had once rejoiced in "the bond of love and confidence" between herself and her son, the Crown Prince, whose diary records their "simple natural cordial relations," were filled with alarm and mortification: but what could they do? The freedom and adulation which had been William's since leaving school had done their work; and those forces which had been stored up in the secret places of his soul—rebellious and resentful forces—burst out, and carried him headlong in their own direction.

William was not his own master. His treatment of his dying father and his unhappy mother during the last months of Frederick's life might be, and have been, attributed to some deep-seated malignity. And yet the very bitterness, the unreasonableness of that quarrel, seem to point to something less obvious; they seem to indicate a profound exasperation of the nerves. The mother irritated the son, the son irritated the mother; and this unhappy state of affairs was further exacerbated by the fact that the father was withdrawn from the scene, and made no attempt to understand it. Moreover, William was, in many other respects, an uncontrolled person. He had a keen, acquisitive, and shallow intelligence, which sought to compensate him, it may be, for his sense of physical inferiority. When he came to the throne, the number of his accomplishments was formidable. He was a general, an admiral, a painter, a composer, a conductor. Commerce, art, yachting, socialism, archaeology, boat-building, education, theology—he spoke with authority upon them all. One looks in vain for any central being whose existence could account for these singular pretensions.

In some respects, it is true, William II seems never to have matured at all, but to have remained simply a gifted child. There were times when he could think of armies as if they were toy soldiers; when navies sprang into being in his excitable imagination and sailed upon seas as measurable as a bathtub; and the whole world, with all its perils and complexities, became little more than a box of tricks, to be opened in the morning and folded away for the night. Or else a histrionic mood would seize upon him, and he would see himself as a Knight in Armor, an impersonation which the slightly melodramatic character of the imperial uniforms did nothing to impede. Or again, having swallowed in two or three gulps the intoxicating doctrines of Bismarck, he would give his own version of the axiom that the means justify the end. He would tell lies with a mischievous zest; were they not necessary for the achievement of his purposes? But what were his purposes? In this respect, he bears a resemblance to Napoleon III; he did not know what his purposes were; but the resemblance is at best a faint one. If we look back at Napoleon III, we can see him as a juggler, manipulating with infinite dexterity a number of highly-colored objects—the Orleanists, the Bourbonists, the Clericals, the Socialists, the Revolution, the Reaction. As the years pass, his expression becomes dismayed. Why is he doing this? At last he sinks exhausted to the floor, and the objects, which had poured in a marvelous arc from hand to hand, scatter in confusion around him. Yes, Napoleon was a juggler: but William—as he tumbled around in international politics—was William ever more than a clown?

It is only just to say that the childish element in William II was not always uppermost. He could be a mature and charming person when the mood was on him; his conversation, on such occasions as it did not sink into a sermon or rise to a philippic, was informed and agreeable. Moreover, there were times when his timidity and his reason would both assert themselves; when he realized with clarity the loneliness, the danger, of his position; when the world was no longer a box of tricks, but an unpredictable jungle; and when even the principle of Divine Right held no comfort. It is not surprising that, after committing a blunder or experiencing a rebuff, the Kaiser would sometimes be found in tears.

There was one flaw in Bismarck's Empire; it was built upon the assumption that Bismarck himself was permanent. It made no provision for the day when death, or the logic of history, or an ambitious and daring Emperor would remove the Iron Chancellor from the scene. Powers were vested in the Emperor, which, so long as he remained amenable to Bismarck's advice, might seem excessive, but not preposterous. But suppose the Emperor was not amenable; suppose he was a man of dangerously veering moods; suppose, in fact, that he was not William I but William II . . .

The position of the German Emperor, the *Kaiser in Deutschland,* was a peculiar one. His title was not, strictly speaking, hereditary; he was Emperor because he was King of Prussia. He had no civil list, his revenues were derived from Prussia. He wore no imperial Crown. On the other hand, if his title was shadowy and his emoluments were non-existent, there was something supremely practical about his executive powers. He could declare war and conclude peace, make alliances, appoint and receive ambassadors; he could call, open, adjourn, and dissolve the Bundesrat and the Reichstag; he could promulgate and execute the laws of the Empire; nominate and dismiss officials; appoint all officers in the German Navy and the Prussian Army, and all the highest officers in the armies of the other states. It was true that his imperial enactments required the counter-signature of the Imperial Chancellor, who thereby assumed the responsibility for them; and that the Imperial Chancellor, if he were also Minister-President of Prussia, was a very powerful man. But the Emperor could dismiss the Chancellor at will. It was true, too, that the Emperor exercised his rights through the Bundesrat; but the Bundesrat—though its composition has fascinated political scientists, and though its nominal powers were enormous—was in actual fact a docile body, dominated by the seventeen votes of Prussia. The Reichstag also had its powers: it could veto and initiate legislation, and, being elected by universal male suffrage, it might be said to represent the nation. Yet above its head, like a Damoclean sword, hung the Emperor's right to dissolve it: and it was continually outfaced by the Prussian Landtag, a gathering that was immoderately susceptible to the claims of privilege and property. In short, the Empire was completely overshadowed by Prussia, a mighty kingdom of bureaucrats and soldiers. And in Prussia the word of the Emperor-King was paramount.

Such a personage, with such powers, would have to be very level-headed if he were to avoid the pitfalls that surrounded him. The fountain of honor, the dispenser of offices and titles, he attracted to him all that was ambitious and servile in the length and breadth of Germany. William II was, perhaps, one of the last men to be able to resist these influences, or even to detect them. But there was another influence at work, more obscure and more deadly. As he bent his ear to the booming compliments of Prince Donnersmarck, or basked in the adroit adoration of Philip Eulenburg, as he jested roughly with his elderly generals and harangued his rigid recruits, William II began to confuse velleity with Will. The words "My Will" appeared more and more often in the speeches that he made on military occasions: it was, he said, the only law. One might have asked whether there was not

some distinction between the law that kept soldiers and statesmen standing stiffly by the hour and the Law that governs the
destiny of a nation. To most Germans, however, even jocular
and critical Germans, the distinction was never very clear.
A belief in Will, as a superhuman force, was inherent in German philosophy; it was a familiar doctrine in the lecture
halls; it crept, with equal facility, into the textbook and the
barracks and the palace. Was not the growth of the Bismarckian Empire, were not the very lineaments of the Bismarckian Emperor, a living expression of the German Will?

Like a glittering weathercock at the apex of the Empire,
William II twisted in the winds. Sometimes he seemed to be,
not only the weathercock, but the breath that turned it; his
gusty personality blew him perpetually to and fro. As time
passed, however, he began to point more often in one direction. An external wind, a damp, cold, prevailing, metaphysi-
cal wind—the German Will—seized upon him and used him
for its own extraordinary ends. But winds, even philosophical
winds, carry voices that are not philosophical at all. William
II began to listen to one voice in particular, sounding more
and more insistently in his ear. He listened in ecstasy and in
trepidation; he even tried to close his ears to it altogether;
but in vain. Not in spite of his executive powers, but because
of them, the voice became his master. It was a very odd voice.
It spoke of world-power, and it used the brisk accents of militarism; but it proceeded from industry and commerce.

At the time of the Vienna incident, it was just beginning
to make itself heard.

IV

Such were the two men, uncle and nephew, whose personal dislike for each other, increased every year by some petty incident, seemed at last to typify a growing coldness between their countries. Meanwhile, to give some point to this assumption, there had arisen in the sky of Anglo-German relations a small cloud, no bigger than a man's hand.

In November, 1883, Germany asked whether the British possessed any claim to Angra Pequena, a port in Southwest Africa, in the waste between Portuguese Angola and the Cape. She received an ambiguous reply. In December, she renewed her inquiries, and a faint agitation could be discerned among the British authorities. The Foreign Office handed this odd business over to the Colonial Office; the Colonial Office referred it to the Cape Government; the Cape Government was surprised but silent. On April 25, 1884, Germany decided to wait no longer, and placed under her protection the trading stations of Herr Luderitz, in and around Angra Pequena. A month later, she protested against the Anglo-Portuguese Convention, by which England recognized the Portuguese claims to territory around the Congo; demanding, at the same time, greater consideration for her interests in Africa. The Liberal Government thereupon dropped the Anglo-Portuguese Convention and recognized the protectorate of Angra Pequena. At this there were alarms and rumors. It was generally agreed that Germany, a land power sandwiched between France and Russia, could not possibly have any colonial aspirations. Why then had she made this *démarche*, and why had the Government yielded? Some said that Bismarck was currying favor with the German public; others that he was about to form a European coalition against England. Questions were asked in Parliament and in the press; there were charges and counter-charges; and all this time the German flag, an agile and irritating piece of bunting, was run up in parts of New Guinea, in Togoland, the Cameroons, and the Sultan of Zanzibar's territory on the east coast of Africa. This process was halted in February, 1885; and in March, Mr. Gladstone was able to say that Germany "becomes our ally in the execution of the great purposes of Providence for the advantage of mankind."

Mr. Gladstone himself, none the less, was not at all sure that Providence had much to do with the scramble for Africa. He disliked the whole business, and so, although the vigor of his oratory remained unimpaired, his imperial policies were apt to be of a hesitant nature. The German demands were not, really, very important: there were other and more momentous issues to grapple with—the Russian move against Afghanistan, for example, or his extreme unpopularity because of the death of General Gordon. This combination of circumstances might account for his Government's readiness to yield to Germany. But, as we know now, there was another reason, more obscure and—in its implications for the future—far, far more sinister. . . .

Defending the Government's Anglo-German policy in the Lords, in February, 1885, Lord Granville delivered himself of a furibund speech. He declared that Bismarck had advised Lord Beaconsfield to seize Egypt, and that Lord Beaconsfield had not seen fit to do so. The same advice had been proffered, he said, to his Government; with the same results.

How then could the Conservatives blame the Government for not taking a course which they themselves had found unacceptable? The speech was considered most undiplomatic; and the German press, inspired by Bismarck, broke out into vehement recriminations. At the same time, oddly enough, Bismarck sent his son, Count Herbert, to London with a conciliatory message. What could this mean? Only a very few people, in very high places, caught the actual drift of Lord Granville's speech. It was not in what it said, but in what it did not say, that its importance resided. Lord Beaconsfield's conscience—the seizure of Egypt—these were just so many words. For the real cause of Lord Granville's fury and Bismarck's agitation one must look elsewhere; and the search ends, at last, in an international Commission, known as the Caisse de la Dette.

At the time of Lord Granville's speech, the Caisse de la Dette was composed of four members—an Englishman, an Austrian, a Frenchman and an Italian. Their duties were to receive revenue on behalf of the creditors of Egypt; while at the same time they watched over the decrees, conventions and protocols which formed, in appalling complexity, the international regulation of the Egyptian finances.

It is only necessary to repeat that the Khedive Ismail, having involved himself in a series of ruinous transactions with a number of shady European money-lenders, had fallen at last into the hands of the European Powers. Such was the logic of nineteenth century finance. Struggling with his own futility and with a set of corrupt ministers, he made one last attempt to assert his independence. He was at once deposed, and the Khedive Tewfik, a more amenable personage, reigned in his stead. And it was just as well for Tewfik that he was prepared to be amenable; for he was only nominally the ruler of Egypt. The real government was the Dual Control, whereby England managed the receipts and France the expenditures of Egypt, with the other Powers watching this uneasy alliance from the sidelines. Arabi Pasha, an Egyptian army officer of *fellah* origins, had also been watching, and at last, in 1882, he judged the time ripe to lead a revolt against this foreign domination. France would not stir against the revolutionaries; and so, while a conference of Ambassadors vaguely discussed the crisis in Constantinople, an English fleet bombarded Alexandria, and an English army crushed the aspirations of Arabi at Tel-el-Kebir. Lord Granville then issued a circular note, declaring that the Dual Control was now at an end; that England had assumed all responsibility for the maintenance of order in Egypt; and that all existing conventions, protocols, and decrees would be respected. He also said that English troops would leave Egypt as soon as their task was completed; a statement which, strange to say, did not reassure the other Powers.

It was this last statement, none the less, which—by begging the question of an outright protectorate—revealed the chink in England's armor. Mr. Gladstone had been caught, once more, in the toils of his own conscience. He realized that the origins of the occupation were shameful; that wherever one turned, one was faced with the sordid and unappeasable specter of Ismail's debts. He believed, too, in the principle of the independence of small nations; it was one of his favorite pronouncements. And yet he knew that if he failed to crush Arabi, he would bring down upon his own head and that of his party a political storm which might be the end of them. He therefore adopted what was, for him, a characteristic course—he advanced upon Egypt looking the other way.

As a result, two incompatible forces emerged and faced each other across the prostrate form of the Khedive Tewfik. On the one hand, there was the Financial Adviser, an Englishman who, while he held no portfolio in the Egyptian Government, had to give his consent to all financial decisions. Since most important acts of government involve some financial questions, it can readily be seen that the Egyptian Government was at the mercy of the Financial Adviser. Behind this functionary there loomed, in undefined majesty, the powerful figure of the British Consul-General.

On the other hand, Mr. Gladstone's reluctance to put Egypt directly under the protection of England had brought about a corresponding increase in the stature of the Caisse de la Dette. The relations between the Egyptian Government and the Caisse de la Dette were, to say the least, intricate. The bond between them was an ingenious piece of legislation known as the Law of Liquidation. By this law the Egyptian Government was "authorized" to spend a certain sum; the rest of its revenues was to go to the Caisse, for the service of the debt. Thus the Government was expected to keep its expenditures within a purely arbitrary limit; a preposterous situation. Should the receipts fall below the authorized expenditure, the Caisse made up the difference out of its surplus; should the Government—as was more likely—exceed the authorized expenditure, it was expected to come to a ruinous agreement with the Caisse. The Law of Liquidation was modified in 1885, but even then the Government was obliged to find £E2 for every £E1 that it spent in excess of its limit.

Nor was this all. If the Government wished to float a loan

or relieve taxation, it was obliged to go cap in hand to the Caisse. And so—while Egypt itself, as a semi-independent entity, ceased to exist—its English masters were themselves bound hand and foot by the complicated treaty rights of other powers and by the Caisse which represented them. Under these circumstances, efficient administration was difficult; and, with a hostile majority in the Caisse, it might become more than difficult; it might become impossible. This is where Bismarck tiptoes into the picture.

The Imperial Chancellor in the early '80's might almost have been said to control the European balance of power. Russia and Austria had made him the mediator of their interminable disputes; Italy had placed herself under the protection of Berlin; and it was with German backing that France, in 1881, obtained the protectorate of Tunis. England had broken with France in 1882, and she, too, looked for German support in her attempt to run the affairs of Egypt. It was an astonishing situation. Bismarck had, as it were, merely to lift an eyebrow, and his obedient allies in Austria would immediately cast their vote against England in the Caisse; while in any larger gathering on the subject of Egyptian finances the voice of Germany—speaking now on this side, now on that—seemed to have the last word. When Sir Evelyn Baring groaned that the center of gravity for Egypt was not to be found in Cairo but in Berlin, he was hardly exaggerating. Even when the Law of Liquidation was modified in England's favor in the London Convention of 1885, this concession was accompanied by two highly significant gestures: Mr. Gladstone would not let England guarantee the whole of a new loan to Egypt, and a German and a Russian were added to the four original members of the Caisse de la Dette.

And so, when the Liberal Government yielded to German demands in Africa, it was partly from hesitation that it yielded, and partly because these demands were enforced by German interference with the finances of Egypt. The English, it is true, did not take Germany's excursion into Africa very seriously; their attention was absorbed by French expansion in Northern Africa and in Indo-China and towards the mouth of the Congo. Yet there was something ominous —some presage of the storm that still hung and gathered, unseen, beyond the horizon—in the manner in which the Germans had achieved their ends. For where Egypt was concerned, England was peculiarly sensitive.

Bismarck had no real desire for a colonial empire. The drift of his thought was political not economic. But, just as he had achieved the unification of Germany by diverting the German mind with a series of dazzling exploits, so now—in the period of consolidation, when wars were neither necessary nor desirable—an occasional adventure was called for. Domestic affairs were far from settled. The disastrous outcome of the *Kulturkampf;* the disintegration of the National Liberals; the rise of Social Democracy—all these were threats to the Chancellor's rule.

He knew that Germany must not be allowed to brood over the loss of her political liberties. It was for this reason that he went into Africa, for this reason that he permitted the press to thunder against England, for this reason, above all, that he instituted his social reforms. He never foresaw the consequences of the protective policies which he had initiated in 1879: to the end of his life, he thought of Germany as a "satiated" power—the arbitress of Europe, not the ruler of the world.

It was here that he lost his grip upon the German Empire. The signs were as yet almost imperceptible, but they existed, for those who cared to look. Bismarck could not or would not see that German maneuvers in Africa might represent, not merely a political diversion, but the beginnings of a search for ores and phosphates and for savage consumers of cheap German goods. After the successes of 1884-5, he seemed willing enough to drop the subject of German colonial ambitions; but his official mouthpiece, the *Kölnische Zeitung*, which had been abusing England as a part of his campaign, refused to keep quiet. Unaccountably, without his permission, against his wishes, it continued to abuse England. The expanding energies of German industry rippled, like a tide, about his feet; and the tide was rising fast.

V

While these political adventures were taking place, one can observe, in a less spectacular region, the quiet beginnings of the clash between England and Germany.

In spite of the enchantments of the Golden Jubilee, England in the '80's was far from being as solid as she could have wished. No sooner had she recovered from the great slump of the later '70's, than another depression set in in the middle '80's, and this was followed by yet another in the early '90's. The reason for this was not clear at the time. Some commentators seemed to think that a shortage of gold was at the bottom of the trouble; others declared that foreign competition and foreign tariff policies were to blame. Both these causes were present in the depressions, but neither was the chief one. The fact was that the world, the economic world, was growing every day—in the development of new countries, in the powers of production, in dramatically improved transport; and it was not able to accomplish this growth at an even pace. No plan existed to observe the due relativity of one thing to another; everything went by fits and starts. It was not surprising, therefore, that these maladjustments should cause depressions; or that the depressions, in that planless world economy, should grow more serious with each recurrence.

If English thinkers were also inclined to believe that the depressions were a sign, not of growth, but of contraction, that was due to a change which had taken place in England's economic position. She no longer held what amounted to the manufacturing monopoly of the world; she had become merely the leader among a group of industrial nations, and her leadership was being threatened every year. Since her economic progress was accompanied by immense dislocations and distresses at home, and by an intensified competition abroad, it was only natural that some people should urge the dangerous remedy of an increased imperialism, and that they should get a hearing. Professor Seeley's book, *The Expansion of England*, the first argument in favor of an imperial protective policy, obtained a wide and enthusiastic following. Among others, the Empress Frederick, incensed by German colonial ambitions, was much struck by it. "How I wish, dear Mamma," she wrote to the Queen, "that you would read that *admirable* little book." The Queen, however, does not seem to have become one of Seeley's public.

It was to allay such ideas as those of Seeley that Lord Salisbury, on returning to power in 1885, decided to create a Royal Commission to Inquire into the Depression of Trade and Industry. The Commission's chief duty was to come out in favor of Free Trade; and in a report published in 1887 the majority of its members obediently did so. Its other duty was to divert public attention from the internal effects of the depression; it looked around for an interesting topic; and in Germany it found one. The competition of German industrialists and traders was, it said, particularly severe. "In the production of commodities we have now, few, if any, advantages over them; and in a knowledge of the markets of the world, a desire to accommodate themselves to local tastes or idiosyncrasies, a determination to obtain a footing wherever they can, and a tenacity in maintaining it, they appear to be gaining ground upon us."

It is only fair to the Commission to say that it did not originate these apprehensions; they had been familiar to the public ever since Germany had gone over to Protection in 1879. None the less, in the last clauses of the sentence quoted above, the Commissioners had once more activated a figure—partly factual, partly imaginary—who was apt to haunt the imagination of English industry and commerce. This was the German salesman, an earnest and diligent person. Wherever one looked, in any corner of the world, there he seemed to be, with his cropped hair and his pink face, his high collars and his formal clothes; and his eyes gleaming from behind his thick spectacles. He sold rice in Lisbon and cheap hardware in Madrid; one found him extending generous credits in

Odessa, and offering to take all sorts of risks in Bucharest; he studied the needs of impecunious peoples in Russia and Asia and Latin America; he carried jewelry and lamps to Tunis. He never refused an order however small. Often he worked for almost nothing; not merely to educate himself, but to benefit the Fatherland, for he was the fruit of many years of triumphant bureaucracy. His goods were often shoddy and his methods were appalling: he dealt in pirated trade marks (his cutlery, for example, often bore the deceptive word "Sheffield"), and false marks of origin. For he seemed to believe, with Bismarck, that the means—even faked cutlery—justified the end.

There was a certain amount of truth in this picture. The intensity of the German salesman was certainly due to the belief that he was serving his country as well as his firm; while his vigor seemed to reflect the impetuous and compulsive nature of German industry. For German industry was growing a little too fast. Too many enterprises were founded on advances from banks; too many great industrial and financial companies were inflating their share and debenture capital so much that any slackening of production would have spelled disaster. Meanwhile, since two-thirds of the population was now living upon wages earned in factories and workshops, the Government became more and more directly involved; and it was upon an elaborate system of private and state support that German industry was built, until the whole nation was pulled into its interests. With its provocative tariffs, with its need to manufacture goods from foreign raw materials and semi-finished products, and the necessity for paying for these imports with more and yet more exports, Germany—a great militarist nation—became inextricably bound up with the world market. Eager, disciplined, shrewd, chauvinistic, and ubiquitous, the German salesman seemed to embody all the phases of this situation.

The rivalries of English and German industry were not, in the 1880's, extreme; indeed, they did not become so until after 1900. England was still far in the lead. But the fact remained that England was being attacked more severely each year. Secure—too secure—in her financial leadership, in the supremacy of her merchant shipping, in the enormous total volume of her national export, she clung to the antiquated methods of the mid-Victorian era. Her salesmen sniffed at little orders; her manufacturers did not study the poorer markets. Credits were inelastic, and the use of English weights and measures bewildered and irritated the users of the metric system. Meanwhile, she was being ousted from the markets of Europe; and her metals and textiles, the mightiest branches—the very root, even—of her industry and trade, were being attacked not only in Europe but all over the world. Germany's output of pig iron, her production of steel and coal, her consumption of wool and cotton increased by leaps and bounds. At the same time, entrenched behind their tariffs, German producers began to encroach upon the open markets of England: iron and steel goods, chemicals, textiles, paper, glass, china poured in impertinent profusion across the North Sea; and raw and refined sugar, the product of German beets, undercut the British refiners of West India cane. It was still, to be sure, only a threat, no more; the English public frowned a little vaguely and thought of other things; and even those who were better informed were consoled by the fact that Germany was—and was likely to remain—far and away the best customer of England and her empire.

Yet even here there was a counterbalancing consideration. In order to offset this unfavorable trade balance, Germany was beginning to increase her merchant marine. And she was doing this by means of heavy subsidies—a method which, to the English mind, was only a little less reprehensible than the faking of trade-marks. All over the world, in Black Sea ports and the Atlantic ports of the United States and Africa; in the Pacific ports of Latin America; in the harbors of Cape Colony, the East Indies, and Australia; in the romantic wharfs of the Pacific Islands and the Asiatic Far East—German shipping appeared in increasing numbers. It did not as yet equal British shipping; but that was not the point. The point was that this sort of thing was beginning to have an adverse effect upon the British re-export business, and that vast English warehouses, once filled with silks and spices and all the tribute of the East, were being slowly emptied, and would never be filled again.

Prince Bismarck found no difficulty at all about fitting these as yet unimportant rivalries into his scheme of things. The African quarrel, the trade expansion—a little cloud, a rising tide—seemed to him to be no more than incidental effects in a process which he believed inevitable—the closer union of England with Germany. As his mind ranged over the European scene he saw there, too, a reassuring picture: the balance of animosities, the thrust and counter-thrust of interests and antipathies. Nor was there in Germany itself anyone to dispute his pre-eminence. Frederick was dead, William was his pupil. The aristocracy had learned who was its master. The great industrialists, surely, were on his side: had he not given them a protective tariff? As for the socialists, a vociferous and increasing group, he knew how to deal with them. From that portentous day when, in 1875, the disciples of Karl Marx wrested the leadership from the disciples of Lassalle at Gotha, he had determined to crush them: and in a law, passed in 1879, he possessed the instrument with which to do it. All was well.

And yet how true were the splendid generalizations of ancient tragedy! To every great man at last may come the time when, through some violent act of his own, the large verdict of Fate will be pronounced upon him. It no longer occurred to Bismarck that he would fall, that he would be dismissed; he saw himself as retiring in the fullness of time and handing the reins of Government over to some person of his own choice. The reins of Government! He had grown so accustomed to pulling savagely on them, and cursing, and cracking the whip! The occasional remonstrances of William I, jolting, in phlegmatic majesty, in the coach behind, had been—he was willing to admit it—a valuable check upon him. But William I had shown no disposition to leave the coach and climb upon the box: and William II ought to be just as amenable.

For the rude old coachman there was now a rude awakening. Suddenly, in the winter of 1889-90, William showed a desire to seize the reins for himself. Bismarck brushed the young man aside: if the Emperor wished to dabble in world politics, let him learn from *him*—from him, who had been a public man before William was born. There were violent scenes in the palace. William wished to give Austria more support in the Balkans; Bismarck, who saw in this a threat to the delicate maturing of his Reinsurance Treaty, angrily disagreed and supported, with oaths, the claims of Russia. On the question of the socialists, they were also at odds; for Bismarck wished to deal a final blow to these obstreperous people, and William, who was momentarily in a progressive state of mind, was anxious to soothe and even to encourage them. The Chancellor raged and threatened to resign—a threat which, he thought in his pride, would certainly bring the Emperor to heel: and William appeared to yield. He needed Bismarck's support in order to get certain military votes through the Reichstag. For a little while longer, he endured the Chancellor's tyranny; and then, summoning all his courage, on March 17, 1890, he dismissed him.

The fall of Bismarck astonished the world. And yet—it is very strange—in the comments of the German press one can detect, amidst the formal compliments to the Emperor, a note of relief. The architect of the German Empire was gone and the Germans, actually, were a little glad. It is easy to understand the happiness of Ministers, who might now become something more than just the agents of Bismarck's will; it is easy, too, to appreciate the satisfied malice of courtiers like Waldersee. As for the public at large, it was not unnatural for it to experience a certain pleasure in the mere fact of change. But none of these things can quite account for the apparent ingratitude of Germany. Why was the country glad at the Chancellor's departure? The reason was an exceedingly complex one, but it can be simply stated. Bismarck was old-fashioned; he was beginning to become a dead weight upon enterprise; he stood for a policy of consolidation: and Germany meant to expand.

Thus William II was launched upon the very tide which

had engulfed the Chancellor. He did not, of course, see himself as the symbol of a rising force in German economy. His actions after his *coup d'état* were, indeed, such as to make one think that he was sailing against the tide. He acquiesced with joy in Lord Salisbury's scheme to exchange the island of Heliogoland for Zanzibar, Witu, and Somaliland. The exchange seemed to favor England; it might almost be said to have undone the work of 1884-5. In return for an island which, when fortified, would protect the Kiel Canal, England had obtained a long stretch of coast north of German East Africa, and vague miles of *hinterland* reaching back to the sources of the Nile. This was a peaceful move; but then— there is no doubt of it—William desired peace. He sought peace, as the Psalmist advised; but he did not follow the rest of the Psalmist's advice; he did not ensue peace. His susceptibility to influences and his craving for personal aggrandizement dragged him helplessly in the other direction; and the forces which had overthrown Bismarck swept him, also, away.

He saw his triumph over Bismarck in a purely personal light. He was now the Master; he had emerged victorious from a dramatic duel in the very secret places of Government. But dramas must be staged and timed: and it was noticed, as an odd and perhaps not a fortuitous coincidence, that Bismarck's downfall took place on the very eve of a visit to Berlin by the Prince of Wales and his younger son, Prince George.

The Kaiser William received his uncle with every honor; he treated him almost as if he were a sovereign. None the less, amidst all the excitement and exaltation that possessed him, there were doubts. The drama had been more than successful—he had stepped forth, apparent Emperor, before the eyes of the very relative whom he most desired to impress —but how was he to explain his motives? As usual, he could not make up his mind: he veered wildly from one explanation to another. He told Queen Victoria that Bismarck had been dismissed because his health had broken down, because his life would have been endangered if he had remained longer in office: and that, when the Chancellor came to say good-by, "we parted under tears and after a warm embrace." To Sir Edward Malet, the British Ambassador, he gave quite another version. He poured into Sir Edward's astonished ears a story of terrible paroxysms of wrath, of times when he almost thought that his Chancellor was about to hurl an inkstand at his head. Bismarck was on the verge of apoplexy, of insanity even: he had to go. Of the two versions, the latter seemed, on the whole, to be nearer the truth. When Bismarck lunched on the 26th with Malet, Lord Londonderry and other gentlemen of the Prince's suite, he was clearly neither apoplectic nor insane; but his language was fearful.

The Queen, the Empress Frederick and the Prince had for some years been united upon one point: they all distrusted and feared Prince Bismarck. And yet—now that the old tyrant had gone—they could almost wish to see him back again. They had grown used to him. As soon as the Prince had a free moment, he hurried off to see the ex-Chancellor. Bismarck— a snarling old man, standing upon the threshold of the last and least dignified stage of his incredible career—received his visitor with eagerness. For a long hour, he abused William; and the Prince listened with grave attention—he rather prided himself as a *raconteur*—and with a particular relish for Bismarck's expletives.

It was most unlikely that in any capital, especially Berlin, such an interview would pass unnoticed. By one means or another, every detail was reported to William, with additions and embellishments. The Emperor—convinced that his uncle was a sinister mischief-maker—trembled with fear and fury. And, indeed, to permit a courtesy call to take on the nature of a confabulation was not very tactful of the Prince. But then the Prince was not the man to forgive a slight; as friends who presumed too far learned to their cost: and he had by no means forgotten his undignified exit from Vienna.

VI

The Kaiser waited for more than a year before he was given a chance—an unlooked for, a splendid chance—to have his revenge. . . .

The details of the Tranby Croft scandal, so bitterly discussed at the time, require no more than a summary relation. The Prince was staying, for the St. Leger meeting of 1890, at Tranby Croft, near Doncaster, the home of a new friend of his, a Mr. Arthur Wilson, shipowner of Hull. He proposed to play baccarat during the evenings, and had brought a box of counters with him, ranging in value from five shillings to ten pounds. "Whist is slow," wrote the poet, "but baccarat bites, baccarat bites and we want to be bit." On the first evening, Mr. A. S. Wilson, the son of the house, thought that he had detected his neighbor on his right in the act of employing an ingenious device known as *la poussette*. That is to say, if the cards were good he pushed more counters across the white line, under cover of his hand; if the cards were bad, he withdrew some counters. This neighbor was Sir William Gordon Cumming, a Colonel in the Scots Guards. Mr. Wilson waited until the play was over, and then he informed his mother, his sister, his brother-in-law, and his other neighbor, a subaltern in Sir William's regiment. On the next evening, therefore, five people watched Sir William; and all agreed that the infatuated colonel had once more made use of *la poussette*. What were they to do?

The Prince, who was banker, had noticed nothing. The other members of the party, which included General Owen Williams, Lord Coventry, and Mr. Reuben Sassoon, were also in the dark. Under these circumstances, it might have been wiser if the five observers had said nothing at all. Putting all considerations of caution or wisdom aside, however, they informed Lord Coventry and General Williams; and Lord Coventry and General Williams told the Prince.

At this point, there was only one thing to be done. General Williams and the Prince should have obeyed the Queen's Regulations (No. 41), which insisted that an officer accused of dishonorable conduct must face a court of inquiry. They seem to have believed that such a course would lead to scandal; and so they summoned Sir William who, after passionately denying the charge, agreed to sign a paper, promising never again to play cards for money. The other signatories, among whom was the Prince, bound themselves never to disclose the story of what had happened at Tranby Croft.

The circumstances which lead up to the scandalous *dénouement* of the Tranby Croft Case have never been perfectly

303

clear. It has been said that the Prince told his current mistress, a lady whose identity is not relevant to this history, and that she let her tongue wag, too. For some time afterwards, in any case, she was known as "The Babbling B——." On the other hand, in a letter to Mrs. Arthur Paget, the Prince seems to suggest that Sir William had broken his agreement, and had been playing "B. at Paris." But whether Sir William began to play baccarat because the story had leaked out, or whether the story leaked out because he had begun to play baccarat, will never be certain. What is certain, however, is that the scandal assumed such proportions that Sir William sued his five original accusers for libel. The case was tried in June, 1891; and since Sir William's counsel was Sir Edward Clarke, who believed in the innocence of his client and had a persuasive tongue, it is just possible that even the evidence of the signed paper would not have convinced the jury. One of the witnesses was the Prince; and as he prepared to leave the witness-box, after a tactful handling, a juryman asked him a direct question. Did he or did he not believe that Sir William was guilty of cheating? The Prince replied that the evidence of five witnesses gave him no choice. A verdict for the defense was the inevitable consequence.

As soon as the case was over, there was a great flare-up in the Press—a final revivification of all that was laborious and respectable in the Victorian age. *The Times* lamented, in a leading article, the gambling habits of the Prince. The radical newspapers, the Church press, thundered day in and day out. Mr. W. T. Stead thought up a device called "The Prayer Gauge," which reckoned up the number of times that the Prayer for the Prince of Wales had been recited in the churches of the Establishment; the result of these orisons being a card scandal. Another gentleman investigated the Prince's activities during the year 1890, and discovered that in the course of nine months he had attended thirty plays, twenty-eight race meetings, and forty social fixtures, as against forty-five official functions and eleven attendances on the cross benches at the Lords. A German newspaper published a cartoon which depicted the Prince of Wales's feathers above the great door at Windsor, and under the feathers was not the historical motto "Ich Dien," but the words "Ich Deal."

The attack was far from insincere. It expressed in its rather venomous and excitable way the genuine distress of a considerable section of the public. Gambling was reprehensible; but for a member of the royal family to gamble in the house of a shipowner of Hull—that was unbearable. It was not the Prince's habits alone that caused offense, but his friends as well. This latter consideration took the form of a piece of reverse gossip: it was stated everywhere that Mr. Wilson, unused to the ways of expensive society, had not wished to have baccarat played in his house, but that the Prince had insisted. This tale was foolish and untrue, but it was somewhat deadly.

The Prince wrote a disingenuous letter to the Archbishop of Canterbury to protest his horror of gambling. "I consider that gambling," he said, "like intemperance, is one of the greatest curses with which a country could be afflicted." The Archbishop, who of course had heard of that box of counters, replied with a humble but scarcely feasible suggestion that this protestation ought to be made public. And there the matter ended.

Indeed, neither excuse nor expostulation would have served.

The animosities of 1871 were flickering, briefly but intensely, into life: and this time the Queen did not share her son's unpopularity. Her subjects viewed her through a haze of adoration. Everything about her, her long hours of work, her rigid standards—the fact that no divorced lady was allowed near her court, that even widows who had married a second time were frowned upon—what a shining contrast it all made to the disreputability of her son! The Queen, to be sure, shared these opinions. For the past few years, she had drawn much closer to the Prince; but now she took her pen in hand and sent him one of her most tremendous wiggings. He sighed; it was perhaps no more than he deserved. But then there arrived another missive from a far less acceptable quarter.

For the Emperor William, unable to resist this god-given opportunity, also took his pen in hand. In a long letter he expatiated upon the necessity of good behavior in royal circles, upon the evils of gambling, and above all upon the evils of gambling with subalterns. This lecture was the last straw. The Prince read it, and flung off in a rage to Homburg, where he remained buried for several weeks.

After such a letter, it was most improbable that the uncle and the nephew would be able to settle their personal differences. They met as infrequently as possible; and whenever they did so, there was trouble. In 1893, for example, William II arrived at Cowes with a new yacht, the *Meteor II*. On the evening after his arrival, he dined on board the Prince's yacht, and during the course of the dinner Sir Henry Ponsonby, the Queen's secretary, appeared with a decoded telegram which he had brought from Osborne. It contained momentous news. The English dispute with France over a French occupation of territory bordering upon Siam had suddenly flared up and seemed about to lead to war. When the Prince read it, his face fell; he handed the telegram to William; and William, slapping his uncle on the back, declared, with a loud laugh, that he would soon be seeing active service in India. There was a dead silence, and then the party broke up.

The Siamese crisis died down as swiftly as it had arisen. The Prince's *Britannia* and the Emperor's *Meteor II* raced for the Queen's Cup which, much to the nephew's glee and the consequent irritation of the uncle, the *Meteor* won handily. On board the *Britannia* that day was Count Philip von Eulenburg, the imperial Minister in Munich. A large, plump, fair man, of a jealous temperament and a malicious disposition, the Count was William's closest friend. Their relationship was of a highly confidential and romantic nature. William addressed the Count with the familiar "Du"; the Count sent William a dagger, engraved with the words *Das Leben ohne Freut ist wohl ein Traurigkeit,* and said that it was right for his imperial master to "stab anyone with it who disturbs our joy." William was in many respects a singularly innocent man, and he never seems to have realized that Eulenburg's relationships with other people might not always be of a spiritual nature. At last, there was a tremendous scandal; the Count's friendships became the sport of the gutter press; and William, in horror, banished the offending Eulenburg forever from his presence.

In 1893, however, Eulenburg was in high favor. He was not the man to make the mistake of praising the Prince; and in his Diary, he sets down a record of their conversation that day. The Prince touched upon the Czar's dislike of "my nephew Willy"; he belittled William's colonial ambitions; abused the German Ambassador, Count Hatzfeldt; and, in short, made himself as unpleasant as could be. Now, it is possible, but not very likely that the Prince—knowing that Eulenburg was malicious and that he had the Emperor's ear—would have committed himself to such an extent. And so one is faced with these alternatives: either the Diary contains a true record of what was said, or else it simply repeats the version with which the inventive Eulenburg regaled his master. Taking everything into consideration, the latter alternative is the more probable one.

The belief that his uncle was a mischief-maker, fostered during this visit to Cowes, was richly nourished by certain events which took place during the winter of 1894. That summer, as it happened, there had been a slight *rapprochement*. The Kaiser, who prided himself upon the few Stuart corpuscles that might still be said to linger in his blood, wished to be made honorary Colonel of a Highland regiment. He confided this ambition to Colonel Swayne, military attaché to the Berlin Embassy; and at the same time wrote to the Queen, asking her if she would allow him to place Uncle Bertie *à la suite* of the Queen's Own Prussian Dragoons. The Prince snatched at this bait. He pressed his nephew's claims upon his mother, who disliked the whole idea, and said so. "This fishing for uniforms upon both sides," she remarked, "is most regrettable." But as the Queen's reluctance increased, the Prince no less steadily raised his demands. He now began to talk about making his nephew a Field-Marshal. Victoria, perceiving that this little incident was becoming important, grew very agitated. She consulted

Lord Salisbury, who thought it would be a good thing to gratify the Kaiser; she consulted Lord Rosebery, who gave an opposite opinion. "What is to be done," she burst out to her secretary, "about this hateful business of Hon. General or Field-Marshal?" At length, she came to the conclusion that she could settle the whole matter by sending a present of kettledrums to her Prussian Dragoons. This solution was, to be sure, an ingenious one; but, somehow or other, it did not satisfy the Kaiser. He waited: and then, when his grandmother was due to arrive in Coburg to attend a family wedding, he dispatched a squadron of the Prussian Dragoons to greet her with a roll on the new kettledrums. The Queen at once relented. Setting aside her own wishes and the advice of Lord Rosebery, she made her grandson Honorary Colonel of the First Royal Dragoons.

The outcome of these slightly ruritanian incidents, with their echoes of the merriment of *La Grande Duchesse*, was that William for a time felt kindly towards his uncle—who was partly responsible for his belonging, as he put it, "to the thin Red Line of England." But, alas, in October a series of events cast a heavy shadow upon this faint patch of sunlight, and, indeed, extinguished it altogether. The Czar Alexander III fell seriously ill, and it was doubtful if he would outlive the month. The Czar was married to the Princess of Wales's sister, and the Czarevitch during the summer had become engaged to the Prince's niece, Alix of Hesse-Darmstadt: it was therefore quite natural that, when the Czaritza asked the Prince and Princess to join her, they should do so. They arrived at Livadia in the Crimea after the Czar's death; but they were in time to take their place on the train which, by slow and barbarous stages, was to carry the body to Moscow.

For three days the cortege, smothered in crape and studded with imperial emblems, crawled towards Central Russia; three times it halted while the priests chanted their intercessions for the dead; at every station, as it rumbled slowly through, crowds of peasants fell upon their knees in prayer. At night it would draw up at some wayside halt, and as it stood there, black and forbidding and surrounded by guards, people swarmed out of the countryside, and knelt for hours in the frost. At Moscow, there was a state service in the Archangel Church. At St. Petersburg the eleven days' journey ended with a tremendous interment in the Cathedral of St. Peter and St. Paul.

The Prince joined punctiliously in every part of that ceremonious journey: at the conclusion of which he stood for hours, clutching a candle, while the indefatigable ecclesiastics of the Orthodox Church sang their interminable requiems. Then, suddenly, the Russian court threw off its semi-Asiatic gloom; the lights and the diamonds blazed once more; the music swelled; the bare shoulders, the fantastic uniforms bowed in obeisance or whirled in the dance. According to the laws of the Russian Church no marriage could be celebrated between Christmas and Easter; the mourning had therefore been suspended for a week; and, amidst appropriate festivities, Czar Nicholas II was married to the Princess Alix in the chapel of the Winter Palace. After his unaccustomed religious exercises, the Prince was in his element; and before the time came to say good-by, the new Czar had grown, it was observed, quite fond of his English uncle.

The Kaiser watched all this with a jealous and suspicious eye. It was true, of course, that the English Government welcomed a chance to make a friendly gesture towards Russia, and saw in the Prince the very person most equipped to make it. Lord Rosebery, Sir William Harcourt, the Liberal and Conservative Press all congratulated him on having done much for the cause of peace; and these congratulations were by no means insincere. At the same time, the relations of Germany and Russia were somewhat obscure. The fall of Bismarck had produced one effect: the Reinsurance Treaty was not renewed, and Russia was slowly drifting towards France. Perhaps this was not William's fault: the geographical dispensations of the Congress of Berlin had made a clash between Russia and Germany in the Balkans almost inevitable, and the Congress of Berlin was the work of Bismarck and Disraeli. Could it be that England was now trying to unite with France and Russia? William did not think so. Anglo-French relations had never been more strained; while every mile between the Adriatic and India testified to the enmity between England and Russia. But then, just as he reached this reassuring conclusion, other thoughts, of a more personal nature, asserted themselves. He was always inclined to put too much emphasis upon the influence of royal persons; nor could he ever quite distinguish between personal slights and international maneuvers. His uncle's success in St. Petersburg filled him with alarm: but how much more sinister was the fact that Nicholas II, on his wedding day, had been made Colonel-in-Chief of the Scots Greys. A Scots regiment! Nicky, who was just a relation by marriage, and had no Scots blood, had been granted a favor for which he, William, had begged in vain! There could be no doubt about where the responsibility lay. It was all his Uncle Bertie's doing; his Uncle Bertie was trying to entice Russia into a friendship with England; was setting in train—that was it, there could no longer be any question about it—nothing less than the encirclement of Germany.

Henceforth, William II began to think of his uncle as a sort of inferior Mephistopheles, suddenly materializing in places where he could do most harm, and disappearing, not with a peal of demoniac laughter and a smell of brimstone, but with a fat chuckle and the fragrance of a rich cigar.

It was not until 1896, with his famous telegram to President Kruger, that William's animosities took on a political form. Up to that time, they had been confined to the lesser realm of jealousies and rudenesses; they had been little more than a quarrel with an uncle who, to be sure, had not shown any inclination to make friends. The exchanges were, on the whole, in the uncle's favor: when William asked the Prince, to his face, whether he had ever seen service in the field, or spoke of him in the presence of some English guests as "the old peacock," the Prince's riposte was of a quieter but more effective kind. He began to use the words "my illustrious nephew"; speaking in solemn tones, and with a broad wink.

From 1896 onwards, the signs of an approaching Anglo-German catastrophe were more and more evident. They showed themselves, not merely in the chancellery but in the trade press, not merely in Whitehall but in *The Hardware Journal*. In 1896, that prosaic but far from negligible publication complained of the "pushing, indomitable growth" of German rivalry; and in the same year, Ernest Williams' *Made in Germany*, a short, spicy, and alarming account of the effects of German progress upon English industry, was anxiously read by large numbers of excited persons. In 1897, public attention seems to have turned towards American progress; but on September 11, *The Saturday Review*, in a strangely prophetic mood, once more reverted to the topic of Germany. "In the Transvaal, at the Cape, in Central Africa," it intoned, "in India and the East, in the islands of the Southern Sea, and in the far Northwest . . . the German and the Englishman are struggling to be first. A million petty disputes build up the greatest cause of war the world has ever seen." In 1898, with the first German Navy Bill, the two countries drew apart at an increasing speed; in 1899, there was a great shipping scare; and in 1900, when the second German Navy Bill gave an ominous significance to German sympathy for the Boers, even the optimism of Joseph Chamberlain was forced to concede that the misunderstanding between the two countries was rapidly becoming complete.

But between 1889 and 1894—between the Vienna incident and its culmination in the marriage festivities of Czar Nicholas II—Anglo-German relations still loomed, an ambiguous mountain, among the fluctuations of world politics. There was an occasional rumble and a puff of smoke: but that was all. During this period the uncle and the nephew take on, as it were, the character of portents; and portents, even small portents, have their place in history. It is not through what they thought and did, but through what their thoughts and deeds anticipated, that the two men struggle together into a singular prominence: quarreling upon the summit of an awakening volcano.

Chapter Nine

EDWARD VII: 1901

ON JANUARY 22, 1901, Queen Victoria died. She had been lingering for several days, insensible and silent, with her family around her; while farther and yet farther away, across England and throughout the Empire, people waited, in astonishment and grief, for the impossible news.

During the last years of her life, the Queen had been much changed and softened: by age; by sorrow—she had wept over the death of children and grandchildren and friends; and by something very different from either—by happiness. Her daily and hourly remembrance of Albert remained with her, but it was no longer so intensely poignant; and as that strange domination passed away from her life, her pleasure in living— which, before Albert's death, had been one of her predominant characteristics—no less steadily returned. It showed itself in a hundred vivid and affectionate ways, but not least in a sense of community with the nation. When, at the conclusion of the Diamond Jubilee celebrations, she flashed this message around the Empire: "From my heart, I thank my beloved people"—she meant every word of it. She had forgotten the miserable days when, so it seemed, the English had shown themselves cold and unsympathetic towards the

memory of Albert—when they had complained of her grief—
when her mourning had repelled them: she simply felt that
she belonged to her people and they to her. How this could
be, she did not bother to inquire: it was enough that it was
so. Nor was this sense of community merely a question of
affection on the one side and of almost superstitious venera-
tion on the other: it manifested itself in a more definite way.
It had become customary with Ministers of late, when faced
with some knotty problem, to say, "Let's take the Queen's
opinion": for they had discovered that the Queen's opinion
invariably coincided with that of the English public. The
Queen, on her side, became less exacting in her relations with
Ministers: and those who study her correspondence over the
last decade of her life will discover that, though in some
respects—in her antipathy to Mr. Gladstone, for example—she
did not unbend, in general she was apt to interfere less with
affairs of State. The stupendous work continued—the meticulous examination of boxes, the signing of papers—but it was
conducted with a moderation unknown in the dark years of
her widowhood or the vehement days when Albert was
alive and she was Albert's voice.

Those most intimately connected with her, in the last
decade of her reign, came completely under her spell. After
the death of Leopold I, she had become head of the Coburg
family, with its intricate European ramifications: but now
she was no longer satisfied with family matters. She showed
an eager interest in the private affairs of her ladies and even,
it has been said, of the palace domestics. And yet, at the
same time, even while she charmed and conquered those
who had anything to do with her, there was not one who
did not stand in tremendous awe of Victoria. An infringe-

ment of etiquette—unpunctuality—an indecorous remark—
produced a terrible metamorphosis in that kind, aristocratic,
and managing old lady. The eyes began to protrude, the
mouth to turn down at the corners: the Queen was displeased. Those who experienced the displeasure of Victoria
never afterwards, to their dying day, forgot it.

The public at large had, of course, no very clear notion of
Victoria's personality. To them she had become England.
They felt that as long as she was reigning over them no violent change or irreparable disaster could overtake them.
There is a story told about her which seems exactly to illus-
trate the spirit which endeared her to the nation. In the early
days of the Boer War, when English generals were losing
battles with a unanimous persistence, one of her Ministers,
during the course of an audience, let fall some discouraging
remarks. The Queen was up in arms at once. "There is no
one depressed in *this* house," she said. "We are not interested in the possibilities of defeat; they do not exist." In that
speech, with its odd mingling of Queen Elizabeth and Jane
Austen, stood forth the Queen whom England found most
admirable: an indomitable woman. Yet her indomitability
did not show itself only in her speech; it stood forth in
another and equally admired respect. She was very old. Her
enormous reign stretched backwards into what, for most of
her subjects, was an era more ancient than antiquity, the era
just preceding their own. Her life was more than a page or
a chapter; it was a whole book of English history. She had
not, it is true, grasped the meaning of half the momentous
events that had taken place during her reign; but this notion,
if it ever occurred to her subjects, would have seemed no

more than appropriate. They saw in her the embodiment of qualities more to their taste than were subtlety or intelligence: she was commonsense, solidity, respectability, anointed and crowned. The fact that she had not changed in any important respect was what gave her her unique importance. Permanence, impermeability—was not wisdom to be found there? Yes, and something more than wisdom. As long as Victoria lived, Time itself . . . the undiscriminating and the unpredictable, which ruined the granite column and twitched the straw from the cottage roof, and was forever hastening from the death of yesterday to the death of tomorrow . . . Time itself had become respectable, moving slowly through the long vague years. Now, in the appalled silence which followed upon her death, one could almost hear the imperceptible noises of hurry and decay once more asserting themselves. And, with Time, Mortality—so long in abeyance—came back: and the people mourned, not only for Victoria, but for themselves.

II

Such feelings are not likely to rule a vigorous nation for long. The immanence of Queen Victoria, it was only natural, became less and less apparent; and she ascended, with a certain rapidity, to the more transcendental spheres of memory. As for the machine of the state, it had to be set in motion—even in the few days in which the Queen had not been able to discharge her duties, a great pile of work had mounted upon her desk, a pathetic reminder of that vanished industry. On the day after her death, the new King traveled up to London, to attend a meeting of the Privy Council at St.

317

James's Palace. Here he gave a brief and impromptu speech which, since there was no short-hand reporter present, had afterwards to be reconstructed from the impeccable memory of Lord Rosebery. It was a felicitous speech, but in one particular only was it significant: the King said that he would take the title of Edward VII.

Thus the last thread which still hung between himself and his father was snapped, and shriveled away into the dust. The Queen had always supposed that he would take the title of Albert Edward. "It would be *impossible* for you to *drop* your father's [name]," she had written some years before. "It would be *monstrous*, and *Albert alone* would *not* do." The Prince had replied with a vague expostulation. "Albert Edward," he said, had a foreign sound, like Victor Emmanuel and Louis Napoleon, and he did not commit himself to a definite promise. His new title was certainly anything but Coburg: and his successors have followed his example.

He entered upon his inheritance—it was to be expected from a man who had been waiting a long time, and who was in his sixtieth year—with a certain zest. When the Queen's body was borne across the waters from Osborne to Portsmouth, the King and the other mourners followed in a second yacht. The King noticed that the Royal Standard was flying at half-mast, and asked the reason why. "The Queen is dead, Sir," was the answer. "But the King is alive," said Edward VII briskly. And it was with the Royal Standard at full mast that he followed the Queen's body, through the lines of warships, into Portsmouth Harbor.

III

The coffin was placed on a gun carriage at Victoria, for the journey through London to Paddington. The vast and stricken crowds were silent except for a most inappropriate noise—in fact, a cheer—that greeted Lord Roberts as he rode by, fresh from his conquests in South Africa. The bands discoursed Handel and Chopin. It was a gray, cold February day.

What was left of the nineteenth century and what was left of the Queen passed together into the shadow and the dust.

The Kings of Portugal and Greece rode in the procession, and behind them among the throng of princes was the burly form of the Archduke Franz Ferdinand: all three were to be assassinated, the last at Sarajevo. Elsewhere in the procession, from the windows of a cab, beamed the King of the Belgians, the wickedest old man in Europe. Though too old and infirm to ride a horse, he was not altogether without vigor; and to solace him during his melancholy stay in London, he had brought a concubine from Belgium. Edward VII, who believed that there was a time and a place for all things, duly noted this arrangement, and the Belgian monarch never visited him again.

The King and his nephew William II rode together at the head of the kings and the princes and the generals. William was, for the moment, very popular in England. Genuinely distressed at the news of Queen Victoria's passing, he had hurried over from Germany; and for two days, he watched

319

with the family beside her bed. Once there was a flicker of consciousness, but the room for the dying Queen was thronged with memories rather than with people: and as the Kaiser leaned over her, she seems to have mistaken him for his father. That he had come so quickly to his grandmother's side seemed, to the warm-hearted English, a touching thing, and on his first arrival in London, before he drove from the station, a man came out of the crowd to his carriage and said simply, "Thank you, Kaiser." William took this as a tribute from the nation, and perhaps, in a way, it was. At any rate, he behaved very well for most of his stay. His best qualities were in evidence; he was kind, gentle, considerate; and, what was more, he and the King were able to discuss affairs without disagreement. At the time, they were both angry with the French.

And then, on the last day, at a lunch in his honor at Marlborough House, he delivered a speech. "We ought to form an Anglo-German alliance," he said, in response to the King's proposal of his health, "you to keep the seas while we would be responsible for the land; with such an alliance not a mouse could stir in Europe without our permission, and the nations would come, in time, to see the necessity of reducing their armaments."

The consternation of his Ministers, the fury of the German public was equaled in degree by the shocked surprise with which responsible English opinion greeted this extraordinary concept of the Balance of Power. But William noticed nothing. He departed in the best of humors, and for days afterwards seriously upset his officers by dining in civilian clothes. It was an English habit.

✦

The King, too, was astounded by his nephew's parting words. What could one make of William? Ever since 1896, with the Kruger telegram, his pronouncements had been of an explosive nature. In that year, when Dr. Jameson rode across the borders of the Transvaal with a few hundred men, hoping to stir up a Uitlander rebellion, there was—it was no more than could be expected—uproar in Europe. In England, too (though Joseph Chamberlain must have had some knowledge of it), this preposterous raid was generally condemned. The raiders were easily surrounded and made prisoner by some Boer commandoes; and when the news of their capture was announced in Berlin, on January 3, William II summoned an Imperial Council. His Chancellor, his Foreign Secretary, and his Colonial Secretary sat with him in one room; beyond the door, in solitude, was the Political Director of the Foreign Office, Fritz von Holstein, a bureaucrat who was, perhaps, slightly demented. One of Von Holstein's peculiarities was to introduce into the nineteenth century some of the more tortuous diplomatic methods of the sixteenth. Another was never, if he could help it, to meet the Kaiser face to face.

After opening the proceedings in a great state of excitement, William agreed that to declare a German protectorate over the Transvaal (his first proposal) might be inadvisable. What then should be done? At length, the Colonial Secretary proposed, the Foreign Secretary drafted, and William eagerly endorsed, a telegram to be sent *en clair* to President Kruger of the Transvaal. It read as follows: "I sincerely congratulate you that you and your people have succeeded, by your own energetic action and without appealing for help to friendly Powers, in restoring order against the armed bands that broke into your country as disturbers of the peace, and in safeguarding the dignity of your Government from attacks from without."

President Kruger was an old man, the unpretentious head of an unpretentious republic. When he was asked if a statue of him might be erected in the capital, he replied that he was perfectly willing, on one condition: the sculptor must carve a depression on the crown of the tophat, as a bath for birds. But, for all his endearing characteristics, there was another side to Oom Paul: he was a man of a gloomy and mystical religious habit, illiberal views, and a wiliness which, though it might do well enough in the market, was somewhat too narrow for affairs of state. When he received such a telegram, from such a source, he may have believed that he could afford to take any risk.

Elsewhere the telegram was received, in the German press with unbounded joy, in the English press with extreme anger. It was, to say the least, odd for the head of a presumably neutral state to make such a provocative gesture; for the relations between England and the Transvaal were of so peculiar a nature, the ties between the peccant Jameson, the Cape Government, and the Colonial Office so ambiguous, that to congratulate Kruger was obliquely to attack England. The Prince, in his rage, asked his mother to give William "a good snubbing"; he was deliberately stirring up bad feeling. But the Queen was wiser. Once again she decided to approach him as grandmother and as Queen; but this time the dual rôle was played in a masterly fashion. She wrote him a letter, one of the most unusual of state papers. "My dear William, As your Grandmother, to whom you have always shown so much affection and of whose example you have always

spoken with so much respect, I feel I cannot refrain from
expressing my deep regret at the telegram you sent President
Kruger. It is considered very unfriendly towards this country, which I am sure it is not intended to be, and has, I
grieve to say, made a very painful impression here. . . ."
William read these words, and experienced—as was so often
his way—a sudden revulsion of feeling. Had he gone too
far? He sent back an incoherent reply. Were not the raiders,
in effect, rebels? "Now to me Rebels against Her Most Gra-
cious Majesty the Queen are to me the most execrable beings
in the world . . ." The Queen was unmoved; but she sent
the explanation to Lord Salisbury, and it was agreed to accept it. William had been using very different language in his
communications with the Czar; and it is more than possible
that the Foreign Office was not unaware of this. But, as the
Queen put it, "sharp, cutting answers only irritate and do
harm . . . William's faults come from impetuousness (as
well as conceit); and calmness and firmness are the most
powerful weapons in such cases."

But it was not long before William II, in spite of the
Queen's application of these powerful weapons, once more
incurred the displeasure of his relatives; though this time, to
be sure, he did not do so in a public manner. The Jameson
raid was a ragged preface to a larger tale. Conditions in the
Transvaal grew more and more confused, and Alfred Milner,
as High Commissioner at the Cape, went to Bloemfontein at
the end of May, 1899, to confer with President Paul Kruger.
The situation was one which involved, not merely the internal state of the Transvaal, but the whole design of South
African relations. The Uitlanders, a group of Englishmen and
Europeans who had come into the republic in 1887 in search

of gold, and who founded Johannesburg, were being severely taxed, while at the same time they were denied the franchise. Now taxation without representation is a very bad thing: but gold-fevers do not produce the most desirable human beings; and the Uitlanders were not merely the products of a gold-fever—they were also backed by the South Africa (Chartered) Company, which controlled the territory of Rhodesia along the Transvaal border. As a further and far more sinister complication, the Company's moving spirit was Cecil Rhodes, who was also Prime Minister of Cape Colony. Such a problem, with its political and economic and ethical elements, could have been settled only by the most delicate negotiations between two very liberal-minded persons. Alfred Milner, alas, a man of an arbitrary temper, was the last person to grasp—or even to desire to grasp—the elusive workings of Kruger's mind: while Kruger, with his passion for lengthy bargaining, could make no impression upon the steely impatience of Milner. The conference broke down, and in October the South African War had begun.

Europe rightly supported the cause of the Boers, and William II, also, lent it his countenance. But William did not countenance the Boers because they were a small nation struggling to be free; he saw in them the possible contrivers of an English débacle. His biographers have noted his desire at this time for a closer union with England; and they have been inclined to describe it in two opposite ways—either as plain hypocrisy or as the pivot upon which his whole curious statecraft turned. And yet, perhaps, it cannot be made to answer to such descriptions: perhaps it was no more than a thread which, appearing and disappearing in the texture of his thoughts, gave them an unexpected color. In December,

1899, two conflicting ideas seem to have passed in turn through his excited mind: a European bloc against England; an Anglo-German alliance, with a chastened England as a kind of "naval Austria." In his indecision, he devoted himself to literary composition, and early in the new year sent his uncle, in rapid succession, two sets of aphorisms or *Gedenkensplitten*, the first of which contained some remarks upon England's perilous situation in South Africa, and suggested that she might need a friend. The Prince's acknowledgment was a little chilly. The second set of *Gedenkensplitten* was of a more menacing nature and included, not only military advice, but a hint that England would be helpless against a foreign Power. Its final, or twenty-second, aphorism was as follows: "Even the best football club, if it is beaten notwithstanding the most gallant defense, accepts finally its defeat with equanimity. Last year in the great cricket match of England *v.* Australia, the former took the victory of the latter quietly with chivalrous acknowledgement of her opponent."

This appeal to the sporting instincts, strange to say, did not produce the expected effect. In that dark and unhappy period—in the last discreditable agonies of "Splendid Isolation"—nerves were strained and sensibilities were acute. The Prince, who was no devotee of football or cricket, retorted with some heat that there was a good deal of difference between a Test Match and a war. The Kaiser was unrepentant. He wrote back to say that he was sorry to have given his uncle "umbrage"; but surely he could see that the aphorisms were dictated solely by a love for England. The Prince, who was now thoroughly exasperated, did not bother to refute this argument and, with a further brief but testy allusion to cricket, let the matter drop. Not long afterwards Sir Redvers

Buller and his colleagues, who had somehow or other confused a campaign on the veldt with maneuvers around Alder-
shot, gave way to Roberts and Kitchener, and the tide of war
began to turn. At the same time M. Delcassé made it clear
that France, at any rate, was not prepared to intervene; and
a curiously elegiac note began to creep into William's correspondence. Such, in brief, was the state of affairs when the
Prince became King.

William was an anglophile for only a brief while. The
civilian clothes were soon put away. In the navy-yards of
Germany the noise of hammering grew louder. The German
railroad promoter was active in Turkey; the German archae-
ologist innocently excavated the site of Troy; the move towards Bagdad, Basra and Koweit had begun. Meanwhile, as
French eyes turned more and more towards the "blue line of
the Vosges," the ambitions of the neighbor across the Channel assumed a less deadly form; and, with infinite reluctance,
England and France drew closer together. . . .

King Edward, like Chaucer's springtime creatures, longed
"to goon on pilgrimages." There was now a definite objective
with which to assuage these longings. In April, 1903, he proceeded by way of Lisbon and Rome to Paris, bringing with
him two equerries and a representative of the Foreign Office.
As he drove through the streets of Paris towards the British
Embassy, the crowds cried "Vivent les Boers!": or else, re-
calling the almost fatal clash of England and France in the
mysterious Sudan, greeted the passing monarch with "Vive
Fashoda!" The unhappy President Loubet, a venerable innocent, quavered a few faltering remarks about the fine turn-

out. "I thought I heard a few hisses," said Edward VII. "But no, I heard nothing, I heard nothing."

In the afternoon, he made a speech at the British Chamber of Commerce in which he touched upon his familiarity with Paris, and declared, with indefatigable optimism, that all differences between the two countries were now at an end. This was not apparent at the *Theâtre Français* that evening, where there was a command performance, and where the King's reception was distinctly chilly. In the interval, it is said, he mingled with the crowds in the foyer, and chatted for a while with a charmer of other days, La Belle Otero. The story may be mythical, but, as such stories sometimes do, it summed up the essential nature of his attack upon Paris. He believed that informality was the key to the city's heart, and it was a key which he handled with consummate skill. If the English and the foreign sides of him could be said to have a synthesis, it was a Parisian one. He was a child of the boulevards. His social sensibilities, always acute, were sometimes exquisite; the politest capital in the world responded; and when, on the fourth day, he drove back from the Embassy to the station, there were shouts of "Vive notre roi" all along the route. It was a personal triumph, and though it has often been given too much importance, as though it were actually responsible for the change in Anglo-French relations, it undoubtedly put a delicate finish upon the more solid labors of Lord Lansdowne, M. Cambon, and M. Delcassé, and destiny.

The Kaiser had been following the early stages of this progress with that passionate interest which he always bestowed upon his uncle's doings. Lisbon was bad enough; but Rome! Rome was his preserve, the sub-center of the Triple

Alliance. He owed the King of Italy a visit, and this was clearly the right moment for paying it. While Edward was in Paris, therefore, William was in Rome. He arrived in a special train, all blue and gold and eagles; and drove about the Eternal City in his state coach, with his Garde-du-Corps riding before and behind; and was accompanied by a military staff of enormously tall men, led by Colonel Plüskow (or Plus-que-haut, as the irreverent Parisians had already dubbed him). It is not unlikely that, as he stepped into his special train on May 5 and turned his face home, he had read in the morning's newspapers of his uncle's triumph in Paris on the day before.

And here, perhaps, we can state, in the contrasts afforded by these two visits, the essence also of the personal disputes between these two men. The King never had a very regal manner, but he had very good manners: the Kaiser, on the other hand, had a very regal manner, but he had almost no manners at all. It was upon this distinction, as upon a barricade, that their personalities clashed. And the clash produced, at times, a most peculiar result. Not always, only sometimes, quite infrequently—but often enough to make their meetings uncomfortable in the extreme—the uncle lost his manners and his tact when they met, and the Kaiser his manner. For the rest of King Edward's reign this was the case. Moreover, after his Parisian triumph, the King continued to go on progress to the courts of his fellow monarchs. It was an exercise which he found especially agreeable, and he entertained the belief—which his subjects endorsed—that he was doing something for good relations in Europe. Whether there was any justification for this belief is, to be sure, doubtful. Europe was in so apprehensive a state of mind in the first decade of the twentieth century that so *mouvementé* a personage as Edward VII was not likely to exercise a calming effect. His nephew, for example, either pursued the King, as in 1903, or else scribbled his exasperation upon the margins of dispatches. He was convinced that his uncle was designing an *Einkreisungspolitik*—a policy of encirclement; and would often allude to him in his conversations as a "Satan" or a "Fiend." The King, on his side, was equally brief but more laconic. Once, after an afternoon with his nephew at Friedrichshof in 1907, he was asked how the Kaiser had been. "Impossible," said Edward VII.

But all this was in the future. Already, in 1901, at the time of the King's accession, their unfriendly relations had been established so firmly that only a miracle could have altered them for the better. The same thing might be said for the relations between their two countries. The fatal concentrations of capital, the fatal expansions of bourgeois imperialism were forcing the insatiable and militarist empire into a collision with the satiated and civilian one. And at the root of Anglo-German rivalry, as it grew out of the '80's and increased in intensity, there lay the germinating enmities of industry and commerce.

This explanation is true; it is an historical fact that cannot be avoided either in relation to the past or in relation to the future; but it does not contain the whole truth. During the past years we have been rather too inclined to examine history in the light of only one of its factors. But recent events, in their mystery no less than their magnitude, have been somewhat upsetting to economic determinism. We find ourselves obliged, once more, to regard the complex and changing substance of history as the result of an infiltration of a number of varied elements. We look into that eternal retort: economics, politics, geography, geology, climate, race swirl together. This concept raises some interesting questions. What place has psychology, for example, in the affairs of men? When we talk of rival imperialisms, as we must, ought we not also to take into account another rivalry—the rivalry of ways of life? In 1901 cannot such a rivalry already be seen, moving, in a somewhat contradictory manner, through the economic differences of England and Germany?

The English way of life has been for centuries—ever since the defeat of the Armada and even before—a question of what kind of adjustment a unified nation can make to the changes that beset it from within and without. Compromise has been—with very few exceptions—the guiding principle in this adjustment. In the fierce dawn of industrialism, for instance, when the philosophies of the eighteenth century stalked explosively among the social consciences of the nineteenth, the most momentous upheavals in English society were embodied in undramatic and bloodless forms—a Reform Bill, a Corn and Customs Bill, a Factory Act. The barricades were almost, but not quite, built; the revolutions almost, but not quite, sprang into being: at the last minute, compromise set in. Compromise may exasperate the historian, but it explains, as nothing else can, the calm continuity of English history. And along with compromise, one has to take into account, as a necessary part of the English adjustment, an unwillingness to grasp facts until some time after they have occurred. The English nation, like the English diplomat, is neither logical nor *doctrinaire*. Now an actual fact is always less compulsive than an anticipated one; and this circumstance may account for the optimistic patience of the English people. Another name for this patience is insularity; and, indeed, the English might have developed a sense of logic if they had not had the uninhabitable seas for their border.

And one can also discern in the English way of life—moving in human relationships or embalmed in the dry spices of law—a deep respect for liberty. If we grow sentimental about this, and try and raise it to the status of a fixed principle, it does not answer at all. It presents a fugitive and even hypocritical appearance: it is perverted into unmitigated individualism; it wanders off and loses itself in colonial wars and Indian jails; it is abolished in a factory or forgotten in a slum. Where the ruling class is concerned it is often (though not always) indistinguishable from self-interest. None the less, it is a vital element in the character of the whole people, it has influenced all the great changes in English history, and has itself been transformed through them; for it is intimately involved with the English sense of self-preservation. In a great crisis, when the English people are faced with an overwhelming set of facts, this respect for liberty, which requires as likely as not a radical reform in institutions, suddenly flares up. It provides them with the only form of survival which, at heart, they understand. For, in spite of its shortcomings, the English way of life is essentially progressive.

In the German past, on the other hand, the centuries have been full of disturbance and disintegration. The Holy Roman Empire, the Reformation and Counter-Reformation, the Confederation of the Rhine, the ingenuity of Metternich—all these have been the agents, not of continuity but of confusion. The confusion, it is true, has been dominated to a certain extent by the circumstance of a single state; by the fact that the rulers of Prussia were obliged to maintain themselves by military and bureaucratic methods. But Prussia's star rose and set in a highly disconcerting manner. It had sunk very low before the War of Liberation in 1807; and even lower in 1848. Indeed, in 1848, a German could complain that he was not a German: he was a Hanoverian or a Hessian or a Saxon or a Prussian or a Bavarian or any one of thirty-nine varieties. He lived in a welter of flags, visas, consulates, and ministries; in a world where absolutist laws prevailed in charming provincial principalities; and where a ruler, with equal facility, suppressed a newspaper or financed an opera. His world cohered only in a Customs Union. Then the Bismarckian Empire rose, four-square and solid, upon the ruins of 1848. It was a remarkable building; and yet, somewhere, in the cellar perhaps, a ghostly voice insisted that it was built upon sand. It had no racial or historical or geographical unity. One could only dispel such a voice, so full of insecurity, by conjuration; and so a very mystical philosophy was evolved to deal with it; and the German Will, after hovering for years in a state of abstraction, at last came into its own. It produced an odd kind of diplomacy which first endeavored to inspire fear in other nations and then, when they seem disposed to resist, complained of encirclement. It produced a way of life—swift, daring, illiberal, authoritarian. From seeking to dominate Europe, and then to turn Germany into a world-power, it has at last—after a great defeat, and a long period of economic depression—decided to dominate and even to enslave the world. Before this amoral Will (now embodied in an outlaw government), which seeks more and more to connect the German people with the forces of nature, and which declares that Germany "is a destiny, not a way of life," the solid and magnificent qualities of the Germans have simply abdicated.

As the two ways drew farther and farther apart after 1900, one could perhaps discern—in the King and the Kaiser—a representation of this divergence. The representation was very slight—the genial uncle, the volatile and vehement nephew—but, slight as it was, it had its importance. Seen through the diminishing glass of time, their quarrel seems to spin away down the years, growing smaller and smaller: but it is not without significance, nor should it be altogether forgotten.

IV

Meanwhile, in January, 1901, Edward VII prepared to move into his new position with no misgivings—even though people were saying that he could never hope to fill Victoria's place—and as smoothly as possible. In his first speech to the Privy Council he declared his intention to be "a constitutional" monarch. Now "constitutional"—as the Prince Consort might have used it—could have meant almost anything; and, considering the ectoplasmic nature of the English Constitution, this is hardly surprising. What Edward VII meant was that he did not propose to interfere too much. He insisted, to be sure, upon his rights to be informed, to encourage, and to warn; and very specially upon his right to be informed: but his autocratic nature found its intimate satisfactions in other ways—in the delights of society, in the performance of ceremonies, and the elaborations of protocole.

He began at once, and literally, to clean house. His two main palaces—Buckingham Palace and Windsor Castle—bore everywhere the impress not only of Victoria but of her Age. As for Osborne, the Queen's favorite retreat after Balmoral, that was a monument to the taste of the Prince Consort. Albert had planned the Pavilion, or central portion, where the frescoes and the shell-shaped alcoves of garter blue testified to his esthetic sensibilities. He had planned the avenue of monkey-puzzlers, the winding walks between the ilexes. The Queen always intended this estate to be handed down from one sovereign to another; but the King, with the advice of his lawyers, decided that her wishes might be overridden. He had his own estate at Sandringham; the two thousand acres of Osborne would be an additional burden; and he did not care for the house at all. The stables, therefore, were torn down and a school for naval cadets rose, at the expense of the Admiralty, in their place; the large wing became a convalescent home for naval officers; and the Queen's private apartments on the first floor of the Pavilion were maintained as a permanent memorial to herself and the Prince Consort. There were some grumblings in the family: the King's two sisters who had residences at Osborne, Princess Beatrice and Princess Louise, were naturally not too pleased; but the King had made up his mind. And so the Osborne which Disraeli had once described as the home of "Queen Titania, gathering flowers, with her Court, in a soft and sea-girt isle," vanished: the convalescent officers, the noisy youths, the public arriving on visiting day erased the imprint of Titania, and abstracted from Dizzy's soaring hyperbole whatever meaning it might once have had.

At Windsor, the Queen's personality, the richness of her

kingdom, and the growth of the Empire were strangely intermingled. Vast cupboards were opened to reveal jades from
the Emperor of China; or a stack of rotting ivory tusks, the
laborious tribute of some African tribe; or rolls of tapestry
and heaps of armor from heaven knows where. Not all such
imperial accumulations were, however, inanimate: in King
John's Tower, in an odor of curry and musk, lived the
Queen's two Indian attendants. Elsewhere, huge rooms
gleamed with gold and silver dinner services; the marvelous
Sèvres and Dresden china of George IV was ranged in endless cabinets; while the varied tastes of that monarch could
be discerned in delicate snuff-boxes, collections of exquisite
French furniture, and golden baskets and flagons of an appalling ugliness. In the Guard Room stood Lord Nelson, a
vigilant bust: he was placed upon a fragment of one of the
Victory's masts, around which had been piled, in ambiguous
tribute, a quantity of curiously decorated horse-harness.

But the Queen's own commemorative longings were most
in evidence. In Windsor the Prince Consort's apartments
had been left untouched, and more than untouched. Though
Albert himself was gone, the details of his daily life were
perpetually renewed. Every evening his clothes were laid
upon the bed, every evening fresh water was poured into
the basin. In the Queen's apartments, above her bed, was a
photograph of Albert's head and shoulders as he lay dead.
And not only Albert was remembered: there were innumerable figures and busts of relatives and friends, in gold and
silver, in marble and plaster and bronze. They crowded
everywhere; and favorite dogs and horses were also among
the assembly. Nor had the Queen permitted her own past to
elude her; mysterious trunks, when opened, were found to

335

be filled with dolls, or with the muffs and the parasols, the bonnets and the pantalettes of her remote childhood. Nothing that she had used or worn or been given had been thrown away. It was a fathomless collection. But at length the contents of Windsor and Osborne were sorted out; the unhung pictures were sent to the National Gallery or to Buckingham Palace; and streams of photographs and engravings poured back to the royalties of Europe, who did not say thank you. Some objects, it is true, were simply discarded. There were plates with pictures of relatives and dogs painted upon them; there was a macabre collection of the childrens' hands, in white marble; there were countless lithographs by Winterhalter and Von Angeli, and copies of inferior paintings from Coburg. One of Osborne's cupboards contained some plaster replicas of a statue of the Queen's faithful gillie, John Brown; and these King Edward, to whom that domineering Highlander had always been particularly rude, is said to have smashed with his own hands. He never forgave a slight.

And in Buckingham Palace, or the Sepulcher as Edward preferred to call it, the curtains were drawn back and the light of a new era fell in harsh surprise upon those dismal interiors. Since 1861, the Queen had never used the Palace for more than two or three days at a time; in plumbing, heating, and illumination it was completely mid-Victorian; while dust and damp nested glumly amidst its splendors. As the King went through its maze of apartments and corridors he came at last—and one can well believe with reluctance—into the private apartments of the Prince Consort. Nothing had been moved since Albert's death: the ink had hardened in the inkstands; intimate letters, yellow with age, lay just as he had left them; the chairs, the desk, the carpets seemed to have been waiting for forty years for Albert to return. In one corner stood the organ upon which he had played to Mendelssohn, but it was perished and voiceless. Had the King ever penetrated these rooms before, for some awful interview with that formidable parent? We do not know. He ordered everything to be packed up and put away with care. And then the electrician, the plumber, and the cleaner, and the Twentieth Century came in.

INDEX

339

Printed in Great Britain by
Lowe and Brydone Printers Limited, London, N.W.10